Salvation begins

Reading Genesis Today

Andrew Reid

AQUILA
PRESS

A book by Aquila Press
Published October 2000
Revised and reprinted October 2007
Copyright © Andrew Reid 2000

Aquila Press
PO Box A287
Sydney South NSW 1235
AUSTRALIA

National Library of Australia
ISBN 978 1875861 83 5

Designed and typeset by Lankshear Design

Contents

Foreword

Andrew Reid has served us well in this splendid commentary on the book of Genesis. Our author has placed himself inside the amazing story line of this the first book of the Pentateuch in a way that tells the whole 'story' from Abraham to the entry to the Land of Promise. Stepping back and seeing a 'wider angle', Andrew Reid sets Creation and Fall against God's gracious work of Re-creation and Redemption in the Second Adam.

Not all commentaries prove helpful today. On one hand they are so lengthy, wordy and technical that the reader does not know where to begin. On the other hand they are shallow and so bent on 'application' that they fail to get inside the text. But Andrew Reid's work is to the point, true to the inspired text and very readable.

The author brings to his work the historian's interest in detail, the literary critic's appreciation for drama, personal characterisation and pace and the pastor's concern to strengthen the church.

I am confident that readers will derive as much pleasure and benefit as I have. Andrew Reid is to be congratulated for his achievement.

Dr Paul Barnett
Series Editor

For Heather, Joel, and Daniel,
who helped me understand and
experience the great richness
and joy of being a created being
in a created world.
'It is not good for the man to be alone'
(Genesis 2:18).

Preface

The book of Genesis has meant so much to me and to my view of who God is and what it means to be Christian in the twenty-first century. I hope that my reflections on it may in some way help you better understand Jesus Christ, the one to whom Genesis points, and that you come to love him more as a result.

As with all such efforts, there are people to thank for their contribution and participation. First, Bill Dumbrell, who lectured me in Old Testament at Moore Theological College, who opened the Old Testament to me for the first time and who taught me, by word and example, how to deal with it as Christian Scripture.

Second, the members of St Matthew's Anglican Church in Shenton Park, Perth who listened to numerous sermons on Genesis with great enthusiasm and encouragement. Not a few found faith here for the first time and many others were established in their faith.

Third, my friends Paul and Anita Barnett, who encouraged me to write again and gave me confidence that I could do so.

Fourth, Andrew Page, who read the manuscript as a trial reader and offered such helpful advice and criticism.

Fifth, my wife Heather, my generous and gentle critic, who kept encouraging me to write even though she knew of the inevitable distraction that would come because of it.

Andrew Reid

Salvation begins

Why read Genesis?

In my mind's eye I often wander out with Abraham to stand and stare at the starlit skies over ancient Palestine. I feel his doubts and fears, but then I see him turn his eyes heavenward at the command of God. In my imagination the tears in his eyes sparkle with the reflection of millions of stars as God promises yet again to fulfill his word. Like Abraham, I get a glimpse of God again—he who is the star maker and promise giver, the One who can turn barrenness into a great nation and who can turn sinful humans into those who are righteous in his sight.

In page after page of Genesis I see this man, his forebears, and his descendants, struggling with the same God and with the same issues as I do. From this book their examples creep into my soul to teach, rebuke, correct, and train me in righteousness (2 Timothy 3:16–17). From this book, world-changing ideas spring with both ferocity and gentleness.

Who?

The book of Genesis is an anonymous work. Unlike many other authors of Bible books, the author of this book gives us no indication as to his identity. Having said this, Jewish and Christian tradition have long ascribed Genesis and the rest of the Pentateuch to Moses (compare John 1:17; 5:46; 7:19, 23). This is understandable in the light of the education Moses would probably have received in the court of Pharaoh and the fact that the Old Testament often records his writing down events, words from God, and the law of God within his lifetime (for example Exodus 17:14; 23:4; 34:28; Deuteronomy 4:13; 31:9; compare Joshua 8:31–32). Perhaps the best that we can conclude is that no matter how the book came to assume its final form, the writings of Moses lie at its core.

How?

Genesis is a highly structured and deliberate work. The clearest evidence for this structure is seen in a Hebrew phrase that occurs throughout the book. The principal part of this phrase consists of a Hebrew word *(tôlēdôt)* that can be translated as either 'genealogy'/'generations' or 'account'/'story'. This word occurs ten times in the book of Genesis and is used by the author as a major device for structuring his book. Usually the phrase has a person attached such as in Gen 6:9; 'This is the account of Noah.' Usually a genealogy or narrative about that person follows after this introduction (see table below).

The tôlēdôt headings in Genesis

Heading	Title	Subsequent Content	Reference
2:4	These are the generations… *of the heavens and the earth.*	**The story** of Adam and his descendants	2:4–4:26
5:1	This is the book of the generations… *of Adam.*	**Genealogy** of Adam to Noah	5:1–6:8
6:9	These are the generations… *of Noah.*	**The story** of the flood	6:9–9:29
10:1	These are the generations… *of the sons of Noah.*	**Table of nations/genealogy** of 10:1–11:9 those descended from Noah	
11:10	These are the generations… *of Shem*	**Genealogy** from Shem to Abraham	11:10–26
11:27	These are the generations… *of Terah.*	**The story** of Abraham	11:27–25:11
25:12	These are the generations… *of Ishmael.*	**Genealogy** of Ishmael	25:12–18
25:19	These are the generations… *of Isaac.*	**The story** of Jacob and Esau	25:19–35:29
36:1, 9	These are the generations… *of Esau.*	**Genealogy** of Esau	36:1–37:1
37:2	These are the generations… *of Jacob*	**The story** of Jacob and his sons	37:2–50:26

In five of these occurrences the formula is associated with narrative. In the other five it is associated with genealogies. However, there are also other indications of structure. For example, the story of the Old Testament as a whole is largely played out in three geographical areas—Babylonia, Palestine, and Egypt. So it is with Genesis—Chapters 1–11 are set in Babylonia, 12–36 in Palestine, and 37–50 in Egypt. When this is combined with the fact that Genesis 1–11 outlines the beginnings of the cosmos while 12–50 outlines the beginnings of Israel, it is clear that the writer of Genesis is interested in writing a world history rather than simply a history of a particular nation. His fundamental concern, while obviously entwined with Abraham and his descendants, is to tell us of his God's concern for, interest in, and plan for, the whole world.

Part of a much larger work

Even to the cursory reader it is clear that the book of Genesis is part of a much larger work. This larger work consists of the first section of the Hebrew Bible, or the first five books of the Bible. These books appear to have been known in Jesus' time simply as 'the Law' (compare Luke 24:44). Today they are collectively known by the term used to describe them in the Hebrew Bible, 'Torah' (meaning 'Law') or by a Greek term known since the second century, 'the Pentateuch', a term that literally means 'compilation of five' or 'fivefold book'.

Theologically, the backdrop for the Pentateuch is set in the first eleven chapters of Genesis. God is the God of the whole cosmos. He creates a world where humans live together in harmony with God, each other, and their environment. However, human independence brings that harmony to an abrupt end and God acts in punishment, expelling the humans from the garden he had made for them. In Chapters 4 to 11 of Genesis we see an increasing avalanche of sin and subsequent judgment by God. What becomes clear is that the large bulk of humanity has no inclination to set things right and that even those who would like to, have no ability to do so.

In Genesis 12 God calls one man—Abram—and gives him great promises. These promises of land, descendants, and blessing have in mind the world spoken about in Genesis 1–11. Through this man and his descendants, God will bring redemption from the situation created in Genesis 1–3. While humans are unable to rescue themselves from their predicament, God seeks their rescue.

From this point on, the focus is on the promises and their fulfilment. The story that follows traces how descendants increase in number, and the land is entered and possessed. Canaan becomes, at least in prospect, a place where God might live with his people as he had lived in Eden and where they might live with him as his holy people.

Because the impetus for these promises comes from the God who created the world, we know that he is a God who is able. Genesis and the books that follow are therefore imbued with hope and anticipation based on the promises and ability of God. They look forward to the day when God might indeed bring about the fullness of the promises to Abraham and thereby bless the world. At the same time, the books that follow also have frustration embedded in them, for the people God chooses to deal with are built of the same stock as the original humans.

The Christian reader knows, however, that Genesis is part not just of the Pentateuch, nor even of the whole Old Testament. Despite the Creator's ability, the promises given in Genesis are never fully fulfilled within Genesis. Nor are they fully fulfilled in the Pentateuch. They reach some sort of fulfilment with the conquest of the land and with kings David and Solomon, but things are never quite as they were in the garden and they are certainly never enduring. Adam's nature appears time and time again to overwhelm the promise, with the result that even the closing pages of the Old Testament continue as the closing pages of Genesis did—in hope that God's promise might be matched by reality.

The Christian reader knows that these hopes are met in Jesus. These great and glorious promises have their 'Yes' and 'Amen' in Jesus Christ (2 Corinthians 1:20). In him, and for those in him, the promises to Abraham are finally assured.

In one sense, then, Genesis is a start waiting for a finish, a beginning waiting for an end. It tells us of a Creator and his plan for redemption. It sets an agenda, outlines the issues, graphically gives them human form, and proposes a solution, but never quite gets to its end. It therefore thoroughly prepares the Christian for Christ, and enriches our understanding of his work and of God's great purpose. Moreover, in its method of presentation—the narrative of people's lives—it lets us into the dynamic of what it means to live in relationship with God, of what it means to be people of faith, hope, and love. It is truly a book for today.

A final note before we start

There are two issues that may cause misunderstanding throughout the commentary and that therefore should be introduced in brief here before we get underway.

First, throughout the bulk of the commentary I have tried to make use of inclusive language. Nevertheless, the application of inclusive language to Genesis 1–3 is particularly difficult because one Hebrew word is used for:

- the name 'Adam';
- 'the man' (as distinct from 'the woman'); and
- 'humanity' as a whole.

I have tried to use inclusive language where possible in commenting on the text of Genesis 1–3. At times, however, it has been almost impossible not to revert to using 'man' in the generic sense of 'humanity' and I have kept such language for ease and clarity. Second, the use of the word 'story'. Throughout the commentary I have deliberately used the word 'story' in reference to much of what happens. Although my dictionary defines 'story' as 'narrative, either true or fictitious' the application of such a term to the narratives of the Bible sometimes causes discomfort to readers who hold to a high view of Scripture. The term is used here for convenience and because it often fits better than 'narrative' or 'account' (although both these terms are used). It is not because I think that the stories are fictitious, but because they are often very carefully crafted literary works of art and not simply historical accounts. They are designed to interest and amuse the reader as well as give them facts. They have plots, character development, drama, and humour. In other words, they are 'stories' in the technical literary sense as well as being historical records.

BEGINNINGS: Of the Cosmos

Part 1

The God who creates
Genesis 1:1–2:3

1

Creation

The book of Genesis was written for a world filled with gods and deities of all shapes, sizes, and dispositions. Each one controlled a different part of human or natural existence. This made the ancient world a place of fear. If you lived in that world you constantly needed to ask yourself whom among the gods you should worship, placate, honour, fear or love. A lot hung on your decision. A wrong answer might mean your crops wouldn't grow, you wouldn't find a husband, your wife might not bear children, and you might not find your proper place in life.

Most of us probably regard this sort of thinking as primitive. Nevertheless, the modern world is no less a place of deities than the ancient world. We might think we are more sophisticated because we no longer worship the sun, the stars, or rainbow serpents. We might not peer at the entrails of chickens looking for answers (although I have known people to peer at tealeaves in the bottom of a cup!) or consult wizards and soothsayers. Nevertheless, we search for somewhere to place our allegiance in return for meaning and identity. Our gods are largely material, social, and ideological. Our lives are shaped by the possessions we own or covet, the social standing we have or aspire to, the ideas that give us form and meaning. We give our allegiance to political ideologies, psychology, various religions, our career, and relationships. One particular television character I have enjoyed observing gives his allegiance to the search for extraterrestrials, and this search very significantly determines who he is and how he fits into the world.

Just as the gods of the ancient world posed threats, so do ours. Deep underneath our search is a fear that if we don't get things right then we won't find our proper place in life. There won't be fulfilment, we won't reach our full potential, we won't succeed.

It was for a world of fear that the book of Genesis was written so long ago, and it is to such a world that it comes today. As we will see, the opening chapter of Genesis addresses these very issues.

GETTING TO GENESIS 1

A bird's eye view of Genesis 1

The basic elements of Genesis 1 are clear:

- God creates the world for humans in six days.
- God rests on the seventh day. (In Hebrew thought the number seven has the sense of importance, completeness and climax, with the implication here that the high point of God's creative work and its final objective is rest.)

These two events make up the first week of human history. The structure of the chapter is built around what was created, and what it was for, as in the following diagram:

Formless Water and Night (1:1–2)			
Form		**Use**	
Day 1:	Light (day and night)	**Day 4:**	Lights in Heaven
Day 2:	Water and Sky	**Day 5:**	Fish and Birds
Day 3:	Land and Vegetation	**Day 6:**	Animals and Humans
Day 7: God Rests			

A note on verses 1–2

In the beginning God created the heavens and the earth. now the earth was formless and empty, darkness was over the surface of the deep, and the Spirit of God was hovering over the waters.

(Genesis 1:1–2)

The New International Version (NIV) follows the oldest and most commonly accepted translation of the original Hebrew words. It fits with the rest of the Bible, which indicates that creation was *ex nihilo* ('out of nothing'; compare Hebrews 11:3).

This interpretation indicates that after the creation the earth was 'formless and empty' (chaotic and dark). This could be so either because that is the way God made it before going on to a further stage, or because something happened to God's original creation to make it formless and empty (the second interpretation may find support in Isaiah 45:18–19). In either case, Genesis 1:1–2 tells us that God made the world we now see in two stages. First, God created the universe as a whole and then, second, he gave order to something that was formless and void.

Putting Genesis in perspective

The writer of Genesis lived in a world where people had grappled with the question of origins. We have discovered various accounts that were written by such people. Their views were probably well known in the ancient world, just as most of us know basically what Charles Darwin said in his book on the question of origins. We may never have read *The Origin of Species*, but we live in a world coloured by Darwin's theories. Even if we don't believe Darwin was right, our neighbour probably does.

Ancient stories of origins look a lot like Australian Aboriginal creation stories. They involve animals, and seas, and bodies of water, and skies, and all sorts of natural phenomena. These natural phenomena are personalised, and become the central figures in stories that are told and retold in highly imaginative language.

The function of creation stories

The style and content of these creation stories indicates that they had a definite purpose or function. This could be:

- To describe how a nation's familiar gods came into being.
- To explain familiar cosmic phenomena.
- To explain how a particular culture's society functioned, and to give some credence to the people who were important, by explaining where their power came from.
- To validate the position of a particular deity in relation to other deities.
- To explain a nation's experience of the lifecycle of the earth, and therefore the religious rituals and celebrations enacted in their religion.

A distinctive presentation

The Genesis 1 account is simple and solemn and in so many ways quite the reverse of the creation stories being told in the world at the time. Were the people who were used to these other creation stories to read Genesis 1, they could not help but notice striking differences. In fact, there are some indications that the writer of Genesis is taking on and speaking against these other accounts. For example, in Genesis 1...

- God doesn't come into existence. He simply is.
- Rather than matter pre-existing God, God pre-exists matter.
- The sun, moon, stars and sea monsters, all of whom were powerful deities according to the creation myths of the surrounding nations, are merely creatures or entities who display God's power and skill.
- Human beings are not an afterthought of the gods, nor are they created by the whim of the gods for their pleasure and service. Rather, humans are central in God's world and the world is provided for them and their use.

By taking a different approach, the writer makes a very clear point. For him, God's creative activity primarily has the whole world in view. This can be seen in the fact that:

- There are no political overtones.
- There are no references to the nation of Israel, Jerusalem or the temple.
- The account does not seek to validate particular people, ideals or institutions.

What comes first with God is the world, not Israel. What will come last with God is the world, not Israel (think about the way the Bible ends in Revelation 21–22, with all the nations and a new creation!).

Genesis 1 is therefore an ancient example of apologetics. The writer is doing something similar to what Paul does in Acts 17. During the course of his wanderings in Athens, Paul notices an altar with the inscription, TO THE UNKNOWN GOD. When he finally gets an evangelistic opportunity to speak to the Athenians, he reminds them of the statue and says to them, 'What you worship as something unknown I am going to proclaim to you.' From this beginning, he proceeds to explain that in fact he proclaims the God who actually made the world and is responsible for the way it functions.

The writer of Genesis is facing a world that worships the creation or the creature. To that world he declares the true God who creates (compare Jeremiah 10:11–12; Psalm 96:5). In a sense he is saying,

'You worship many gods and think that they are responsible for the world and society. You are misguided. There is one true and living God who is the creator of all these things you worship and who stands over all others. He alone is worthy of worship. This, and not the mythological world represented in your stories of origins, is the true reality.'

The power of words

And God said... and it was so.

Another striking characteristic of the biblical account is creation by the spoken word of God. There is no hint of magic as in the mythological accounts, but in its place the record of God speaking an effortless, omnipotent, unchallengeable divine word that accomplishes what he commands. The power of the word of God doesn't come from its magical content, but from the person who speaks it. The God of Genesis 1 is the Creator, with all creation subservient to him. He only has to speak and it obeys.

Male and female

In many other ancient accounts sexual differentiation existed before the world came into being and all the gods were themselves male or female creatures. This is not so in Genesis. The very association of gender with God is utterly alien to the God of the Old Testament. Sexual differentiation between men and women is something God created.

The pinnacle of Creation

> **So God created man in his own image, in the image of God he created him; male and female he created them. God blessed them and said to them, 'Be fruitful and increase in number; fill the earth and subdue it. Rule over the fish of the sea and the birds of the air and over every living creature that moves on the ground.'**
>
> *(Genesis 1:27–28)*

Remember that we saw that the final objective of God's creative activity is rest. Nevertheless, it also has a secondary objective—humankind. Humans are the pinnacle of the created world and the world is made for them. They are made to live in and rule over God's created world and they are made for rest with him.

But what is the function of human beings in God's world? Verses 27–28 make this clear by saying that they are created 'in the image of God'.

In the Ancient Near East, setting up a king's statue (or 'image') was equivalent to proclaiming his dominion. It declared him lord over the area in which the statue was erected (compare Daniel 3:1, 5–7). So, when God creates humanity in his image, he is saying that humanity is God's statue—the evidence that God is the Lord of creation.

But this is not all. These verses also make clear that humanity is not just a passive statue. Humanity not only represents God's rule but also exerts God's rule. This is what verse 28 means when it talks about the subduing of the world. Psalm 8, a commentary on this passage, makes the same point—humanity is God's ruler over God's world.

Since humanity's rule derives from God it also must draw its shape from God. Psalm 145 and many other psalms tell us that God's rule always has the best interests of his subjects in mind. So humans must also be characterised not by arbitrary despotism, but by loving care that has the best interests of those being ruled as its primary concern.

Therefore, 'image' in Genesis 1 points to humanity's function as ruler of the rest of creation. This is primarily what it means to be the image of God. Genesis 1:26 indicates that this function is not given to any individual, but to humankind as a whole.

As we go on in Genesis we will see just how humans rule. We will find that humans can use the materials of the world to make things. For example, they can produce musical instruments and learn the arts of playing harp and flute (Genesis 4:21). They can mine and fashion minerals and iron (4:22), cultivate the vine (9:20), and invent materials which make it possible to put up giant buildings (11:3-4). But, as we shall see, these very same inventions can easily dominate humans and rule them rather than the reverse. So it is that the good gift of wine can deprive Noah of his willpower and put him at the mercy of his son's shamelessness (9:21-27). The very act of constructing a grand building draws humans into the intoxication of selfpraise (11:4b), or into other projects motivated by fear (11:4c).

Wherever the things that they are meant to overpower overpower them, humans become inhuman. This is graphically portrayed in Daniel 2 and 4. King Nebuchadnezzar is spoken about in language reminiscent of Genesis 1 and Psalm 8 (Daniel 2:36-38)—he is God's appointed ruler. However, he then lifts himself up and praises himself, rather than the God who gave him dominion (Daniel 4:28–30). God's judgment is that he becomes a beast of the field (4:31–33), no longer 'human' in the true sense. It is only when he lifts his eyes to heaven, acknowledging the givenness of his dominion and the humanness of his humanity, that he is restored (4:34–35).

The nature of God

> **And God said, 'Let there be light,' and there was light. God saw that the light was good, and he separated the light from the darkness. God called the light 'day' and the darkness he called 'night'. And there was evening, and there was morning— the first day.**
>
> **And God said, 'Let there be an expanse between the waters to separate water from water.' So God made the expanse and separated the water under the expanse from the water above it. And it was so. God called the expanse 'sky'. And there was evening, and there was morning—the second day.**

(Genesis 1:3–8)

Polytheism, the belief in many gods, produces a confusing array of ethical values. Where gods compete for the worshipper's allegiance and devotion on the basis of their various characteristics and interests, there will inevitably be different conceptions of what is good and what is right. This is complicated by the fact that the gods of the creation myths were often morally indifferent, and pagan worshippers had no assurance that the decrees of their god/s would be just. Moreover, in the ancient world the gods were innately capricious and so any absolute authority was impossible.

The picture is very different in Genesis 1. As he goes about his work, God is without peer and competitor and doesn't have to engage in battle with other deities to assert his right to rule. The sun and the moon are not rivals, but creations. He is omnipotent—he speaks and it is done.

In addition, God is presented as a lawgiver. He divides light from darkness and land from sea, naming them and appointing stars for signs and for the fixing of time. Boundaries are set for the natural order. The animate creation is commanded to perform in a certain manner. Species have set roles. The seventh day is made holy. The God of Genesis is not morally indifferent—morality and ethics constitute the very essence of his nature.

And it was good!

> **God saw all that he had made, and it was very good. And there was evening, and there was morning— the sixth day.**
>
> *(Genesis 1:31)*

The Hebrew word 'good' used here can have a broad range of meaning. Here it appears to have the sense of something suited for the purpose for which it is being prepared, corresponding to its goal. In other words, the creation is good for that for which God intends it. The world which God created is the world in which history can begin and reach its goal and so fulfil its purpose. But what is its purpose?

The seventh day

> **By the seventh day, God had finished the work he had been doing; so on the seventh day he rested from all his work. And God blessed the seventh day and made it holy, because on it he rested from all the work of creating that he had done.**
>
> *(Genesis 2:2–3)*

It is clear from Genesis 1 that the days of work have their goal in a day that is different from them. There are two sorts of days—the everyday and the special—and the everyday reaches its goal in the special. Notice that the word *shabat* meaning 'to cease from labour' is used here. The idea of the Sabbath is linked to this passage and we will discuss this further in Chapter 2.

Notice verse 3 where God blesses the day, endowing it with the potential to be the day which he has intended for human experience. He then hallows it, or makes it his own day. The clear hint here is that if other parts of creation were designed for humans, so was the Sabbath (compare Mark 2:27). By implication, just as God's work was not his goal, so work is not the goal for humans. God's goal is the eternal rest foreshadowed in the rest of the seventh day. Similarly, rest is God's goal for humanity.

WRAPPING THINGS UP

'Who' not 'How'

One of the great modern problems with interpreting Genesis is that we want the passage to answer our questions. Our question is often, 'How did God create?' This is because we live in a world that is interested in the 'how' question, and where everyone has an answer to this question.

Although the writer of Genesis is not totally uninterested in the question of 'how', it does not appear to be his primary interest or the primary interest of his ancient audience. He lived in a world where everyone wanted to know, 'Who created?' Genesis offers an answer to this question. The true and living God is the creator of the universe, even of the things that some of his creatures worship as gods.

The fear of living

Do you remember where we started? We talked about the fear that ancient people had about living. What does Genesis 1 say to the people of God as they look out at this world?

Genesis 1 says these things:

- The things other people worship are not gods.
- They are the creation of the one true God.
- They have no spiritual influence and power.
- They offer no threat.

- They are merely physical entities under God's dominion, placed in their proper position by God, doing his will.

This message is just as relevant to us in our world. God's word to us is that the things other people worship have no power. God, the creator of heaven and earth, is the only one who can give purpose. He alone sustains the universe. He created human beings and he created their minds that think up their ideas. He created their relational ability that forms their social structures and he created the wood and steel out of which their material gods are carved. Truth and significance are only found in the one true God.

A powerful word

There is one final message to draw out of this passage. What was one of the most striking things about God as he went about his work in Genesis 1? What is the thing that overwhelms you at every turn as you read the passage? Surely it is the fact that God speaks. God is not hidden and inaccessible but known and accessible in his word. He is the speaking, communicating, relating God. And in Genesis 1 we are told how life is to be lived before this God. Life in his world is not a hit and miss affair. Life is shaped by the God who speaks. The message is clear. If we want to know how to live life in this world then we need to firstly be listeners to his word. Being created, formed, shaped, and guided by the word of the living and true God is the core of life in his world.

2

Thinking it through (i)

Perhaps as you were reading Chapter 1, you found that some of your questions weren't even mentioned. Genesis 1 raises huge issues and questions that call out to be addressed. The early part of this book has some chapters called 'Thinking it through', where I hope to address at least some of the questions I find people asking when I preach on these passages. The aim is to give some guidelines as to how we might think about such issues from a biblical perspective.

CREATION AND EVOLUTION

A framework for thinking

Nearly all of us who have read Genesis 1 cannot avoid thinking about the issue of creation and evolution. For some it might be the biggest question arising from this chapter.

This is a very technical topic. Experts in theology, linguistics, geology, science, biology, and a number of other disciplines have spent much time arguing over it. Every one of us who enters the discussion will find that there are elements that we are not equipped to grapple with. For example, I am a theologian and historian, not a biological scientist. I am therefore hampered in my ability to grapple with the scientific technicalities of this argument. Others will feel out of their depth in other areas.

Having said this, my understanding of the debate can be represented by the following diagram.

THINKING ABOUT CREATION AND EVOLUTION

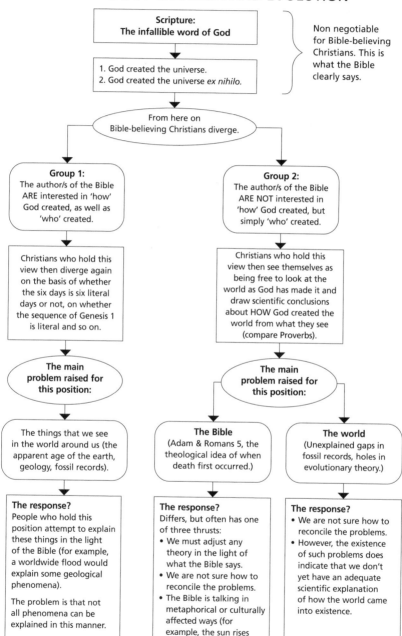

Scripture:
The infallible word of God

1. God created the universe.
2. God created the universe *ex nihilo*.

Non negotiable for Bible-believing Christians. This is what the Bible clearly says.

From here on Bible-believing Christians diverge.

Group 1:
The author/s of the Bible ARE interested in 'how' God created, as well as 'who' created.

Christians who hold this view then diverge again on the basis of whether the six days is six literal days or not, on whether the sequence of Genesis 1 is literal and so on.

The main problem raised for this position:

The things that we see in the world around us (the apparent age of the earth, geology, fossil records).

The response?
People who hold this position attempt to explain these things in the light of the Bible (for example, a worldwide flood would explain some geological phenomena).

The problem is that not all phenomena can be explained in this manner.

Group 2:
The author/s of the Bible ARE NOT interested in 'how' God created, but simply 'who' created.

Christians who hold this view then see themselves as being free to look at the world as God has made it and draw scientific conclusions about HOW God created the world from what they see (compare Proverbs).

The main problem raised for this position:

The Bible
(Adam & Romans 5, the theological idea of when death first occurred.)

The world
(Unexplained gaps in fossil records, holes in evolutionary theory.)

The response?
Differs, but often has one of three thrusts:
• We must adjust any theory in the light of what the Bible says.
• We are not sure how to reconcile the problems.
• The Bible is talking in metaphorical or culturally affected ways (for example, the sun rises and sets).

The response?
• We are not sure how to reconcile the problems.
• However, the existence of such problems does indicate that we don't yet have an adequate scientific explanation of how the world came into existence.

The diagram may seem simplistic in places and undoubtedly it doesn't cover every position held on the debate, but I think it captures the essence of the debate and helps us get some perspective on how we might deal with it.

At the top of the diagram I've noted which elements I believe are non-negotiable for those who believe in the authority of Scripture. Scripture makes clear that God created (Genesis 1), and that he created *ex nihilo* (Latin for 'out of nothing'—Hebrews 11:3). In my experience, it is after this point that Christians who believe in the authority of Scripture diverge in their interpretation of the Bible.

The first group of people (the left-hand side of my diagram) say that the authors of the Bible are significantly interested in 'how' God created as well as 'who' created. However, within this group there is disagreement on a number of issues (for example, whether the six days of Genesis are literal or metaphorical, and whether they are in order or not).

A major problem with a literal understanding of the six days is the way the world *seems* to be. Even the most cursory modern observer will recognise that the world looks a lot older than the age you'd get from calculating the numbers in the Bible (approximately six thousand years). For example, I recently heard of some scientists who had detected light from an explosion that happened billions of years ago. Now, what do we do with such reports? If you believe that the universe is less than 10,000 years old then you can't dodge these findings—you have to explain them. You might explain it by saying there are flaws in the scientific method. Alternatively, you might say that the travelling light was put in place by God after or during the act of creation. No matter what your explanation, an explanation is needed.

Many of the people who hold this position put forward explanations that in turn are based on the Bible. For example, some maintain that the massive pressure exerted by the waters of the worldwide flood of Genesis 7 can explain some of the geological and biological phenomena we observe. However, not all contradictory phenomena can be explained this way (such as the light from the exploding star). In the end, those who hold this position don't have answers to everything. There are still some things that they have to take on faith.

But let's examine the right-hand side of the diagram. The second group says that the Bible is not principally interested in 'how' God created but simply in 'who' created. The implication is that we are therefore free to look around at the world and see what it looks like to us. We can freely arrive at some scientific hypotheses as to how it came to be this way.

The writers of the Bible sometimes take this approach themselves, particularly in the wisdom writings (such as the books of Job, Ecclesiastes, Song of Solomon, Proverbs and some of the Psalms). Such writers observe the world and notice the questions raised by it. Moreover, they notice that the questions raised aren't all answered in God's word, or even that the seem to contradict God's word. They then begin to feel free to draw conclusions from their observations.

However, there are some problems with this position. The first is that the Bible itself seems to treat at least some aspects of Genesis 1–3 as literal. For example, some have noted that although it might be possible to understand Adam in Genesis as a representative human being, Paul in Romans 5 speaks about Adam as an historical human being. If he was an historical human being then apparently there was no death in the world before him. If so, what are we to do with fossil records that presuppose death? Again, there are varieties of responses to such difficulties and many of those who hold such a position do exactly what those from the other side do—turn to Scripture for further help.

Another problem with this second position is that the principal theory humans have used for the last 100 years, the theory of evolution, simply doesn't explain all the facts. For example, the fossil record with its massive jumps in evolution between species doesn't seem to fit well with a theory that relies on gradual change. The point is that evolution does help explain some of the 'how', but it doesn't explain everything. We simply don't yet have an adequate scientific explanation of how the world came into existence and how we as human beings (intelligent and different from the animals) came into being.

I hope you'll see from this cursory overview that both sides of the debate have problems. At some point in the argument each side has to say, 'I take it from here on faith'. Most of us have probably already done this, finding ourselves on one side of the debate or the other, and with differing degrees of conviction as to the certainty of our position.

What really matters?

This is where we get into trouble. Many people are uncertain on this issue while others are very certain. Many Christians, for example, draw the line at a literal six-day creation, essentially claiming that this is the only legitimate Christian position.

As you can see from my diagram, I draw the line at a very different position, a position I believe can be supported from Scripture—that is, that God created the universe and that he did it *ex nihilo*. After this I am not sure that there can be any certainty and so I say, in effect, 'I'm happy to debate it with you, but I simply don't know.' I have no philosophical, theological, or scientific problem with God creating everything in six days. I know from Scripture that God is able to do whatever he likes. However I'm just not sure that God in his Word requires me to take this position. It would be wrong for me to judge another Christian on any standard other than the one God states in his Word.

Let me take a step back and draw a bit more from those wisdom writers I mentioned earlier. They give us a model for approaching this troublesome issue. You see, when they read what they had of the Old Testament, they knew that the Old Testament made clear that 'What a person sows, that shall they reap'. However when they observed the world they saw that things didn't always work out this way—the good were often poor and died young, and the bad often died old and wealthy. So, what did they do? They thought about it, they argued with God about it, and they came up with some tentative conclusions. However, in the long run their general position was that they didn't know the complete answer, but they knew that God knew and that his answer was right (the book of Job is a good example of an extended exploration of this idea).

This is similar to the problem we've been talking about with creation and evolution. We know God did it, but when we look at the world it is often hard to match what we see with what we understand of the Bible. When this is the case we must be wary of being like Job's friends and coming up with simplistic and dogmatic answers. This issue is more complicated than at first it seems. Therefore, before making definitive statements, let's think carefully, knowing that there are problems with everyone's position.

No to evolutionISM!

I do believe that there is one 'no' that needs to be said. In Romans 1:18–25 Paul talks about human nature and the created world. He says that God has revealed himself in the created order but that the universal human reaction is to 'suppress the truth by their wickedness'. He talks about how humans, who know about the real God, 'exchanged the glory of the immortal God for images made to look like mortal man and birds and animals and reptiles'. This picture is one of suppressing truth and replacing it with a fake.

Often I hear evolutionism being used like the idol Paul talks about in Romans 1. That is, evolution becomes a philosophical idea that enables us to avoid having to face up to the real God. One of the reasons Christians react so strongly to evolution is because many in our world have gone overboard with evolutionism, because of the freedom it gives them from what is thought of as the tyranny of God. Underneath it all, our world doesn't want God. Anything that allows humans to get out of having to live with the idea that God made them is welcome. At this point, evolutionism becomes an idol.

THE SABBATH

The second issue we look at in this chapter is that of the Sabbath. For some of us this is not a contentious issue, while for others it is. It is clearly an issue in the Bible and so it is good to think about it biblically. In doing so, God may challenge our present thinking.

The God we see in Genesis 1 is a worker. His work is energetic, joyful, innovative and creative. The results of his work are good. Nevertheless, the purpose or goal of that work is not more work but rest—a seventh day of rest.

The Hebrew word here is *shabat* (from which we get the word 'Sabbath') and it means 'to desist from labour' or 'to pause'. Literally, therefore, the passage says that God ceased from his labour. However, this is problematic given that the rest of the Scriptures indicate that God continued to work— at saving, rescuing, remembering. Jesus makes this clear when he says in John 5:17 that 'My Father is always at his work to this very day...' Because of this, perhaps a better way of thinking about Genesis 1 is that God 'paused', or took a break from his creative work on the seventh day.

This break from work is taken by God and sanctified or set apart. God makes the seventh day different from every other day and makes it part and parcel of the way the cosmic order is structured. Such ordering, like the rest of his creation, is good.

It is very important to note that we are not talking here about sabbath with a capital 'S'. No passage in Genesis does this. There are no stories of Abraham, Isaac, Jacob, or any of the other patriarchs practising Sabbath observance. The institution of the Sabbath doesn't come in Genesis 1 but in Exodus 20 at Mt Sinai when God says, 'Remember the Sabbath day by keeping it holy...' (Exodus 20:8–11; Nehemiah 9:13–14; Ezekiel 20:10–12).

Various passages in the Old Testament explain why God instituted the Sabbath:

- Exodus 20:8–11 (quoting Genesis 2) says that the Sabbath is a day for *ceasing* (pausing) from work (and therefore being refreshed—Exodus 23:12).

- Deuteronomy 5:12–15 says it is a day for *remembering* God's act of rescue/redemption.
- Exodus 31:12–17 says that the Sabbath is a day that functions as a *sign to Israel and God*. (Just as God sanctified the day of rest and sewed it into the nature of the cosmos, so too he sanctified Israel and made it part and parcel of his purpose in the world.)

Notice the impact of these references—this day is a day **for** humans. It is for their good, their benefit.

The idea of rest is developed as we move through the Bible. In the Old Testament the word 'rest' gradually comes to have a larger meaning separate from the idea of the Sabbath.

For example, in Joshua 21:43–45 (compare Joshua 1:13, 15) 'rest' is used to talk about the situation where all the promises of God to Israel are fulfilled (where they have the land and there are no more enemies or wars). This state is reflected in such passages as 1 Kings 4:25 which pictures the idyllic situation where all Jews are so at peace that they can sit down under their vines and fig trees and reflect on what God has done for Israel. The idea of rest here means ceasing from waiting and striving to enter the Promised Land. It is living in peace in the land of God's choice and under the loving rule of God.

Psalm 95 gives us more insight into the idea of rest as it applied to entering the Promised Land. It tells us about the wilderness experience of the people of Israel before they entered the land, reminding us that the people of God were hard hearted (they didn't trust that God knew what he was doing and had their best interests in mind). The end result of their hard heartedness was that the generation that rebelled was not allowed to enter the Promised Land.

In the New Testament Jesus talks about rest (Matthew 11:28–30). He sees people struggling with the weight of living in the world and he calls out to them to rest. The rest that he invites them to is not a one-in-seven-days rest, but the sort of eternal rest that God spoke about in Genesis 2.

Jesus doesn't talk about ceasing from labour (he still wants them to carry his yoke, the cross), but about shifting burdens. The rest he talks about is a rest of substance.

The book of Hebrews addresses the superiority of Jesus when compared with the way of the old covenant, even with the great people of the Old Testament. In Hebrews 4 the writer takes a look at Joshua and the rest that God gave Israel through him, and he compares this with the rest found in Jesus.

In Hebrews 4:4 he says Genesis 2 makes clear that rest existed before the Promised Land. He then reminds us that Psalm 95 was written some time after entry into the Promised Land and yet it still urges people 'Today, if you hear his voice, do not harden your hearts.' He surmises that if God is still urging people to enter God's rest, then God's rest wasn't completed by entering into the Promised Land (Hebrews 4:8–11). In other words, God's rest can be entered today. This rest is the same sort of rest experienced by God—the ceasing from work as God ceased from work (4:10).

The larger context of Hebrews seems to indicate that the works being talked about here involve trying to make yourself pleasing to God, by staying in the Jewish system of keeping and doing laws. This would explain Hebrews 4:3 where the writer says that 'we who have *believed* enter that rest'. Lastly, the writer urges the people to 'make every effort to enter that rest' (4:11).

When you think about it, it's a strange way of speaking, isn't it? *Strive, make every effort*, to enter God's *rest*. The writer is urging these people to go against the tide that says that the way to find peace with God is to keep rules and regulations and traditions. Rather, the way to find rest is to believe in Jesus, to cast all our burdens upon him, to cast off the yoke of the law and take on the yoke of the cross where Jesus met all God's requirements for us.

Let's try to tie all this together.

Point 1: There is a rest we **must** enter—God's rest, the rest of accepting God's work and rejecting our own, the rest of receiving what God has done for us. We enter this rest by believing in Jesus. Notice that the Sabbath is not the important thing—the Sabbath came after Genesis 2. The rest offered in Jesus is eternal security with God, the Genesis 2 and Revelation 22 sort of rest. Sabbath observance in the Old Testament was a foreshadowing of what would be ours in Christ. The Sabbath rest is fulfilled in Christ. The vitally important thing for us is the rest we have in Jesus rather than rest on Saturday or Sunday.

Point 2: God has made the world in a particular way, with six days of work followed by a seventh day of rest. God has sewn into our nature a cycle of life that we ignore to our peril. We are people who need rest—God has made the universe and us this way. Moreover, the nature of this rest is clear. It is the cessation of work, a day free from work, a day of not doing the things that we do every day.

So, we learn from creation by taking a pause in our activity. But we also learn from redemption. As redeemed people we know that true rest is found in dependence upon God, in faith in Christ. For this reason, I take it that we should follow the example of the Jews when we take a day off, and make sure that one of the principal things we do is reflect on God and his salvation. Perhaps this might mean taking advantage of extended times of more relaxed prayer or Bible study or meditating on Scripture.

Point 3: Since it is the principle that is set by Genesis 2 (6 days work + 1 day rest), and not the specifics, I'm not sure that we need to be concerned about being too literal. Rather, I would suggest that the principle be work plus rest in godly proportions, in godly doses, and in regular bursts. Sometimes modern work demands long stretches of work—commensurate breaks should be taken. Sometimes accumulated years of work need special leave (for example, as I write this book I am spending a year out of parish ministry to rest after eighteen years of very active ministry). We should major on the principle rather than depending on law.

However, there is still one thing that needs to be said on the issue. Sabbath observance appears to be the only one of the Ten Commandments not repeated in the New Testament.

It is clearly fulfilled in Christ in a particular way. My conviction is that we are not under the Old Testament law of Sabbath observance.

Having said this, we need to remember Romans 14, which indicates that the early church had problems. Some people kept special days, some didn't. Different Christians did have, do have, and will have different practices with regard to this issue. Some will keep the Sabbath strictly. Some will be rigorous about 1 in 7. Some will say that they don't want to keep any days strictly. Each of these options seems to be acceptable from Scripture.

Nevertheless, not all these options are healthy. Not all are wise. Not all are theologically astute. But all are acceptable. God has given us freedom in this area. We are not under law but grace. Therefore we should act like it and not judge our neighbour as though we were under law. As Paul urges us on this very issue, let us accept each other as Christ has accepted us (Romans 15:7).

BEGINNINGS: Of the Cosmos

Part 2

The story of Creation
Genesis 2:4–6:8

3

Life in the garden

This is the account of the heavens and the earth when they were created.

(Genesis 2:4)

As we noted earlier, the words 'This is the account of...' are crucial in the book of Genesis. The principal part of the phrase consists of a Hebrew word that can be translated as either 'genealogy'/'generations' or 'account'/'story'. This word occurs ten times in Genesis and is used by the author as a major device for structuring his book. Usually the phrase has a person attached, such as in Genesis 6:9, 'This is the account of Noah.' A genealogy or narrative about that person follows after this introduction.

Since it seems likely that the phrase functions the same way here as elsewhere in Genesis, these words form the heading for the next section of the book (although the reference to the heavens and the earth and their creation also binds this story to the previous chapter). In many ways, it appears as though this heading therefore not only looks back, but introduces:

- the section from 2:4–4:26 (i.e. until the next 'this is the account of' heading in 5:1), which could be described as 'the origin of the nations';
- the origin of Israel's ancestors in 2:4–11:26; and
- the whole of the Pentateuch.

The section that follows immediately in 2:4–4:26 falls into three distinct narrative parts (the garden of Eden in 2:5–3:24; the murder of Abel in 4:1–16; and the family of Cain in 4:17–26) and recounts the primeval history of humanity—the accounts of Adam and his sons.

THE GARDEN OF EDEN (2:5–3:24)

Structure
The Garden of Eden account falls into two halves: the creation of the man and his wife (2:5–25) and the temptation and fall (3:1–24). The way these two halves fit together can be seen in the following schema:

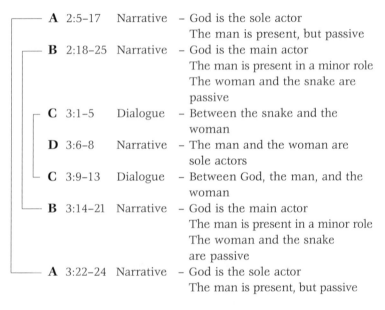

A	2:5–17	Narrative	– God is the sole actor The man is present, but passive
B	2:18–25	Narrative	– God is the main actor The man is present in a minor role The woman and the snake are passive
C	3:1–5	Dialogue	– Between the snake and the woman
D	3:6–8	Narrative	– The man and the woman are sole actors
C	3:9–13	Dialogue	– Between God, the man, and the woman
B	3:14–21	Narrative	– God is the main actor The man is present in a minor role The woman and the snake are passive
A	3:22–24	Narrative	– God is the sole actor The man is present, but passive

The scenes match each other with scene D forming the centrepiece. In this scene the human actors are alone and neither God nor the snake are mentioned. Adam and Eve stand alone before the tree of knowledge and Eve decides to take the snake's advice and ignore God's command. For his part, Adam accepts the fruit offered by his wife in defiance of God's command.

Now we can see how the heading offered in 2:4 fits. These chapters provide an introduction to the rest of Genesis (and the whole Bible!) and a background for it. We will find that the people we hear about throughout Genesis are like the people we find here. Not only that, but the goals God will set for those people will be shaped by the incidents here.

The creation and nature of humanity

The LORD God formed the man from the dust of the ground and breathed into his nostrils the breath of life, and the man became a living being.

(Genesis 2:7)

This verse and the subsequent verses give us a different perspective on humanity from that revealed in Genesis 1. Here, as in Chapter 1, the man is a created being. He is created whole with no division into parts such as body and soul. He is also created frail—he is made of dust and only has life because of God's intervention. Nevertheless, because of this life he is full of potential and promise.

As a created being, Adam finds himself in a number of relationships. First, he is related to God. Adam lives as the creation of God. He receives his form, function (in the 'image' of God—Genesis 1:27), and life (Genesis 2:7) from God. However, although the man is in the image of God, it is clear that there is a huge difference between them in essence. God is utterly independent from man while man is totally dependent upon God. The man's primary relationship is with God, and it is characterised by complete dependence.

Now the LORD God had planted a garden in the east, in Eden; and there he put the man he had formed... The LORD God took the man and put him in the Garden of Eden to work it and take care of it.

(Genesis 2:8,15)

Now the LORD God had formed out of the ground all the beasts of the field and all the birds of the air. He brought them to the man to see what he would name them; and whatever the man called each living creature, that was its name. So the man gave names to all the livestock, the birds of the air and all the beasts of the field.

(Genesis 2:19–20a)

Second, Adam is related to his environment, both animate and inanimate. As far as the inanimate world is concerned, he is *adam* (Hebrew for 'man') and was taken out of *adamah* (Hebrew for 'earth'). He is created out of the earth (2:7), works the earth/soil (3:23), and will, after the events of Chapter 3, eventually return to the earth at his death (3:19).

As far as the animate world is concerned, he is like the animals in that he is created out of the earth (2:19). He is unlike the animals in that they do not receive the divine breath of life. They are offered to Adam as a help, and in this way are comparable to other human beings. In another way they are very different from Adam, as is demonstrated by his naming them and ordering them (2:19–20).

> **But for Adam no suitable helper was found. So the
> LORD God caused the man to fall into a deep sleep;
> and while he was sleeping, he took one of the man's
> ribs and closed up the place with flesh. Then the
> LORD God made a woman from the rib he had taken
> out of the man, and he brought her to the man.**
>
> *(Genesis 2:20b–22)*

Third, Adam is related to other humans. Against the background of being told that things are 'good' in Genesis 1, we are told in verse 18 that there is something that is 'not good', that is, the man's aloneness. God recognises that not even the intimacy of relationship with him is sufficient for the man. Humans need relationship with other humans and so God in his generosity works to end the man's aloneness, reaching a climax in the creation of the woman.

Her unique closeness to him is demonstrated by the fact that she is not created from the earth, but from the 'side' of the man himself ('rib' is probably better translated 'side' here as in the rest of the Old Testament). She is 'a suitable helper', whom he describes as 'bone of my bones and flesh of my flesh'. She is called *ishah* ('woman'), for she was taken out of *ish* ('man').

Having been made out of the man's side, the woman is declared in her essential nature to be the equal of man even though she is created as his helper and complement (compare Genesis 1:27–28). The origin of the woman also explains the Old Testament concept that man and woman in marriage are bound together as though they were blood relatives or kin. In fact, the marriage bond is even stronger than that between parent and child since 'for this reason a man will leave his father and mother and be united to his wife' (Genesis 2:24).

The man and his wife were both naked, and they felt no shame.

(Genesis 2:25)

These three relationships—with God, with the environment in which God placed them, and with other humans—characterise human existence. The essence of human existence is relationships. Moreover, this last statement from Genesis 2:25 tells us that these relationships are good and unclouded by sin. There is no need to cover up here, because there is nothing to cover, nothing of which to be ashamed.

The temptation

Now the serpent was more crafty than any of the wild animals the LORD God had made. He said to the woman, 'Did God really say, "You must not eat from any tree in the garden"?'

(Genesis 3:1)

As we move from Chapter 2 to Chapter 3 there is a marked change in mood. Harmony gives way to discord and mutual trust to suspicion. This contrast is emphasised in two particular areas...

- In Genesis 2 there is a God-established order that follows the pattern of: God → Man → Woman → the environment (animate and inanimate).
- In Genesis 2:15–17 the man and woman were given...
  A vocation: to care for and till the garden (2:15).
  A permit: to do virtually anything and everything (although the permission here concentrates on food—2:16).

> **A prohibition:** not to eat of the tree of the knowledge of good and evil (2:17).

What happens in Chapter 3 throws all this into chaos. First, God's established order is overturned. An animal (in the person of the serpent) seizes the initiative. The woman is deceived and assumes a position of prominence that is not hers. The man is enticed. God is placed in a situation where he must perform his strange work of judgment. The punishments handed out by him strike the serpent, the woman, and the man at the root of their roles within creation. It is clear that sin is not simply a moral lapse—it strikes at the very core of God's created order for his world.

Second, God's instructions for humans are overturned. The serpent talks about the prohibition given by God as though it were not a command but an option. The result is that the woman takes and eats against God's instruction (3:6,17). The permit is also perverted—the humans decide that they can do whatever they like with no exceptions. Last, the vocation of 2:15 is neglected. There is now no mention of tending and feeding and caring for the environment. Human concentration is now on self, and on what they presume to be freedom.

The effect of all of this is that God's order is overturned by his creation. The created world strikes out at all levels, and attempts to supplant God and his role in his world.

Understanding the tree

What happens in the garden revolves around 'the tree of the knowledge of good and evil' (2:17; 3:5,22). Although the phrase is enigmatic, we can get some help in understanding it from the rest of the Old Testament. The concept of differentiating between good and evil is found at a number of places in the Old Testament (such as Deuteronomy 1:39; 2 Samuel 14:17; 19:35; 1 Kings 3:9).

- Deuteronomy 1:39 talks about children who are under a particular age, the age when they 'know good from bad'. The implication is that 'knowledge of good and evil' has to do with making moral judgments.
- 2 Samuel 14 is particularly helpful. In this passage David is asked to perform his kingly duty of pronouncing judgment on a particular case where there appears to be compassionate grounds for waiving the requirements of law. David is asked to give his ruling ('word'—14:17). The woman says that David is able to do this since he is like an angel of God in 'discerning good and evil'. The implication is that David is able to give such a word because he is acting for God. In other words, he is the one who can determine what is good and what is evil in this situation.
- 2 Samuel 19:35 is not unlike Deuteronomy 1:39, although the ability to 'tell the difference between what is good and what is not' has to do with age rather than youth, with physical sight and hearing rather than moral perception. It is the ability (or lack of ability) to sense good and bad food, to hear male and female singers, and so on.
- 1 Kings 3:9 is similar to 2 Samuel 14. Here, the ability to 'distinguish between right and wrong' has to do with governing or making decisions on behalf of God and his people.

The concepts found in 2 Samuel 14 and 1 Kings 3 are particularly helpful in our understanding of Genesis 2 and 3. The opening chapters of the Bible make clear that God is the King over all the world. He made the world and humans to live in it, and he is the one who determines what is good and what is evil. By eating the fruit, Adam and Eve are saying that they don't want God to be in that role. Rather, they want it for themselves. In taking the fruit, the man and the woman are grasping at being God. This is why God says humans have 'become like one of us, knowing good and evil' (3:22)—they put themselves in the role of God, becoming the determiners of their own good and evil.

What happens with the tree in the garden shows us the essence of sin—to discard the rule of God and choose to determine by yourself what is good and what is bad for you. The presence of the tree, and the subsequent eating of it by the man and his wife, is therefore a declaration that there is the possibility that humans may defy the divine word. They are free moral agents. However, their freedom simply magnifies their responsibility.

Verdict and sentence

Then the man and his wife heard the sound of the LORD God as he was walking in the garden in the cool of the day, and they hid from the LORD God among the trees of the garden. But the LORD God called to the man, 'Where are you?'

He answered, 'I heard you in the garden, and I was afraid because I was naked; so I hid.'

And he said, 'Who told you that you were naked? Have you eaten from the tree that I commanded you not to eat from?'

(Genesis 3:8–11)

The sense of disharmony reaches its pinnacle in this passage. There are a number of things that stand out in the conversation between God and the couple.

First, they are afraid of God and of facing him. Sin has tainted their view of God. No longer is he the wise ruler who always has their best interests in mind and who is to be trusted. Instead, he is now viewed as a tyrant to be feared.

Second, notice the use of the word 'I'. What happened with the tree of the knowledge of good and evil was all about self and self-determination. This is highlighted in this passage where the ringing refrain is 'I'—'I heard ... I was afraid ... I was naked ... I hid ... I ate ... I ate' (3:10–13). Any preoccupation with God and his purposes has been discarded. Now the preoccupation is with self.

As for punishment, the three parties are dealt with individually. The snake is cursed and consigned to life on its belly in the dust. Hostility between it and humans will be constant and ongoing. Anyone who sees a snake will at once stamp on its head and whenever a snake sees a person, it will attempt to strike and set its poisonous fangs into the person's heels. Not only will the snake (an animate part of creation) suffer a curse, so also will the inanimate (the ground—verse 17). This second curse comes because of the actions of Adam.

For the woman, in her role as wife and mother, she will experience pain and suffering. In childbirth, there will be pain. In her relationship with her husband there will be conflict. Though she is created to be the man's companion, she will find herself continually at odds with two opposing forces. On the one hand she will long for independence (one meaning for the phrase 'your desire will be for your husband' is that she will desire his position of authority). On the other hand, she will find herself inextricably drawn to a husband (the other side of 'your desire will be for your husband'). As a result, she will often find herself in bondage to a harsh and exploitative rule (because the man is now sinful and prone to abuse his position of authority to his own advantage). The end result is that those who were created to be one flesh will now find themselves tearing each other apart.

Lastly, the man must labour as a farmer, producing food by the sweat of his brow, all the while realising that in the end he will return to the dust. Physical death is his eventual destiny. The potential that was there in 2:7, when the dust had the breath of life blown into it, is blown away. Dust will beget dust. In Genesis this banishment from life takes concrete form in the banishment of humankind from the garden (3:23–24) and thus from the tree of life.

These verses show us the reality of the world under sin. Because of sin, the woman who was made for the worship of God will so often turn to the worship of a man. Because of sin, the man who was made for the worship of God will so often turn to the worship of work. Rather than finding fulfilment in God they will search for it among the created order.

Behind these chapters stands the Old Testament understanding of God who:

- is a great King (Psalm 95:3–5);
- rules with justice (Psalm 96:10–13) and grace (Psalm 145:8–9); and
- is the source of all other rule (Genesis 1:27; Daniel 4:34–35).

We could summarise what has happened in Genesis 2–3 in two diagrams (see following pages). In the 'before' picture, God richly blesses his creation and makes it good. The world is arid but God the gracious and loving king in his goodness makes it into an exquisite garden, forming man, animals, and woman. In the 'after' picture, we see what happens when God's design is broken by human independence and God the just king must act in judgment (albeit tempered with mercy).

DEATH

In our calmer or more distracted moments it may be easy and even attractive to think that death is merely the common destiny of all humans. It is our lot, the natural thing. Such thinking is not so attractive in the face of the death of a loved one. Then we get a glimpse of the truth of the matter as Genesis paints it—that death is an abomination, a horrible absurdity, and the very antithesis of the way things were meant to be.

It is clear from Genesis 1 that although death may have been natural in the world as a whole, it was not natural for Adam and Eve in the garden. Their natural state was the way God planned things for them—life with God, life with each other, life in God's company in God's world. The natural state for humans was a world where relationships and friendship could grow and foster. They also had access to the tree of life that would perpetuate such a state.

Humans broke this natural state through their bid for independence, and God responded in judgment. His punishment for their sin was to add a further unnatural element—death. The wages of sin is death (Romans 6:23).

Those who have lost a loved one know death's sting. They know the pain of turning to talk to someone, only to remember that the person is no longer there.

BEFORE

God's intention for his created beings is that:
- He is the one who determines good and evil, right and wrong.
- Humans exercise their God-appointed role of ruling under God's rule (1:27–28).
- Humans live in their God-ordained order:
  God → Man → Woman → the environment (animate and inanimate).
- Humans live in right relationship with all elements of their world...

With...	Characterised by...	Expressed in...
God	Dependence	Obedience and trust
The other sex	Complementarity and unity	Marriage (2:21–25) and joint rule (1:27–28)
The environment	Rule	Animate—naming of animals (2:19–20) Inanimate—tilling the earth (2:15)

Where humans focus on God and his kingly rule there is:
- Harmony
  - with God (they are in the garden with him)
  - with each other (they have no shame with each other)
  - with the environment (both animate and inanimate)
- Blessing and prosperity
- Life (access to the tree of life)
- Freedom (to eat anything, do anything, even choose to disobey)

AFTER

Because God's intention for his created beings is broken by human independence:

- They seek to be their own determiners of good and evil, right and wrong.
- They seek to rule outside of God's overarching rule.
- God's ordained order is reversed:
  the environment (the snake) → Woman → Man. The end result is that God's rule is expressed in punishment rather than benefaction.
- Human relationships are out of plumb at every level...

With...	Characterised by...	Expressed in...
God	Independence	Disobedience and doubt Worship of man and work
The other sex	Disunity	'Desire for husband but he will rule over you'
The environment	Breaking out from rule	Animate—antagonism with snake Inanimate—thistles and painful toil

Where humans focus on themselves and ignore God's kingly rule there is:

- Disharmony
  - with God (they hide from God and are banished from the garden)
  - with each other (blaming each other, wanting the position of the other, cruel rule)
  - with the environment (both animate and inanimate)
- Dysfunctional relationships
- Death (spiritual and eventually physical)
- Slavery (they can't even choose to do good, every inclination is now toward evil—Genesis 6:5)

The end result is anxiety, shame, fear, bondage, alienation, and judgment.

Death is awful because it breaches what we hold most valuable. It terminates relationships. The known and loved person can no longer be communicated with, or be shown love.

Physical death acts therefore as a potent symbol of our spiritual state. We were created for life—relationship with God. We rejected life and chose to break relationship with God. We are therefore dead to God. Physical death symbolises that spiritual state. What death does to our relationship with all that we value in the physical world, is what already exists between us and God spiritually because of sin. We are dead to God (compare Ephesians 2:1–10).

Such thinking also helps us understand the rather enigmatic phrase 'the second death' that appears in the book of Revelation (2:11; 20:6,14; 21:8). At the moment all humans face a first, physical, death because of Adam's sin and their own. Nevertheless, there is a further death that awaits some. On the last day those who belong to God in Christ will finally and fully receive the life that they already have in prospect, because of the work of Christ and their relationship with him. Those who have rejected Christ and therefore chosen to be dead to him will be banished from God's presence forever, receiving in death what they had wished for in life. The symbol of physical death will have its final and full reality.

From this we can see why those who do not belong to Christ have every reason to live in fear of death (Hebrews 2:15)—it is only a small token of a terrifying spiritual reality. On the other hand it is also clear why those who have received salvation by grace through faith might regard death as mere sleep (compare 1 Thessalonians 4:13)—its sting has been taken away in Christ. They have come to know the fountain of life (Psalm 36:7–9 compare John 4:10) and their relationship with him can never be taken away. Whether they are awake or asleep, they are with the Lord (1 Thessalonians 5:10).

THE NATURE OF GOD

Most of what has happened as we have looked at these chapters has focused on humans. Nevertheless, there is much to say about God here also. First and foremost the picture of God is one of his primary concern for humans and their wellbeing. Before sin, this is seen in what God provides. After all, it is the human for whom the world, the animals, and other people are created ('It is not good for the man to be alone'). Concern for humankind and their welfare stands at the centre of God's activity.

Similar concern for humankind and their wellbeing is apparent after they sin. The man and the woman are threatened with death on the day that they eat (2:17), but their lives are not taken away on the day that they sin. In fact, the punishment of the woman indicates there will be a future, when it refers to childbirth. God also clothes them and, in banishing them from the garden, protects them from eating the fruit that will preserve forever their fallen state.

As we will see later, this restraint from anger, and the desire to bless, continues throughout Genesis. God is the God who richly blesses, and he has human wellbeing at the forefront of his goals for his world. He is also a God who restrains his anger when humans refuse to believe him. He returns to bless and recreate even when he has been rejected and his rule flouted.

4

Thinking it through (ii)

Genesis 2 gives us an opportunity to take a look at some vexing practical and theological issues, to do with men and women, marriage, and work. These issues are at the core of our existence. The fact that God addresses them in the creation account indicates that they are also very important to God.

In any section of Scripture it is vital that we do not simply seek to have our own questions answered. We must also come seeking to discover what is important for God, why it is important for him, and how he thinks we should be thinking about such issues.

GOD, MEN, AND WOMEN

When the Lord God made the earth and the heavens —and no shrub of the field had yet appeared on the earth and no plant of the field had yet sprung up, for the Lord God had not sent rain on the earth and there was no man to work the ground, but streams came up from the earth and watered the whole surface of the ground—the Lord God formed the man from the dust of the ground and breathed into his nostrils the breath of life, and the man became a living being.

Now the Lord God had planted a garden in the east, in Eden; and there he put the man he had formed ...

The Lord God took the man and put him in the Garden of Eden to work it and take care of it. And the LORD God commanded the man, 'You are free to eat from any tree in the garden; but you must not eat from the tree of the knowledge of good and evil, for when you eat of it you will surely die.'

The LORD God said, 'It is not good for the man to be alone. I will make a helper suitable for him.'

(Genesis 2:4b–8, 15–18)

Male and female (1:27)

Even though the issue of men and women arises primarily from Genesis 2, Genesis 1:27 gives us a correct perspective. Many ancient languages, Hebrew included, have a word that is used to talk about humanity as a whole ('man' or 'mankind'). This word is different from the term that is used for the male sex. This broader term is the one that is used in Genesis 1:27, and so what is being said in this verse is that God created humanity split into men and women. Humanity is male **and** female. Together they are in the image of God, and together they are given their function to rule over the world under God's rule.

Although not stated explicitly, the implication of verse 27 and the following verses is one of equality. Both men and women are equally created by God, are equally human (both male and female are included in the term 'man'), both image the divine as much as the other, and are addressed without distinction by the command in verse 28. We can see from this that men and women are in essence equal. They are both part of 'man', and there is no distinction between them in terms of their standing or status before God.

At the same time, Genesis 1:27 also indicates a distinction between men and women. The reference to both of them implies that their roles in life are not identical and that being in the image of God is as much about them in distinction from each other as it is about their equality before God.

Genesis 2

Genesis 2 picks up this latter point and gives it further explanation. The implication is that although men and women are in essence equal, there is a particular ordering of their existence. This is seen in the following references.

In Genesis 2:7 and 22 we are told that the man is created first and that from him the woman is created. The rest of Genesis helps us with this in that it clearly indicates that being born first brings with it some privileges, rights, and duties (e.g. the stories of Jacob and Esau and the sons of Jacob). Paul, who was much closer to Genesis and a culture where being firstborn was important, seems to consider that being formed first does mean something in terms of order (compare 1 Corinthians 11:8–9 and 1 Timothy 2:13). However, the rest of Genesis also clearly indicates that we need to be careful in terms of reading this in such a way as to cut across issues of equality of status before God; after all, the narrative often tells us that the line of blessing flowed other than through the firstborn.

There has been extensive debate around the concept of naming in Genesis 2 and its implications. My reading of the text is that the narrative context implies that the same activity is going on when the man names the woman in verse 23 as that which has gone on in naming the animals in verse 19 and that this is the same activity that is engaged in by God in Genesis 1. If this is the case, then the naming does imply some sort of leadership or authority in relation to the woman. However, these same observations need to be read in the context of the strong notes of equality in the same context. For example, the woman is seen to 'correspond' to the man; she is formed from the 'side' of the man; and she is 'bone of his bone, flesh of his flesh', that is she is of the same substance as him. In fact, it may be that in using a name derived from his own name, the man is acknowledging her as his equal.

Finally, as we saw in our 'Before' and 'After' summary above, the way in which the narrative functions as a whole does seem to require an ordering in the roles of the man and the woman, even before sin occurs.

Avoiding mistakes

When we look at these two different perspectives we have a framework for our thinking on the issue. We can see that it is important to avoid two mistakes. The first mistake would be to stress Genesis 1 over Genesis 2 and say: 'Men and women are equal before God **therefore** let's have nothing to do with distinctions between them.' The second mistake would be to stress Genesis 2 over Genesis 1 and say, 'We are different **therefore** there is no essential equality between us.'

Unfortunately, in the modern western world, role determines value (we will touch on this again when we consider the issue of work later on). If someone has an important role, it is seen by us to imply an essential superiority (for example, the boss is **in essence** better than the worker). The God who speaks in the Bible does not think or speak this way. He is happy to have people who are in essence equal exercising different roles and even different authorities. A great part of the debate among Christians about the role of men and women in the church and the family hinges on a misunderstanding of this concept, and a willingness to accept the world's way of thinking and speaking rather than God's way. Although it may be difficult, we must learn to think of the issue the way God does.

We saw earlier that God's ordained order of authority is God → man → woman → created order and that the nature of sin is to break or reverse this order (serpent → woman → man → God). Though our constant desire will be to break this order, we must resist it. God, who created the world, knows how best to live in it, and he says that this is the order he desires.

The effects of sin

Linked to this is Genesis 3:16b which appears to give a description of how relations will function between the sinful sexes in marriage—men will 'rule' and women will 'desire'. There is some debate as to what it means for the woman to desire her husband, and it is probably best to hear echoes of two thoughts here—the woman will desire her husband and also the woman will desire her husband's position of authority. If the latter meaning is included, then the Bible is here hinting at the effect of sin on God's design for humans to rule his world together. On the one hand, sin causes the man who is in the stronger position of authority to abuse his position by 'ruling' or dominating rather than serving. On the other hand, the sin causes the woman who is in the weaker position of authority to abuse her position by seeking to get into authority. Throughout the Bible these are the dangers that people in authority and submission are urged to avoid. Such breaches of order destroy God's structure for his world and undermine its proper functioning.

There is more in these verses about the effect of sin on men and women. Humans were created to relate to God and serve him. In Genesis 3:14–19, we see that the focus of the man becomes work, and the focus of the woman becomes the man and family. It appears that under sin these are the things they will use to form their identity and give them meaning, rather than God. And as we know from experience and human history, these foci can so easily become idolatrous and full of pain. Many a man has and will die, both physically and spiritually, worshipping work. Many a woman has and will die, both physically and spiritually, worshipping a man and family.

Despite this grim portrayal of the effects of sin, there is positive news for men and women. Verse 15 describes how men and women, in cooperation, will together bring about the defeat of the serpent. At some point in the future, a human offspring will cause the serpent's downfall as his head is crushed.

The impact of the person and work of Jesus

Philippians 2:5–11 tells us of a human who did what Adam didn't do (or who didn't do what Adam did). Here is Jesus, a human who doesn't reach out at being God (even though he is God) but who lives in submission to God. Jesus is therefore a model for all who find themselves in a position of submission. It is not demeaning and nor should it be demoralising. A position of submission is to be gratefully received from God, and to be lived by hearing God's word and doing it.

In Mark 10:35–45 Jesus also gives us a model for all who find themselves in a position of authority. His model of rule is very different from the natural human one that is foremost in the mind of the sinful disciples, who want to lord it over others. The sort of rule that humans should exercise is again lived by hearing God's word and doing it. In this case, it means being willing to become a servant of those over whom you exercise authority, and all for their good. Real authority is about service, not domination.

The impact of the person of Jesus is therefore profound. In his authority and his submission he gives men and women a model of how they are to act in their particular roles. The man must not seek to dominate his wife, but love her by being the servant of her best interests. The woman must not desire to leave the position of submission, but welcome and accept her husband's willing and self-sacrificial service of her best interests.

However, this is not our natural disposition after the fall. This is where the work of Christ on the Cross comes in. Genesis 3:16 is not God's wish for our good—he does not want the situation where men dominate and women desire (compare Ephesians 5:21–33). Because of the work of Christ, we have now been forgiven, and are able to understand God's purpose for us. The Cross has changed our attitude to life. We want to live life as God intended in Genesis 2, rather than as Genesis 3 people.

However, the Cross has not changed the situation of Genesis 1 and 2. Men and women in the New Testament are still viewed as equal in essence before God (compare Galatians 3:28–29) and they are still different in terms of their role (compare 1 Corinthians 11:3–16). The Cross does not therefore change our status or God-appointed role as men and women, but should change our practice of living.

A noticeable absence

Genesis 1–3 contains a glaring omission in its description of the roles of men and women. While it talks about our roles in terms of authority and submission, it does not appear to talk about them the way we often do. For example, there is no command that men must be the providers and women must stay at home or in the kitchen.

As we read on in the Bible it appears that these specifics vary depending on the culture. For example, the godly woman of Proverbs 31:10–31 is hardly the stay-at-home-minding-the-kids sort of woman. It appears as though she is the chief provider of the family and that her husband performs a non-paid legal or religious role within the larger community. On the other side of things, when God talks about his role as father to Israel in Hosea 11, it is not the fatherhood of the absent worker, but of one who is there to teach the child to walk and to feed the child. The language used of his role in relation to his child is the language of nurture. Here are two situations that give the opposite of what is often taught—a woman who provides and a father who nurtures.

The point is that we are in great danger of taking our own cultural stereotypes and reading them back into the Bible. There is no doubt that the Bible tells us a lot about our roles within marriage and the family. We just need to ensure that we don't make God say more than he does!

MARRIAGE

But for Adam no suitable helper was found. So the LORD God caused the man to fall into a deep sleep; and while he was sleeping, he took one of the man's ribs and closed up the place with flesh. Then the LORD God made a woman from the rib he had taken out of the man, and he brought her to the man.

The man said, 'This is now bone of my bones and flesh of my flesh; she shall be called 'woman', for she was taken out of man.'

For this reason a man will leave his father and mother and be united to his wife, and they will become one flesh.

The man and his wife were both naked, and they felt no shame.

(Genesis 2:20b–25)

Genesis 1–3 talks much of men and women in relationship, and while we can distil certain things that apply in general to the relationship between men and women and God, the institution of marriage sits under the surface of much of that discussion. This becomes explicit in Genesis 2:24 when we are told of a man leaving his father and mother and becoming united to his wife, thus becoming one flesh. God created marriage, and like everything created by God it has our good in mind.

An exclusive relationship between one woman and one man

This passage, which sets out God's ideal for marriage, clearly says that it is an exclusive relationship between one man and one woman. There are no multitudes of men or women, but simply one man, one woman, one unit. Although polygamy was practised in the Bible, it appears that monogamy is God's ideal (compare the rest of Genesis where most polygamous situations are torn with strife).

Publicly enacted and recognised

In marriage a man leaves his mother and father and cleaves to his wife. In effect, the couple publicly says to the world, 'This is where we are going to be from now on. We are now a new family unit.'

Such an association can't be done surreptitiously. It is a public event. Hence, nearly every culture in the world has a way of publicly recognising marriage. In most western cultures at this time, we do it through signing a piece of paper in a public place before witnesses. This piece of paper then becomes public property—a public declaration that a man and a woman are now husband and wife. Because we Christians know that God wants marriage to be public, we take advantage of these commonly accepted cultural means of recognising marriage. There is nothing God-ordained about these means—they are just the way that our particular society does it. Other societies do the same thing in other ways.

Permanent in nature

This passage appears to indicate that kinship is established through marriage. The man and the woman are joined and become 'one flesh'. She is 'bone of my bones and flesh of my flesh'. Elsewhere in the Old Testament 'my bone and my flesh' is used to mean something like 'my blood relation, my kinsman' (for example, Genesis 29:14–15; Judges 9:2; 2 Samuel 5:1; 19:12–13). The implication, therefore, is that marriage creates the same sort of kinship as exists between brothers. A brother is a brother forever. Two brothers may fall out with each other, they may never even have met each other, nevertheless, they are brothers or kin. Nothing can change this. It is permanent. Such thinking would explain why Jesus speaks so strongly against divorce and remarriage in the New Testament (compare Matthew 5:31–32; 19:1–12).

Designed for mutual support and encouragement

People get married for all sorts of reasons. However, the Bible is clear that God's primary motivation for marriage is companionship. God saw that it was not good for the man to be alone. There are many other great benefits of marriage, but at its very core marriage is about relationships and therefore about companionship. There may be times when you come home to a husband or wife for other reasons, but the guts of marriage is about coming home to talk over coffee, to share a meal, to belong to someone else, to be not-alone. God knows about the joys of such belonging. After all, he is the God who is Father, Son, and Holy Spirit. He is relational himself, and he has made us in his image.

Consummated and characterised by sexual union

The term 'one flesh', along with being 'united' implies physical and sexual union. This sexual union is really the enactment, or 'consummation' of all the other things that marriage is. In sexual union the couple is saying, 'We are joined together in a special sort of way. We are joined to each other in a way that we are not joined to anyone else.'

The final note in Chapter 2 is important. Here in the garden where everything was the way God wanted things to be, nakedness was not to be feared or to be ashamed of. God made sex and he made it good. This attitude is reflected in the rest of the Bible. In fact, God in his sovereignty has left one book in the canon of Scripture—the Song of Solomon— with apparently little other purpose than to rejoice in the relationship between a man and a woman, and particularly to rejoice in their sexual relationship. Where two people love each other and are bound to each other in the sort of relationship envisaged in Genesis 2, then there should be great fun and great sex. Sexual intercourse in marriage is the God-ordained expression of the natural and good instincts that he has given us.

The gift of children

Genesis is clear that part of the purpose of marriage is procreation. In chapter 1, men and women together are to 'be fruitful and increase in number' and it may very well be that this is a significant part of what it means for the woman to be the man's 'helper' (2:20). The clear sense is therefore, that the union of a man and woman in marriage will result in the blessing of children.

Nevertheless, what is the 'usual' is not always the way things are in a fallen world. Hence much of Genesis is caught up with the great difficulty of infertility and the ways and means used by various people to deal with it.

And as with all matters of human suffering where there is an apparent conflict between what should be and what is encountered in reality, there are no solid answers given on this issue. However, as we shall see, God is clear that even when such great difficulties are encountered, there are appropriate and inappropriate ways to think and act.

WORK

Work and rest: God-like in principle

We have already touched on the topic of rest. Genesis 1 and 2 also talk about work. The God we meet in Genesis 1 is a worker. Joyously, energetically, and exuberantly he works as a creative artist, cosmic gardener, and divine craftsman. Three times in Genesis 2:2–3 we are told that what he had been doing was 'work'.

God is one who works and rests. Work and rest are therefore God-like in principle. It is not strange that when God creates humans in his image they too are made to work and rest. The work they are to do is spelled out in two or three places. They are to rule over the world, filling it and subduing it (Genesis 1:26–28). The man is to work the garden and take care of it (2:15). The fall does not change these mandates. It simply makes them tainted, painful and frustrating (bearing children in pain, working the field with sweat, conflicts over rule). Later in the Bible, a one in seven days rest is also commanded (compare Exodus 20:8–11).

The point is that we have it in our nature to work and rest, and these are meaningful acts of service and worship in themselves. To work and rest is good and God-like.

Work and rest: under the curse

Unfortunately, our experience of work and rest is far from God's ideal, because we live in a sinful, selfish world. Under sin, human beings become dominated by work rather than by God, with the result that their position in the world becomes determined by what they 'do' rather than by who they are in relation to God. Work becomes an end in itself. Rest becomes idleness and laziness, and is filled with self-gratification rather than reflection on God's nature and work in creation and redemption. Work and leisure grow out of proportion, and begin to dominate and harm genuine life.

Rescuing work

We have already explored the issue of how we should view rest as Christians. As with the issue of rest, the coming of Christ reorients our perspective on work.

The first thing to note from the New Testament is that the word 'work' is used of God's work of saving the world from the consequences of Genesis 3. We are told that God is at work and that this work, the work of his Son, and the work of his people is to make sure that Jesus is known and worshipped (John 4:34,36; 17:4; Acts 15:38; 1 Corinthians 15:58; Philippians 2:30). In some senses then, it is right to say that the Christian's main work is to do the work of God, which is to tell people about Jesus. In the Bible this is the only work for which it is worth working until you drop (compare 1 Corinthians 15:10).

However, this is not the only work that is talked about in the New Testament. In the New Testament, ordinary work is also important (compare 1 Thessalonians 4:11; 2 Thessalonians 3:6–15) and our attitude to it has been totally transformed by what Christ has done. Life is now filled with meaning, and therefore even work is an act of worship. As Christian workers build God's church, they do so knowing that God is watching, and that their work will be tested to see of what stuff it is made (1 Corinthians 3:5–15). As slaves serve their masters they do so with all their heart, knowing that they too are working for the Lord, not for humans (Colossians 3:22–25). Masters treat their slaves fairly and rightly, knowing that they too have a Master in heaven (Colossians 4:1). In fact, whatever work Christians find themselves in, they do it all in the name of the Lord Jesus, giving thanks to God the Father through him (Colossians 3:17).

The Christian approach to work is therefore quite radical. Because work is an act of worship or service of God, it is not filled with shoddy workmanship, or even with good quality work produced half-heartedly. The Christian does not engage in endless time wasting, dishonesty, or thievery. Christians serve employers honestly and well. This goes for any and every work they do, either paid or unpaid. Christians serve Christ in their work.

This balanced attitude to work was another discovery from Scripture that informed much thinking during the sixteenth century Reformation. There had been a tendency in pre-Reformation thought to think that only the 'spiritual' tasks were a 'vocation' or 'calling' from God. Fuelled by such passages as Genesis 1:28, Ephesians 6:5–9, and Colossians 3:17, the reformers concluded that not only was work to be done as if it were for Christ, but also in the consciousness that work in itself is pleasing to God. It fulfils our creation mandate to subdue the world for the 'service' of humanity. In such a view, God actually cares about work. Such thinking led to the view that any work could be a 'vocation'—a calling from God. The humblest job was lifted to a new level because it was God-given. God cared about it.

However, it must be said that Christians know that any work is only part of their service of Christ. Work can never be the whole of life. Jesus is Lord, and our 'vocation' in its fullest sense is to serve him in all dimensions of life. Work or its benefits must never dominate and become more important than the Lordship of Christ over all of life. To allow them to dominate is to engage in idolatry.

Perhaps a fitting conclusion to our thought on work and leisure would be to take a look at Luke 10:38–42. In this story Jesus visits two sisters, Martha and Mary. Martha is busy about the household making preparations for meals and the like. She is busy with her work. Mary is seated at the Lord's feet, listening to all that he says. Martha becomes upset and asks Jesus to instruct Mary to help her with her work. Jesus replies, 'Martha, Martha, you are worried and upset about many things, but only one thing is needed. Mary has chosen what is better, and it will not be taken away from her.'

The goal of creation is not work, but rest (the rest of reflecting on God, his word, and his works). Jesus tells us here that what really matters is hearing and reflecting upon God's word and God's works. This is the good part. Unfortunately for many of us in the western world, we have forgotten this better part, neglecting it for vain idols. It is time that we found time to sit at our Lord's feet to listen and reflect.

5

In exile with the first family

THE NATURE OF SIN

Since the events of the previous two chapters are so crucial, it is helpful to summarise what they taught about the nature of sin. First, it is evident that the sudden appearance of sin cannot be traced back to God himself. The picture in Genesis 2–3 is clear—evil is a product of human behaviour, and the human predicament is the effect of human disobedience.

Second, although it is possible to view sin as the breaking of a rule, this is not the core of what sin is. Sin is essentially disregard for God, who always had human interest at heart and who had showered humankind with blessing.

Third, sin amounts to a bid for independence, and as such is against our created nature. We were not created to live autonomously but in dependence and trust. To strike out for independence against our nature is to reap anxiety, shame, fear, bondage, alienation, and judgment. It is to cut ourselves loose from life itself, which can only be found in trusting our Creator (compare Proverbs 9:10—'the beginning of wisdom is fear of the LORD').

Fourth, there is a tendency for the sinner to conceal and disguise sin.

Fifth, sin distorts the core of human existence—relationships. Humans were created for life with others. With sin comes the tendency to blame the very same people we were created to relate to, and a subsequent fracturing of those relationships.

Sixth, as we shall see in the stories that follow, sin is not committed in a vacuum. It grows uncannily and rapidly, spreading like a drop of oil on water. Genesis 2 and 3 therefore tell the story not of two individuals so much as the first people among many.

Lastly, the consequences of sin are disastrous. They are physical (toil, pain, death), relational (alienation, anxiety, fractured relationships), and spiritual (alienation from God). With one small act humans have put themselves into deep trouble from which they cannot escape.

CAIN AND ABEL (4:1–16)

Adam lay with his wife Eve, and she became pregnant and gave birth to Cain. She said, 'With the help of the LORD I have brought forth a man.' Later she gave birth to his brother Abel.

Now Abel kept flocks and Cain worked the soil. In the course of time Cain brought some of the fruits of the soil as an offering to the LORD. But Abel brought fat portions from some of the firstborn of his flock. The LORD looked with favour on Abel and his offering, but on Cain and his offering he did not look with favour. So Cain was very angry, and his face was downcast.

(Genesis 4:1–5)

Humans were created for relationships—with God and each other and with the environment in which God placed them. Where the story of Chapters 2 and 3 concentrated on relationship with God, this one focuses on our relationship with each other.

In the first few sentences everything seems fine—Adam and Eve, with God's help, begin to fulfil part of their creation mandate to fill the earth (1:27–28). Eve lives up to her name (3:20) and the two sons exercise their God-ordained role of dominion over the animals and the earth (1:28). This work is done in the context of relationship with God, and expresses itself in worship of him. This is where things go wrong.

The passage does not explicitly tell us why God favours one offering over the other. The five general explanations offered are:

- God prefers shepherds to gardeners (an unlikely position since working the soil was a command given to Adam in 2:15).
- Animal sacrifices are more acceptable to God than vegetable offerings (again unlikely given that later laws include both sorts).
- God, who knows the heart (1 Samuel 16:7), knew that the motives of one brother were more honourable or righteous than the other (this interpretation draws on Hebrews 11:4).
- The quality of the offerings reflects the attitude of the heart. Cain simply offered 'some of the fruits of the soil' while Abel offered the 'fat portions from some of the firstborn of his flock'. Later sacrificial law emphasises that only perfect, unblemished animals should be offered in sacrifice (compare Leviticus 1:3; 22:20–22). This is the most common ancient and modern interpretation.
- God's motives are unknown, and his preference for Abel's sacrifice reflects the mystery of election, which is inaccessible to us.

Perhaps the best way to approach this issue is to understand this passage as opening up a theme that will run all the way through the book. In a number of places God and his people choose younger brothers over older brothers (Jacob over Esau, Joseph over his brothers, Ephraim over Manasseh). No explanations are given for these choices, and turmoil often erupts as a result.

Cain's downcast face reveals a deep sense of rejection or dejection. He obviously cares what God thinks of him and his sacrifice. For his part, God is concerned for Cain and offers guidance to him as to the appropriate way to respond. The options are clear—on the one hand, Cain can accept what has happened and respond rightly. On the other hand, he can bow to temptation (portrayed in 4:7 as a predator eager to force its way into Cain's existence). Each choice will have results—acceptance by God on the one hand and dominance by sin on the other. God is clear; Cain must not allow sin to rule his life.

Cain follows his father in deciding that he knows better than God as to what is in his best interests. He murders his brother, and death enters the world at the hand of a human (not at the hand of God who promised death as punishment for sin in 2:17).

In the ensuing interrogation, Cain tries to hide and shift the blame: 'I don't know. Am I my brother's keeper?'—implying that surely it is God's role to 'keep'. With no clear confession, God proceeds to sentence Cain for his crime. Though there is no command against murder, God's intention of harmony between humans is clearly shattered by this act.

The punishment given to Cain amounts to a heightening of the punishment given to Adam and Eve. Cain will be driven from the ground and it will not yield anything at all for him. Cain's life will be that of a rootless wanderer.

Cain's response indicates that he knows that the sentence has overwhelming implications. After all, what will be left for him if his relationship with God is shattered ('hidden from your presence') and his relationship with the environment is dissolved ('you are driving me from the land')? Surely these things will put his only other relationship, with other human beings, in jeopardy ('whoever finds me will kill me').

God disagrees with Cain's assessment (perhaps the 'Not so' of verse 15 also questions whether God will indeed be inaccessible to him), but lightens the punishment by promising that if anyone should kill Cain they will themselves experience severe retribution ('suffer vengeance seven times over'). God will be Cain's keeper, in contrast to Cain's failure to be his brother's keeper.

We should not leave this story about Cain and Abel without one further observation. The act of worship that begins the story is a voluntary act. These two men sacrifice without a command to do so, implying an innate, instinctive, and spontaneous desire to worship. At the same time, it is this very same religious act that draws out the most awful violence. It was not to be the last time in the history of the world that religion stirred up the greatest and most vehement violence among human beings!

THE DESCENDANTS OF CAIN (4:17–26)

This passage is notable in a number of ways. It records the genealogy of Cain—seven generations in all. It also records the origin, development, and growth of cultural advances— urban life (17), animal husbandry (20), and the development of various forms of musical instruments (21). Perhaps the seven generations of Cain in their creativity provide a small mirror of God's creativity in his seven days.

The story of Lamech illustrates the violence of Cain stepping up one more notch. With Cain and Abel it was God who avenged a death, by punishment that was tempered with mercy. Not so with humans. Lamech will punish by death for only an injury, and he will do it himself (and boast about it in song before his women!). This is a far cry from Genesis 1:26–28, where human rule was to be exercised under God and reflect the nature of his loving rule. Humans are using intensified violence in an increasingly unruly way. With progress of human 'civilisation' has come progress in sin and its effects.

Yet despite all this violence, and human efforts to burst out from under the rule of God, those same humans cannot escape the fact that they are created beings. They are born to worship, and some will find the right person to direct that worship to. Some will worship the true and living God (compare the reference to 'Yahweh' or 'the LORD' in 4:26).

FROM ADAM TO NOAH (5:1–32)

When we come to the genealogies in the Bible most of us tend to skip over them. They are, however, often very important. The following diagram, which illustrates the structure of the first eleven chapters of Genesis, shows that the genealogies provide a framework for the events and stories of those chapters. The author of Genesis obviously thought genealogies were significant.

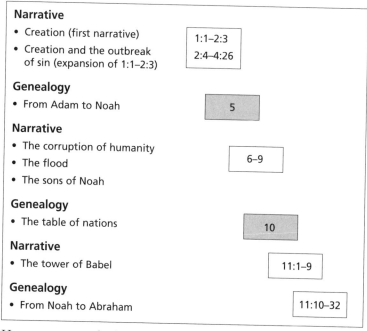

Narrative
- Creation (first narrative) — 1:1–2:3
- Creation and the outbreak of sin (expansion of 1:1–2:3) — 2:4–4:26

Genealogy
- From Adam to Noah — 5

Narrative
- The corruption of humanity
- The flood
- The sons of Noah — 6–9

Genealogy
- The table of nations — 10

Narrative
- The tower of Babel — 11:1–9

Genealogy
- From Noah to Abraham — 11:10–32

However, genealogies are not just structuring devices. They also contain important information, as we will see when we take a closer look at the content of Genesis 5.

The heading and structure of the account

> **This is the written account of Adam's line.**
> **When God created man, he made him in the likeness of God. He created them male and female and blessed them. And when they were created, he called them 'man'.**
>
> *(Genesis 5:1–2)*

The heading is reminiscent of Genesis 1:28, with its blessing and command to fill the earth and subdue it. The implication of the command is that part of what it means to be human is to be fruitful. Hence, when the genealogies tell us about humans reproducing, they are telling us how God has blessed humans by giving them the ability (compare 4:1) to fulfil his command.

After the heading we are introduced to Adam and his descendants. The structure of each generation can be reduced to this form:

When A had lived 'x' number of years, he became the father of B.

And after he became the father of B, A lived 'y' number of years.

He had other sons and daughters.

Altogether, A lived 'z' number of years.

And then he died.

Were you to read these accounts of generations out loud, as they were intended to be read, then you would hear the constant refrain 'and then he died'. Therefore, if one side of the genealogies demonstrates the blessing of God in enabling humans to be fruitful, the other side demonstrates that humans live under the curse of God. All human life ends in death, and this death is not the natural state for humans. Death is the outward and visible sign of an inward and spiritual state of separation from God. It is therefore a sign and symbol of human sinfulness. This is confirmed by the words of verse 29 at the end of the genealogy. Where Genesis 5 began with the positive observation that humans increased in number and filled the earth, it ends with a reminder that humans live in painful labour under the curse of God.

Genealogies therefore perform an important theological function. They show us the double-sided nature of life. Human life is about blessing—living and creating like God, and enjoying life in community with others. Human life is also about standing under the curse and judgment of God, out of kilter with God, other humans, and the environment.

A note on age

One of the problems for us as we read these genealogies is the incredible ages of the people we read about. What do we make of this? My own view is that it is not possible to come to a firm conclusion. Nevertheless, I think there are some observations that should shape our thinking.

- There is no indication that we should take the ages as anything but literal ages (although this does not preclude a symbolic interpretation).
- Long lifespans are a common feature of other Ancient Near Eastern accounts, and the Genesis ages are very conservative compared with many other accounts (one Sumerian king is listed as having reigned for 43,200 years!).
- Suggesting that the years were shorter than ours doesn't really work, since the flood story seems to indicate that the years in Genesis were about 360 days long. Moreover, if the ages are reduced, then the time at which Adam appears will have to be calculated as significantly later than 4004 BC.
- There is symmetry between this genealogy and that of Genesis 11 (ten generations before the flood and ten generations after the flood). This may indicate that when Genesis 5 says that A became the father of B, it means that A became the father of the line that culminated in B. Similar use of symmetry is seen in the genealogy of Jesus in Matthew 1. Here, three sets of 14 generations are listed (we know from other genealogies in the Old Testament that three kings, three generations, and 60 years stand between Jehoram and Uzziah in Matthew 1:8).
- The Bible records a notable decrease in lifespan as it progresses (here they range up to about 1000 years, in Genesis 6 human age is restricted to 120 years, Abraham dies at the age of 175, and Psalm 90:10 talks about 70 years being the normal span of life). It is possible that a theological point is being made about the progression of human sin and God's corresponding judgment (compare Genesis 6:3).

61

A BIRD'S EYE VIEW AGAIN (6:1–8)

When men began to increase in number on the earth and daughters were born to them, the sons of God saw that the daughters of men were beautiful, and they married any of them they chose. Then the LORD said, 'My Spirit will not contend with man forever, for he is mortal; his days will be a hundred and twenty years.'

The Nephilim were on the earth in those days— and also afterward—when the sons of God went to the daughters of men and had children by them. They were the heroes of old, men of renown.

The LORD saw how great man's wickedness on the earth had become, and that every inclination of the thoughts of his heart was only evil all the time. The LORD was grieved that he had made man on the earth, and his heart was filled with pain. So the Lord said, 'I will wipe mankind, whom I have created, from the face of the earth—men and animals, and creatures that move along the ground, and birds of the air—for I am grieved that I have made them.' But Noah found favour in the eyes of the Lord.

(Genesis 6:1–8)

As we prepare to consider these opening verses of Genesis 6, it is helpful to reflect upon what we have seen so far. Genesis 4 occupies a very important place in the book of Genesis. On the one hand, it looks forward to themes that will become more and more important within the overall story. For example, the situation of the younger son inexplicably having favour over older sons, and the consequences of this for family life, will dominate large sections of the final two-thirds of Genesis.

On the other hand, the story looks back to themes already raised. The structure of the story in Genesis 4:1–16 is very like that of Genesis 3. Both deal with a crime and its punishment. The content of the chapters and the theological issues dealt with are also very similar. In Chapter 3, sin disrupts the relationship between a man and his wife and between humankind and God. In Chapter 4, sin brings hatred between brothers and separation from God.

There is, however, a progression here as well. The sin of Cain appears more high-handed and aggressive. Cain is far less compliant when confronted by God, rejecting God's initiative time after time, and grumbling about his sentence. Cain's descendant, Lamech, goes even further in his arrogance (4:23–24).

As we look at these chapters together a pattern of action is beginning to emerge. The pattern is:

- God places humans in a particular situation with particular duties or responsibilities.
- The humans reach out for independence from God rather than dependence upon him—they sin.
- God confronts them with what they have done.
- God punishes their sin.
- God pulls back from the harshness of the punishment promised, and alleviates it in some way—mercy triumphs over judgment.

This pattern prepares us for what is about to come. In the opening eight verses of Genesis 6, we have a rather strange account of intermarriages between the 'sons of God' and the 'daughters of men'. No explanation is given as to the identity of the 'sons of God' (commentary explanations range from angelic beings to pre-flood kings from the godly line of Seth), but it is clear that the liaisons are inappropriate as far as God is concerned. This inappropriateness is emphasised by repetition of words used by Eve earlier. As Eve 'saw' that the fruit of the tree was 'good' and therefore 'took' it, so the sons of God 'saw' that the daughters of men were 'beautiful' (literally, 'good') and therefore 'married' (literally, 'took') any they chose. Moreover, it is clear that God's intention was for order in his created world. Every species was to propagate according to its own kind (Genesis 1:11,12,21; compare the later laws against crossbreeding of animals and intermarriage with foreigners). Whatever is happening here, God's intention for humans is being broken and boundaries are being crossed.

Just as with previous incidents, God sees his creation breaking out from under his rule, and again he promises punishment. Now their life span will be limited to 120 years, roughly a sevenfold reduction of the lifespan of pre-flood people. However, despite punishment, the practice continued (verses 4–5) and God 'sees' again.

The indictment of verse 5 could hardly be stronger—God made humans for good but **every** inclination of the thoughts of their hearts is **only** evil **all the time**. There is not much room here for exceptions—human sinfulness is not just about occasional sinful actions, but a deep, ongoing, and thorough disposition away from God and toward evil. The contrast is profound—God is so passionately disposed toward humans that he is like a grieved lover or bitterly disappointed parent, while humans are so passionately disposed to rebel against God that they utterly ignore him.

As with Genesis 3 and 4, God decides to act in judgment —he will wipe humanity from the face of the earth. Nevertheless, Genesis 3 and 4 also led us to expect that God may not carry out the fierceness of his judgment. He may alleviate punishment and allow his mercy to triumph over judgment. Our hope finds fuel in the last words of this section, for 'Noah found favour in the eyes of the Lord'.

BEGINNINGS: Of the Cosmos

Part 3

The story of Noah
Genesis 6:9–11:26

6

The flood

This is the account of Noah.　　　　*(Genesis 6:9)*

This is the second time we have met the phrase 'This is the account of...'. The first time was back in Genesis 2:4, and we noted there that this phrase is used by the author as a major structuring device for organising his book. It therefore signals that we are entering a new section of Genesis. This section will continue until we encounter the next similar phrase in Genesis 10:1.

This chapter also marks the beginning of a change in pace for our commentary. Up until this point we have gone into significant detail about each passage. This was because of the foundational nature of those early chapters, for the book of Genesis and also for Christians. From now on, however, we are going to move fairly fast, looking at the big picture, and slowing down occasionally to consider significant points in more detail.

As we go about this, large slabs of the text of Scripture will not be specifically referred to, and there is a danger you won't read them. Don't get caught in this trap! Remember to read the passages themselves before, during, and after you've read the commentary. This commentary is to help you read the Bible, not to be a substitute for it.

WE ALL KNOW THE STORY

The story of Noah must be one of the best known stories in the Bible. Many of us know its major elements well—the godly man Noah, the wickedness of the surrounding people, animals and birds entering the ark two at a time, 40 days and nights of rain, long days in an ark, doves, ravens and rainbows. We will not get bogged down in some of the tricky details that exist in this story. Rather, we will concentrate on a 'big picture' view.

One of the clues to understanding any sort of literature is to read the beginning and the end. In these sections, the author often indicates how he meant you to understand what happens in his story. This is particularly so with this story, which appears to be quite symmetrical in its structure.

The beginning of the story (6:1–6)

Genesis 1–3 frames the larger context of this story. There we learn that God created humans to live dependently upon him, their creator. Unfortunately humans steadfastly refused to do this. The end result is that God and humans are in conflict, engaged in a battle for supremacy over human destiny. We see the product of this conflict in the all-pervasive wickedness of humankind (Genesis 6:5).

The bottom line is that God created things 'very good' (1:31) but humans in God's world are 'very bad'. What will God do about this?

Genesis 6:6 tells us that God is greatly grieved at the situation. His heart and the hearts of humans are set on opposing courses. His heart is filled with pain at their evil, while they delight in it. However, because God is righteous and cannot allow evil to remain, he decides to act and to judge. He is grieved that he has made humans and that they have ruined something beautiful (6:7).

There is one bright spot in all of this—Noah. Somehow Noah is different. He is righteous. In other words, he trusts God and walks in friendship with him (6:8–9).

The end of the story (9:1–7)

Then God blessed Noah and his sons, saying to them, 'Be fruitful and increase in number and fill the earth. The fear and dread of you will fall upon all the beasts of the earth and all the birds of the

air, upon every creature that moves along the ground, and upon all the fish of the sea; they are given into your hands. Everything that lives and moves will be food for you. Just as I gave you the green plants, I now give you everything.

'But you must not eat meat that has its lifeblood still in it. And for your lifeblood I will surely demand an accounting. I will demand an accounting from every animal. And from each man, too, I will demand an accounting for the life of his fellow man.

'Whoever sheds the blood of man, by man shall his blood be shed; for in the image of God has God made man. 'As for you, be fruitful and increase in number; multiply on the earth and increase upon it.'

(Genesis 9:1–7)

We have looked at the beginning of the story, and now we flip to the end of it in Chapter 9. In the intervening chapters we hear how God saves this one righteous man and his family (Chapters 7–8). He then starts again with humans, repeating the commands and blessings of Genesis 1. Noah and his family are to 'be fruitful and increase in number and fill the earth'. All creation is given into their hands.

God appears to be grieved that he has been so thorough in judgment, and promises that such a judgment will not happen again. As an indication of his resolve and a reminder of his covenant and promise he places a rainbow in the clouds (9:8–17).

Nevertheless, there are indications in the language of these verses that God knows very well what evil is in human beings, and that the flood hasn't removed this from their hearts. In Genesis 8:21, God smells the sacrifice, rejoices in it, but reminds himself that still 'every inclination of man's heart is evil from childhood'. Immediately after urging Noah and his family to fulfil the creation mandate, God talks about the spilling of blood and the accounting that will be required when a person kills another. God's fears are immediately illustrated following the promise and covenant. Although we can't be sure exactly what the problem is in Genesis 9:20–27, it is clear that something terribly wrong happens that breaches relationships and propriety. One human being treats another human being very wrongly. The flood has evidently changed nothing in the human heart.

Is there a centre to the story?

For forty days the flood kept coming on the earth, and as the waters increased they lifted the ark high above the earth. The waters rose and increased greatly on the earth, and the ark floated on the surface of the water. They rose greatly on the earth, and all the high mountains under the entire heavens were covered. The waters rose and covered the mountains to a depth of more than twenty feet. Every living thing that moved on the earth perished—birds, livestock, wild animals, all the creatures that swarm over the earth, and all mankind. Everything on dry land that had the breath of life in its nostrils died. Every living thing on the face of the earth was wiped out; men and animals and the creatures that move along the ground and the birds of the air were wiped from the earth. only Noah was left, and those with him in the ark.

(Genesis 7:17–23)

What we have seen so far in Genesis somehow reaches its climax in this story. In Genesis 1 and 2, God creates and forms a bond between himself, humans, and the created order. Genesis 3 reverses this, Genesis 4 heightens the reversal, and Genesis 6 demonstrates its climax. God's resolve in Chapter 6 can be seen as a decision to reverse creation (compare 6:7; 7:23). There is a return to a watery chaos such as was seen back in Genesis 1.

But God remembered Noah and all the wild animals and the livestock that were with him in the ark, and he sent a wind over the earth, and the waters receded. Now the springs of the deep and the floodgates of the heavens had been closed, and the rain had stopped falling from the sky. The water receded steadily from the earth. At the end of the hundred and fifty days the water had gone down, and on the seventeenth day of the seventh month the ark came to rest on the mountains of Ararat. The waters continued to recede until the tenth month, and on the first day of the tenth month the tops of the mountains became visible.

(Genesis 8:1–5)

As we have seen, Genesis 9 looks almost like a new creation. There are new promises, a new (or renewed) covenant, and new blessings (and a new start to sinfulness soon after!). This process of renewal or re-creation springs out of the chaos of 7:22–24, when God 'remembers' Noah and all those with him in Genesis 8:1–5, and causes the water to recede. Just as in Genesis 1, there is a separation of the sea and the land again (8:1,7,13). There is a command to multiply (8:17) and the structure of day and night is restored (8:22).

The remembering of God in 8:1 is pivotal in the story and appears to operate in the same way as the word of God does in Genesis 1. God remembers and re-creation begins.

So, what is the principal goal of this story?

This story is not primarily about animals and arks. Nor is it primarily about morality. This story is about **theology**—that is, about who God is and who we are. It is making very serious comments on these issues.

About God, it says:

- God is just and holy. Sin is an affront to him, which is what you'd expect of a God who is good. Sin must therefore be punished, which is what you'd expect of a God who is just.

71

- God's commitment to creation costs him a great deal, in terms of grief, pain, and betrayal. Even judgment seems to be alien to him and contrary to his most basic character (Isaiah 28:21). Therefore, God is much more like a troubled parent than an angry tyrant.
- No matter what, God will not abandon his purpose for creation. His purpose is good and God will do what is possible to bring about that good.
- God always seeks a way out of judgment and harshness.

These truths about God are foundational. They will be played out time and time again in the Old Testament. Human sinfulness will continue to plummet to new depths and God will respond with the same patterns we see here. These same patterns will reach their height in the Cross of Christ, where God is the one who is just and who justifies those who have faith in Jesus (Romans 3:26), and where God's mercy triumphs over his judgment. About humans, we learn that:

- The fundamental human disposition is to refuse to be God's creation or to honour him as God.
- We humans prefer to have our own way, and to anticipate a future determined by ourselves rather than God. We believe we know what works for our good, and we are not sure that God knows.
- There are some humans who seek to accept that they are creatures and want to let God be God. However, 'every inclination' of the human heart is evil even here (8:21). God may dwell in heaven but he doesn't have his head in the clouds—something much more than a flood will be needed to change human nature.

What are the implications?
This story is a salutary reminder of where human hope must find its focus. Humans can never inherit God's future and God's purpose through their own initiative. Human nature is inclined away from God and his purposes.

The Bible is clear that our hope is not based on the possibility of humans making it happen. If we are trusting that humans will gradually get better, we'd better think again. They haven't, and they won't! Human hope must look outside itself to God, and hope for him to do something.

It is here that the flood helps us, for it reminds us that the only thing not overwhelmed by the flood is God's commitment to his creation. The central verses in the whole story are therefore those that occur in the midst of the flood, when the world has been overwhelmed by God's judgment and the consequences of sin. In Genesis 8:1 God '**remembered** Noah and all the wild animals and the livestock that were with him in the ark, and he sent a wind over the earth, and the waters receded'. Later, God promises that he will always 'remember' his 'everlasting' covenant between him and all living creatures (Genesis 9:15–16). In the Old Testament, for God to 'remember' means that God will act on behalf of his people. To remember is to see human need and to act to save (compare Exodus 2:24). Human hope is found in God remembering that we are but frail dust, unable to save ourselves. Psalm 103 captures it this way:

> The LORD is compassionate and gracious, slow to anger, abounding in love. He will not always accuse, nor will he harbour his anger forever; he does not treat us as our sins deserve or repay us according to our iniquities.
>
> For as high as the heavens are above the earth, so great is his love for those who fear him; as far as the east is from the west, so far has he removed our transgressions from us. As a father has compassion on his children, so the Lord has compassion on those who fear him; for he knows how we are formed, he remembers that we are dust.
>
> *(Psalm 103:8–14)*

7

After the flood

As I write this chapter I am sitting in my study at home in Perth. Outside is a balcony that overlooks a small garden of Australian native trees, a narrow, dead-end street, and a series of sporting fields lined by tall eucalypts. This has been our home for the last twelve months. In that same twelve months, I have helped a congregation sell one church building, buy another, renovate it and move into it.

This last year has taught me a lot about buildings. Having a home of your own somehow means something. It conveys a sense of belonging and of security and refuge. It panders to that deep-seated need within us all to flee the transitory and to seek security in something tangible.

This personal tie to buildings mirrors a problem that God's people have had throughout history. Most meeting places for God's people have had very humble beginnings—tents in the wilderness, places of prayer beside rivers, school classrooms, and the like. But then, as the gospel is preached, more people come and casual meeting places are no longer adequate. People begin to feel reputable and crave something more stable, and so they build buildings. Those buildings make demands, chew up time, money and resources. This problem alone might be manageable if it were not that the people of God begin to put their trust and security in the buildings. For the people of God, as with us individually, buildings often convey safety, security, and comfort. At this point the children of a moving God often lose direction.

The issue of buildings is the issue that rises to the surface in these chapters of Genesis. For the first time, we find humans building significant structures, and we come across

74

some important concepts that will keep recurring throughout the Scriptures and on into our own day. Before we get on to the Tower of Babel in Chapter 11, we need to look at the genealogy of Genesis 10.

THE GENEALOGY OF GENESIS 10

This is the account of Shem, Ham and Japheth, Noah's sons, who themselves had sons after the flood.

(Genesis 10:1)

A new account

Genesis 10 begins with that phrase we have already noticed from Genesis 2:4 and 6:9—'This is the account of...'. Here again we have the use of that special Hebrew word that divides the book into sections of interest. As we were introduced to the 'account of the heavens and the earth' after the first act of creation, so now we are introduced to the world that will exist after God's act of re-creation in the flood and afterwards. This is the history of the world 'after the flood'.

The focus of the list

The genealogy can be broken up in the following manner:
Verses 2–5   about Japheth and his descendants
Verses 6–20   about Ham and his descendants
Verses 21–31   about Shem and his descendants.

There is a double introduction to the sons of Shem and a specific introduction to Eber (which may be linked to the term 'Hebrew') who is the ancestor of Abraham and Israel.

The scope of the list

Many of the names recorded here stand for whole nations, or groups of peoples that descended from them. The scope of these people groups stretches from Crete and Libya in the

West to Iran in the east, and from Arabia and Ethiopia in the south to Asia Minor and Armenia in the north. They are a diverse group geographically, sociologically, politically, and commercially.

Seventy peoples

Notice that seventy people groups are mentioned (if the aside on Nimrod in verses 8 and 9 is omitted). Given the importance of seven and seventy in the Bible this is surely not an accident. Perhaps it indicates that the entire known world has been included, or that all peoples spoken about share a common unity. The general thrust would then be that no matter where these people are from, and regardless of their cultural and social and religious differences, they belong to a shared humanity. They belong to one world created and fashioned by God.

Filling the earth

Underneath all of this is the sheer size of things now. There are whole nations occupying the world. God's charge to fill the earth (1:28 and 9:1,7) is surely being fulfilled.

THE TOWER OF BABEL (11:1–9)

Now the whole world had one language and a common speech. As men moved eastward, they found a plain in Shinar and settled there.

They said to each other, 'Come, let's make bricks and bake them thoroughly.' They used brick instead of stone, and tar for mortar. Then they said, 'Come, let us build ourselves a city, with a tower that reaches to the heavens, so that we may make a name for ourselves and not be scattered over the face of the whole earth.'

But the LORD came down to see the city and the tower that the men were building. The LORD said, 'If as one people speaking the same language they

have begun to do this, then nothing they plan to do will be impossible for them. Come, let us go down and confuse their language so they will not understand each other.'

So the Lord scattered them from there over all the earth, and they stopped building the city. That is why it was called Babel—because there the Lord confused the language of the whole world. From there the Lord scattered them over the face of the whole earth.

(Genesis 11:1–9)

A different perspective

Genesis 10 has a somewhat positive tone. Genesis 11:1–9 offers a different perspective on the same facts and figures recounted in Genesis 10. It shows the downside of human growth and development, as it shows the character of the peoples mentioned in the genealogy.

A unique story

This story is unique in the ancient world. We have other creation narratives and we have other flood narratives, but to this date we do not have any other Tower of Babel stories from the rest of the ancient world. This story is special.

Context

Before we have a look at the story itself, it is important to notice its context. Chapter 10 has outlined the descendants of Noah. Interestingly, the order of Noah's sons in verse 1 is reversed in the subsequent account with the result that Shem is the last son whose genealogy is described. Within that genealogy we are told that the line of Shem extends through Eber (10:24), where it branches into two; Peleg and Joktan (10:25). However, again the order is reversed and chapter 10 goes on to tell us about the descendants of Joktan, while we have to wait for the second half of chapter 11 to hear about the descendants of Peleg. The implication of this framework in genealogies is that the line of Shem → Eber → Joktan leads to the tower builders in 11:1–9 while the line of Shem → Eber → Peleg leads to an alternative; Abram and his descendants.

The other, not so obvious, connection between the two genealogies and the story of the tower builders of chapter 11:1–9 is found in a play on words. The Hebrew word for the name 'Shem' is identical to the word for 'name' used in 11:4 when the tower builders seek to 'make a name for ourselves'. This in turn is contrasted with the Abram account in 12:2 where God says to Abram that he will 'make your name great'. Again, we are being told of two ways of interacting with God and two alternative futures.

It should also be noted that there are numerous wordplays and repetitions throughout 1:1–9 and an intricate structure to this story. Structurally its centre is found in the words, 'the Lord came down' in verse 5.

The situation (11:1–4)

The situation painted in the first four verses is straightforward. Humans have a common language and a common resolve—to 'build ourselves a city, and a tower that reaches to the heavens, so that we may make a name for ourselves and not be scattered over the face of the whole earth'. The humans in this story are unified in their desire to make their own honour and glory paramount, rather than the honour and glory of God.

However, there is something else going on here as well. The passage tells us that they are seeking to avoid being 'scattered over the face of the whole earth'. Underlying this building project is a unity in fear—fear of what the future might bring. These humans don't like insecurity, and so they attempt to secure their own future as a unified community, isolated from the rest of the world.

In other words, the tower is a symbol of humans making themselves the focus of life and security rather than God. They cling to each other, in hope of a better future. However, Genesis 8–9 told us that the only hope for humans was in God's intervention.

A judicial inquiry (11:5)

It is at this point that we are told, with deep irony, that 'The LORD came down to see the city and the tower that the men were building'. In verse 4 humans decided to ascend to the heavens. Despite their ascent, God is still a far way off in verse 5—he has to descend to the city. Moreover, his descending appears to have the purpose of making an inquiry.

Reversal (11:6–9)

The results of the inquiry are outlined in verse 6. A consultation among the Godhead or some angelic council is undertaken and a decision is made—to descend again for judgment.

It is important to understand what is going on in verse 7. It is not that unity itself is a problem, but what motivates it and empowers it. Human unity here is for the purpose of isolation and self-preservation. Such unity goes against God's expressed purpose of 'filling the earth and subduing it' (1:28). The people here don't like that notion. Instead, they want to stay in one place and secure their place in the world in this one place. They are therefore engaging in a creation-threatening task, and so God must judge.

Again, notice how gracious God is in judgment. While his judgment does indeed create difficulties, it works toward preventing projects that could be carried out by self-serving, self-preserving, united humans. God puts a limit on how humans may destroy the creation, and makes it so that they have no choice but to obey God's creation command. In other words, God creates confusion and diversity in order to help unite people in their mandate to care for the creation.

The issue

The issue in this passage is that God has a good purpose for his world (1:31). This purpose involves an outward focus for humans, living rightly with God, themselves and the environment in which he has placed them. The people in this passage have an alternative purpose—doing what works for them. However, if God were to allow them to pursue this, the result would be losing God's purpose for them. In other words, they will save themselves but forfeit their own souls. And so it is that God protects humans from their own self-centredness by driving them out.

THEOLOGICAL REFLECTION: TWO FOCI

This story in its larger literary context shows us two ways of being human. The first way to go is the way of the tower builders, the descendants of Joktan. This is the way of deciding to be the determiner of your own destiny (i.e. to make a name for yourself). This is the way that we saw Adam and Eve choose and it ended, as this story does, in judgment. The second way to go is the way of the descendants of Peleg, that is to allow God to determine your destiny (i.e. to allow God to make a name for you). This is the way Abram goes, and it ends in being blessed and in being a blessing to the world (12:3).

In the rest of the Bible these two options are highlighted in the language of cities. We are told the stories of two cities, representing two different approaches to life. On the one hand, there is Jerusalem or Zion, which represents a way of life focused on God and God's purposes. On the other hand, there is Babylon or Babel, the city mentioned in our passage, which represents a way of life focused on humans and human interests.

From Genesis 11 all the way through to the closing passages of the New Testament, we are told the story of these cities. Babylon/Babel is always seen to be under judgment, because of its disposition and actions. Jerusalem/Zion is often in danger of turning into Babylon, but will eventually be victorious if it hangs on to its God-centredness.

The way the Bible ends is to tell us about the end of these two cities. In the last pages of the book of Revelation, Babylon is seen to be a harlot who is judged by God and driven out of his presence. Jerusalem is a bride who is married to the Son of God.

The presentation of these two cities throughout the Bible operates as a choice. The hearers of Scripture are asked to define their allegiances. To which city do they belong—the city of the tower builders on the plain of Shinar, who seek security in themselves and their own purposes, or the city whose builder and architect is God? Which future will be theirs—judgment or blessing?

THEOLOGICAL REFLECTION: TO THE NATIONS

One thing that is evident from Genesis 1–11 is that God has the whole world in mind. The Bible does not start with Israel but the whole world. The Bible will end with the whole world. This is important to remember as we launch into the story of Abram in chapter 12. God's choice of Abram has the whole world in mind (12:3). This is where God is going in his world. However, as the story of God's work progresses in the Bible, that focus will often drop from view as we focus on the descendants of Abraham. Nevertheless, it will surface again in the New Testament. We will find hints of it in the ministry of Jesus and then it will be explicit in the commissioning of the apostles in Acts 1:6–8.

With this background in mind, it is helpful to reflect on one of the other great passages in the Bible that talks about languages—the events of the day of Pentecost recorded for us in Acts 2. The context is the commissioning of Acts 1:6–8. The people of God are to go into all the world to bear witness to Jesus, through whom the people of the world might be forgiven and restored to God. In Acts 2, a group of people who are united in their knowledge of the events surrounding Jesus and his coming are gathered in a room. The Holy Spirit is poured out on them and they speak in other tongues. In other words, the language barriers which might prohibit the effective speaking of the gospel are taken away in a symbolic reversal of Babel. The disciples are thereby united—not in doing their own thing their own way, not in 'making a name for themselves or self-preservation and self-focus. Rather, they are united in the preaching of the gospel of true unity—unity with God and his purpose of making the name of Jesus great in the world. God gives these people the ability to speak across cultural and political barriers, because there is now the message of God's kingdom, which is God's common goal for all humanity.

THINKING ABOUT US

As we have seen, constructing and possessing buildings is always a risky venture for the people of God. God's people are like all people on earth. Although they should pursue God's purposes, they sometimes slip back into wanting what ordinary people want: security and tenure. The evidence for this can often be seen in our attitude to careers, money, relationships, families, church buildings, and the like. This shift away from centring on God and his purpose and becoming inward looking is often slow and subtle. Nevertheless, it is very real, and the result is that the people of God don't do what God brought us together to do. We fail to fill the earth and subdue it through the preaching of Christ crucified. Instead of going to all the nations, we stay at home and focus on building comfortable houses, careers, families, and church buildings. It is not that these things are wrong in themselves, but simply that we give too much importance to them. Faced by such a shift of focus, we ask for judgment from the God who would drive us out so as to restore us to true unity in his purposes. Persecution was needed to drive the early Christians out of Jerusalem into all the world. May this not be necessary for us!

BEGINNINGS: Of Israel

Part 4

The story of Abraham
Genesis 11:27–25:18

8

God does it again

The constitution of a nation is a very significant document. It outlines the fundamental principles that govern how that nation came into being, the values that shape it, and the manner in which it seeks to govern and direct its affairs. At the time I write, my country has a constitution which does not really reflect all of its history and traditions. It does not take full account of the long history of habitation of Australia by indigenous people. You could be excused for thinking that our land was empty before European explorers arrived.

Similarly, many people who read the Bible (and even some that write about it), seem to think that the history of Israel begins with Genesis 12. This is not the position of the writer of Genesis. As far as he is concerned you cannot understand Abraham, the human hero of the next section of his book, without understanding Genesis 1–11. Who Abraham is and how God interacts with him is shaped fundamentally by the events of those earlier chapters. Abraham's life provides answers to the questions posed by those earlier events. The history of Abraham must not be considered on its own—it is part and parcel of the history of the world.

That history has been somewhat bleak so far, hasn't it? We have heard of a good and great Creator who made the world to be a good place. We have heard of humans who seem determined not to live rightly with God, and how God has responded by justly punishing while at the same time offering undeserved mercy. The last incident we looked at— the Tower of Babel—has captured many of these themes, and sets the scene for God's next great action in human history.

THE GOD WHO CREATES

> This is the account of Terah. Terah became the father of Abram, Nahor and Haran. And Haran became the father of Lot. While his father Terah was still alive, Haran died in Ur of the Chaldeans, in the land of his birth. Abram and Nahor both married. The name of Abram's wife was Sarai, and the name of Nahor's wife was Milcah; she was the daughter of Haran, the father of both Milcah and Iscah. Now Sarai was barren; she had no children.
>
> Terah took his son Abram, his grandson Lot son of Haran, and his daughter-in-law Sarai, the wife of his son Abram, and together they set out from Ur of the Chaldeans to go to Canaan. But when they came to Haran, they settled there.
>
> Terah lived 205 years, and he died in Haran.
>
> The LORD had said to Abram, 'Leave your country, your people and your father's household and go to the land I will show you. 'I will make you into a great nation and I will bless you; I will make your name great, and you will be a blessing. I will bless those who bless you, and whoever curses you I will curse; and all peoples on earth will be blessed through you.'
>
> *(Genesis 11:27–12:3)*

Another important beginning

This passage begins with yet another of those 'this is the account of...' sayings. This time we are being introduced to the account of Terah, the father of Abram. As we proceed it will become obvious that this is really the account of Abram, who dominates the story at least until the next similar introduction.

The genealogy of Shem and Terah

We have already noted how important genealogies are in these introductory passages to the Bible. Genealogies show the sign of God's blessing in that it is only with God's help that humans are able to multiply (compare Genesis 4:1).

Genealogies also remind us that all human life ends in death, instead of life as God intended. Death is therefore a sign of sin and its consequences, a reminder that God has judged humanity because of sin.

We know from past references to Shem that he is the one through whom the godly line flows. Here we find that Shem's line ends with Terah. Unfortunately, we also find that Terah's line ends with Abram's wife Sarai, who is barren. It is as though Sarai's barrenness is a symbol of where all humanity ends when it is left on its own—unable to invent its own future and crying out for God to change things. Into such helplessness comes the word of God.

God's creative word

'Leave your country, your people, and your father's household and go to the land I will show you. I will make you into a great nation and I will bless you. I will make your name great, and you will be a blessing. I will bless those who bless you, and whoever curses you I will curse; and all peoples on earth will be blessed through you.'

(Genesis 12:1–3)

The promises here are comprehensive in scope. God promises Abram a land. He promises the husband of a barren woman that he will give him children ('make you into a great nation'). He promises that instead of a curse there will be blessing.

In Genesis 1 we saw God's first creation through his powerful word. Now God is speaking again, and this time it is to create a different sort of humanity—the people of God. This time, the universe is not chaotic, empty and void. Instead, there is a void in the life of a human being and his family, emptiness in the womb of a particular woman. Into such emptiness, God speaks a creative word that will form a nation from this couple.

This is the God we know so well already from the pages of the Bible. He is the God whose nature is to create something out of nothing, and bring life and blessing where there is curse and death. As Paul puts it in Romans 4:17, this is the God who 'gives life to the dead and calls things that are not as though they were'.

Do you believe in a creator?

The God of the Bible is a creator. His whole relationship with his world is one of creating and re-creating. God did not stop creating after seven days, but continues throughout history. Even now, as we read God's word or hear the gospel proclaimed, God continues to create.

This is why it is that when the Bible talks about God's work of saving and redeeming his people it often uses the language of creation (compare 2 Corinthians 5:17; Revelation 21:1–5). The way God redeems or saves is by doing what he has always done—creating anew. The mechanism he uses for such re-creation is his word—this is the way he has always done it.

This, then, is why the Bible starts with creation—not because it happens first, but because creation is the guarantee of salvation. If God can create then God can save.

Let's think about this from a New Testament perspective for a moment. In Ephesians 2 Paul writes:

> As for you, you were dead in your transgressions and sins, in which you used to live when you followed the ways of this world and of the ruler of the kingdom of air, the spirit who is now at work in those who are disobedient. All of us also lived among them at one time, gratifying the cravings of our sinful nature and following its desires and thoughts. Like the rest, we were by nature objects of wrath.
>
> *(Ephesians 2:1–3)*

Before we became Christians, we, as human beings, stood under the wrath of God. We were dead, like Sarai's womb and like all other human beings. But then Paul says:

> But because of his great love for us, God, who is rich in mercy, made us alive with Christ even when we were dead in transgressions. It is by grace you have been saved.
>
> *(Ephesians 2:4–5)*

And no doubt Abraham could echo the words of Paul in Ephesians 2:8–10:

> For it is by grace you have been saved, through faith—and this not from yourselves, it is the gift of God—not by works, so that no-one can boast. For we are God's workmanship, created in Christ Jesus to do good works, which God prepared in advance for us to do.

The doctrine of creation is therefore a doctrine of great encouragement. As we strive to live as God's people we often find ourselves in despair at our own sinfulness. We know that our lives are not all that we would like them to be, let alone what God would like them to be. If we did not believe in a God who could create, then we would have every reason to despair without hope. However, we have hope because God is the Creator and will continue to create, even in us. He does such creation and re-creation **through his word** as it is read and heard.

GOD'S GREAT PROMISE

The verses at the end of Genesis 11 and the beginning of Chapter 12 are not important just because they look back and remind us about God the creator. They are also important because they encapsulate much of what is yet to come in the Bible. In the first three verses of Chapter 12 we have a call by God for Abram to leave, followed by five statements by God about what he will do.

'I will make...'
'I will bless...'
'I will make...'
'I will bless...'
'I will curse...'

First, the repeated 'I will...' makes clear that God is behind all that is about to happen. God's future, and the future of the world, finds its genesis in God. It is not the world's doing. It is the gift of God.

Second, note that there are three principal elements of the promise of God to Abraham:

- Land ('...go to the land I will show you.');
- People ('I will make you into a great nation...'); and
- Blessing ('I will bless you...').

These three promises shape the course of history as it is portrayed in the books of Genesis to Deuteronomy. For this reason we will find ourselves coming back to them time and time again as we move through the chapters of Genesis. We will largely focus on one promise in these chapters—the promise of children—and we will have to leave it to the rest of the Old Testament books (and indeed, the New Testament as well) to take up the rest of the promises and finish the story. Jesus and the New Testament authors are convinced that the fullness of these promises is only reached in Jesus Christ. The promise of land is rarely mentioned specifically, but the New Testament does talk about some of the ideas associated with it. For example, in the Old Testament you knew you were safe in the land when you had the Temple, which indicated God's presence. In the New Testament, the Temple is Christ himself. John 1:14 tells us that the Word became flesh and 'made his dwelling' among us (literally 'tabernacled' among us). In Jesus Christ, God is with us, and through him we are made members of heaven, that spiritual land promised to the people of God. The New Testament also deals with the promise of children. It tells us that Christ is the 'seed' or descendant of Abraham. It also applies that description to a whole new group of people, drawn from both Jews and Gentiles, who are the people of God.

The promise of blessing also finds its fulfilment in Jesus, who is the 'light of the nations'. He is the one through whom the Gentiles, who were formerly without God and without hope in the world, can come near to God.

However, it is clear that even with the coming of Jesus the promises to Abraham are not finished. That's why the last pages of the Bible return to the language and thought of Genesis 12. At the end of the book of Revelation, great hordes of people are seen praising God amid great blessing, and there is a new heaven and a new earth where humans can live in untainted relationship with God. All this is possible because of a Lamb who has been slain but still lives—Jesus Christ—for it is in Jesus Christ that all the promises of God have their 'Yes' and 'Amen' (2 Corinthians 1:20–22).

GETTING SOME PERSPECTIVE ON ABRAHAM

The presentation of Abraham and his descendants that stretches from this chapter through to the end of Genesis is full of events that seem bizarre to modern Western people. These events are easier to understand if we remember that Abraham is part of a group of Bedouin-like peoples that have existed in various parts of the Middle East for many centuries. Such cultures are strongly tribal, and often consist of a number of groups of people who consider themselves related through the male line and descended from a common male ancestor. The tribe and each of its sections is presided over by a sheikh, who is considered the senior member in wisdom and experience, if not always in age.

Bedouin life is nomadic. When there is minimal rainfall in the winter, the tribes wander about the desert in search of water and pasture lands. There are usually favourite watering holes or fertile places that are visited year after year, generation after generation. The organisation of the tribe is somewhat fluid, with sections frequently splitting off and recombining, and with outsiders occasionally attaching themselves to the tribe.

The practices of these tribal groups give us some helpful insights into Abraham. He is like a Bedouin sheikh, wandering the deserts of ancient Palestine in search of some new existence. Fundamental to this new existence is the call of a new God, different from the gods worshipped by his father and other ancestors (compare Joshua 24:2–4). This will be an exciting and intriguing story.

FOLLOWING A MOVING GOD

> So Abram left, as the LORD had told him; and Lot
> went with him. Abram was seventy-five years old
> when he set out from Haran. He took his wife
> Sarai, his nephew Lot, all the possessions they had
> accumulated and the people they had acquired in
> Haran, and they set out for the land of Canaan,
> and they arrived there.
>
> Abram travelled through the land as far as the
> site of the great tree of Moreh at Shechem. At that
> time the Canaanites were in the land. The Lord
> appeared to Abram and said, 'To your offspring I
> will give this land.' So he built an altar there to the
> LORD, who had appeared to him.
>
> From there he went on toward the hills east of
> Bethel and pitched his tent, with Bethel on the
> west and Ai on the east. There he built an altar to
> the Lord and called on the name of the Lord. Then
> Abram set out and continued toward the Negev.
>
> *(Genesis 12:4–9)*

Capturing God

Before we take a close look at these few verses, it will be
helpful to remind ourselves of some key characteristics of
the God who reveals himself in Scripture.

No image (Exodus 19–20)

One of the striking things about the God of the Bible is that
he allows no physical likeness of himself to be made.
Therefore, unlike the other gods of the ancient world, you
could not actually go somewhere and find an image or statue
of him. This in itself is significant, for if you have no image
of God then you can't tie him down and domesticate him.

No building (2 Samuel 7; 1 Kings 8)

Not only does God not allow himself to be tied down in an
image, he also eschews the whole idea of a temple. In 2

Samuel 7, David has just been appointed king of all Israel. He has captured Jerusalem and made it his capital city, and has brought the Ark of the Covenant up to that city. In a gesture that is undoubtedly that of a godly and pious man, but probably is also an attempt to tie God's presence and blessing to his kingship, David makes plans to build a temple for God. God responds by sending Nathan the prophet with a message that God has not been dwelling in a house for some time, and has no inclination to do so. He has been 'moving from place to place with a tent as my dwelling'.

God does, however, allow David's son, Solomon, to build a temple in Jerusalem. At the consecration of the building Solomon says:

> But will God really dwell on earth? The heavens, even the highest heaven cannot contain you. How much less this temple I have built!
>
> *(1 Kings 8:27)*

This point is very important. The God of the Bible resists all attempts by humans to tie him down, either with an image or in a temple. He will not be captured in this way.

But a Word (Exodus 19–20)

Nevertheless, God does allow himself to be captured—in his word. This is illustrated quite graphically in the construction of the tabernacle and temple. In the ancient world, when you journeyed into the inner recesses of a temple you expected that in the most inner sanctum you would find an image of the god who was worshipped there. When you journey into the holiest of places in the Jewish tabernacle or tent you find the strangest thing—a box. If you opened the box, your principal find would be a set of stone tablets with ten commandments inscribed on them.

This is a very powerful non-verbal communication from God, and tells us about one of his primary characteristics. If you want to find the God of the Bible, he is found in his word. God ties himself down only in his word.

With a purpose

The second characteristic about God is one we have seen much of already in Genesis. God is a God with a purpose. We saw this in Genesis 1–3, and we have seen it yet again in his promises to Abram in Genesis 12:1–3. In the broadest of terms, this purpose is to return people to relationship with him and each other.

Returning to Abraham

When God comes to Abram in Genesis 12 he speaks, promises, and demands. The demand on Abram is that he leave. And so it is that Abram trusts God. Despite his barren wife, he trusts that God will give him children. Despite the fact that the land he has been promised is occupied by Canaanites, he trusts that God will give him the land. Despite appearances to the contrary, Abram trusts God to fulfil his word, and wherever he goes he builds altars as an expression of his trust.

More than that, Abram obeys. He actually leaves the things that had given him security. Unlike the tower builders of Chapter 11, he forsakes security and stability voluntarily. From now until the end of his life he will be a wanderer, finding security in the word and purpose of God rather than elsewhere. Previously, Abram's life had consisted of the tangible. Now he lives by trusting a God he can't see and who cannot be tied down in an image or a temple. He goes where this God goes, and follows where he leads.

In this attitude, Abram becomes a model of the true believer. The true believer is like him—a sojourner, a traveller, a wanderer, a pilgrim. The true believer has no fixed focus for his or her security, except in God and his word and purpose.

Jesus

This theme is taken up in the person and ministry of Jesus. When we meet Jesus in the Gospels, he is a man whose life is a constant journey shaped by the word and purpose of God. This is seen clearly in such places as Luke 9:51–62, where Jesus fixes his eyes on Jerusalem and on the suffering that awaits him there. He does this because this is where God's purpose will reach its zenith.

This lifestyle is also enjoined upon the disciples of Jesus in Luke 9:57–62. They are to be like their leader, who has no place to lay his head and who keeps his eyes on the goal without looking back. Jesus expected that his disciples would be like him—constantly on a journey, shaped by the word of God and the purpose of God. They would free themselves from the things that held them back so as to be available for God and his purpose.

And us

Let's summarise where we have been in this chapter, and see how we can take into our own lives some of the great ideas that are found here.

First, we have a God who is into creating. He loves making something out of nothing, and creating life where there is lifelessness.

Second, God goes about this creative work by speaking words and promises.

Third, in Genesis 12 God saw the human predicament, and spoke a word that he knew would create life and light. That word consisted of three promises directed to Abram that addressed his own particular needs. That word, however, was also directed to all humanity and would meet their need for salvation.

Fourth, the promises to Abram are eventually fulfilled in Jesus. He is God's means of providing life where there is death, and salvation where only damnation can be expected.

Fifth, when Abram heard God's great promises, he was willing to leave everything he held dear in order to align himself with God's great purpose expressed in those promises.

Sixth, the way we do today what Abram did in his day is to align ourselves with Jesus. Such an alignment means taking up our cross and following Jesus. It means being willing to lay aside the things that give us a fading security, and place our security and our hope for the future in the hands of Jesus alone. Although this seems to be committing ourselves to a tenuous existence, it is in fact the only existence with a future. This is the point the writer of Hebrews makes. God is proud to be called the God of people who have such an attitude:

> By faith Abraham, when called to go to a place he would later receive as his inheritance, obeyed and went, even though he did not know where he was going. By faith he made his home in the promised land like a stranger in a foreign country; he lived in tents, as did Isaac and Jacob, who were heirs with him of the same promise. For he was looking forward to the city with foundations, whose architect and builder is God.
>
> By faith Abraham, even though he was past age—and Sarah herself was barren—was enabled to become a father because he considered him faithful who had made the promise. And so from this one man, and he as good as dead, came descendants as numerous as the stars in the sky and as countless as the sand on the seashore.
>
> All these people were still living by faith when they died. They did not receive the things promised, they only saw them and welcomed them from a distance. And they admitted that they were aliens and strangers on earth. People who say such things show that they are looking for a country of their own. If they had been thinking of the country they had left, they would have had opportunity to return. Instead, they were longing for a better country—a heavenly one. Therefore God is not ashamed to be called their God, for he has prepared a city for them.
>
> *(Hebrews 11:8–16)*

9

Abram and Lot

GREAT EXPECTATIONS AND HARSH REALITY

Life is full of great expectations. All of us have them—expectations about our children, exam results, marriage partner, job applications, and a myriad of other aspects of our lives. The experience of life, however, is that expectations and reality do not always neatly coincide. Sometimes reality falls far short of expectation, sometimes it is matched, and, on rare occasions, it is exceeded.

In our last chapter we were introduced to Abram. We saw God make a new start with him, which created expectations. What will happen with this man? Will there be a change? Will reality match our great expectations of this man? These next few verses will begin to give us some indication.

The exploits of God's man

A problem and a plan

Now there was a famine in the land, and Abram went down to Egypt to live there for a while because the famine was severe. As he was about to enter Egypt, he said to his wife Sarai, 'I know what a beautiful woman you are. When the Egyptians see you, they will say, "This is his wife." Then they will kill me but will let you live. Say you are my sister, so that I will be treated well for your sake and my life will be spared because of you.'

When Abram came to Egypt, the Egyptians saw that she was a very beautiful woman. And when

Pharaoh's officials saw her, they praised her to Pharaoh, and she was taken into his palace. He treated Abram well for her sake, and Abram acquired sheep and cattle, male and female donkeys, menservants and maidservants, and camels.

But the LORD inflicted serious diseases on Pharaoh and his household because of Abram's wife Sarai. So Pharaoh summoned Abram. 'What have you done to me?' he said. 'Why didn't you tell me she was your wife? Why did you say, "She is my sister," so that I took her to be my wife? Now then, here is your wife. Take her and go!' Then Pharaoh gave orders about Abram to his men, and they sent him on his way, with his wife and everything he had.

(Genesis 12:10–20)

Abram's occupation of the promised land is facing a problem—there is drought and famine. Abram begins to grow worried, and makes a plan to solve the problem. The plan involves his family making a move down to Egypt, and the telling of a half-truth about Sarai (Sarai shares the same father as Abram but not the same mother—Genesis 20:12).

This situation is Abram's first problem of faith. God had promised him land and blessing. The action Abram takes, however, casts doubt on his faith in God's ability to fulfil his promise. If Abram was confident of God's blessing of him and his family in the land, he would have had no need to flee to Egypt and lie about his wife.

Abram's actions result in dire consequences. Sarai is taken into Pharaoh's household and serious disease is inflicted upon the household. Pharaoh responds by sending for Abram, questioning him closely, and expressing his grief at the way Abram has treated him. Like everyone in the ancient world, he undoubtedly regarded adultery as a serious offence (in Egypt, as elsewhere, it was punishable by death). In the Hebrew, the words to Abram are short, sharp, and full of condemnation—'Here ... wife ... take ... go!' However, even in condemnation, Pharaoh acts with leniency, not exacting revenge, and not withdrawing the gifts he had given.

The meaning of the story

As readers of the story we know God's commitment to Abram. We see that commitment in action as God blesses Abram, by protecting Sarai and stopping Pharaoh from having children by her, and by giving him many material possessions. God curses Pharaoh by putting a disease upon his family. This commitment to Abram remains despite Abram's lack of faith. Although Abram is faithless, God remains faithful (2 Timothy 2:13).

Let's not forget, however, that this is not an isolated story—it is part of the larger story that began with Genesis 1. Human nature has constantly been revealed as leaving much to be desired. This incident demonstrates that Abram is a true descendant of Adam, still doing things his own way and not trusting that God has his best interests in mind. This is confirmed by verse 18 where the words, 'What have you done to me?' strongly echo those uttered by God to Eve in Genesis 3:13 ('What is this you have done?') and to Cain in Chapter Genesis 4:10 ('What have you done?'). There is expulsion from the Garden of Eden in Genesis 3, from the ground and its fertility in Genesis 4, and here it is expulsion from the land of Egypt. Like all human beings endowed with promise and potential, Abram has failed.

There are a number of results that spring from Abram's failure. In the first place, instead of the nations being blessed as a result of Abram (12:3), the Egyptians are cursed. Second, instead of Abram's presence being the cause of praise for God and his people, Pharaoh condemns the people of God and charges them with dishonesty and deceit. This Egyptian king shows himself to be nobler than God's man, who is not even able to keep the most basic moral requirements of right relationships. Pharaoh can't get rid of Abram fast enough. He doesn't want to have anything to do with the people of God.

Living as God's people

The story is poignant and very modern. As God's people we bear God's promises, and yet we also bear Adam's nature. Our resistance to God's purposes, our trust in ourselves, and our pursuit of our own interests are often catastrophic. Our failure to live up to who we are in Christ is paraded before us and the world in a variety of ways. How often do we hear the name of Christ maligned because of the failure of his people? Far too often the words of Pharaoh are the words of the world—'What have you done to us?' The prophet Zechariah prophesied that the people of the world would come to the people of God and say, 'Let us go with you, because we have heard that God is with you' (Zechariah 8:23; compare Isaiah 2:1–4). This is God's intention, but all too often the world just wants to get rid of us, and God's name is defiled and profaned among the nations because of us.

ABRAM AND LOT

Blessed are the peacemakers (13:1–18)

The first five verses of this passage tell us that Abram is now a wealthy man, who has left Egypt and journeyed until he comes to rest in Bethel. Verses 6-7 tell us about the downside of being a nomad and becoming numerous and wealthy—disputes are inevitable. The result is that it becomes obvious that the party should split up. Abram should go one way and Lot another.

The mechanism for this parting is set out in Genesis 13:8–13. Although Abram has the right of first choice because of seniority, he lets Lot choose. Lot looks around, sees the well-watered plain of the Jordan and chooses it. This land does not appear to be within the land of Canaan (note the contrast in verse 12—'Abram lived in the land of Canaan while Lot...'). It is also in the same general vicinity as the two notoriously evil cities of Sodom and Gomorrah. Lot's choice therefore appears to place him at some distance from the scope of God's blessing and promise.

Finally, the Lord speaks to Abram and calls him to look at the land he is being given. The words of God build on the previous promises of 12:1–3. Where before the land was simply 'this land', now it is '**all** the land that you see'. What had seemed a particular promise to Abram is now broadened to include 'you and your offspring forever'. 'I will make you into a great nation' becomes 'I will make your offspring like the dust of the earth, so that if anyone could count the dust then your offspring could be counted'. Finally, and symbolically, Abram is to walk through the land and take possession of it.

This passage stands in contrast to the immediately preceding passage regarding Abram's sojourn in Egypt, and presents the other side of that story. Here Abram sees problems in relationships and seeks to preserve those relationships, by allowing Lot to choose a share of the Promised Land. It is a large sacrifice to make in the pursuit of peace. As it is, Lot chooses a more temporary and transitory wealth over the eternal promises of God. The result of Abram's trust in God, and his willingness to preserve relationships, is God's reaffirmation of the promises in an even more abundant form.

While Abram's earlier model was not one to emulate, this time is different. Here Abram is not anxious for his life, and is content to rely on the promises of God. Moreover, he acts like God, for whom peacemaking and reconciliation are central aspects of his character. Such people are like Jesus, the Prince of peace, who bought our reconciliation at the cost of his own life. As he himself said, 'Blessed are the peacemakers, for they will be called sons of God' (Matthew 5:9; compare James 3:18).

The battle of the kings (14:1–24)

The story in Genesis 14 is one of the strangest in the whole book of Genesis, even though it is straightforward enough in its details. The maps on the following pages outline the main elements of that story.

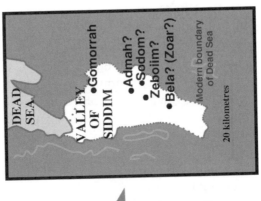

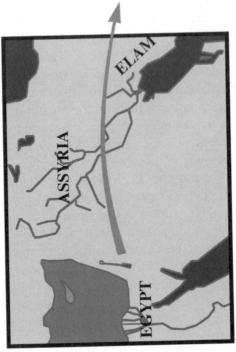

1. There are four local kings in the Valley of Siddim (Bera, king of Sodom; Birsha, king of Gomorrah; Shinab, king of Admah; Shemeber, king of Zeboiim).

2. These kings and their people are subject to Kedorlaomer, the king of Elam (a mountainous region east of the Tigris and Euphrates Rivers).

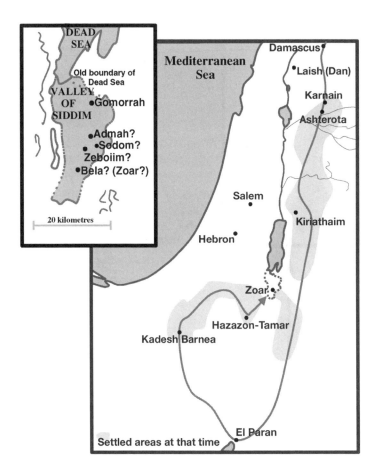

3. After twelve years the four kings from the Valley Siddim form a coalition and decide to rebel against Kedorlaomer. They get away with it for a year.

4. In the fourteenth year Kedorlaomer and his allies come West to suppress the rebellion. Their warrior bands kill, burn and plunder the cities on their way.

5. Kedorlaomer's party then engage the rebels in battle. The four rebel kings are defeated. In the subsequent looting of Sodom and Gomorrah, Lot (Abram's nephew) and his possessions are taken.

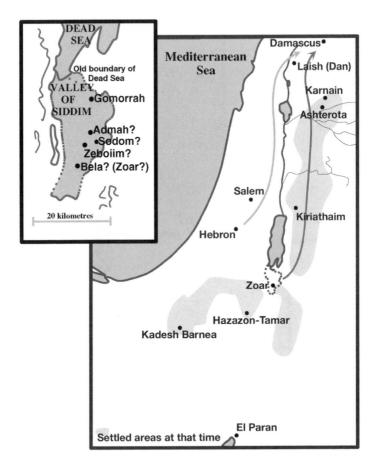

6. An escapee from the battle brings news to Abram who is living in Hebron. He calls together his allies—three Amorite brothers—and his 318 trained men and quickly journeys north to Dan. He attacks the five kings and pursues them to a place just north of Damascus. Abram defeats the kings from the East and recovers all the stolen goods and people, including Lot and his possessions.

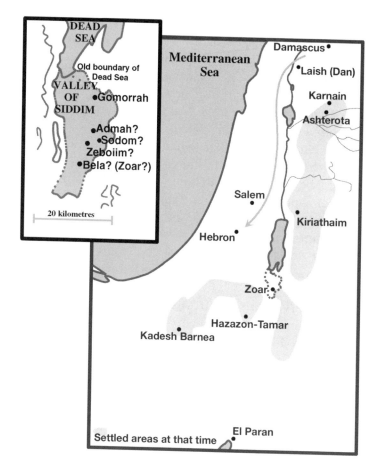

7. Abram journeys south again where he is met by Melchizedek, king of Salem (king of Jerusalem) and the king of Sodom.

This last event—the encounter with Melchizedek, king of Salem (king of Jerusalem), and the king of Sodom—is quite strange. Melchizedek is someone about whom we have heard nothing before. He appears to be a worshipper of the same God that Abram worships. He seems to have the superior part, since he is the one who is offered an offering and from whom a blessing comes.

The king of Sodom offers to hand over the entire spoils of war to Abram, who reacts indignantly, almost insultingly, swearing before the Lord that he will not take so much as a thread or sandal or strap or anything belonging to the king. It appears that he does not want it said that anyone made Abram rich. God alone is responsible for this, and Abram's wellbeing and prosperity are not the result of military or political machinations but the gift of God.

Some observations about history

For some time now it has been fashionable to criticise the Bible for its historicity. For example, an article in *Time* magazine on 18 December 1995 said:

> There is no direct evidence, other than in the Bible, to suggest that Abram's exploits—his rejection of idolatry, his travels to Canaan, his rescue of his nephew Lot from kidnappers in the Canaanite city of Laish (later renamed Dan)—ever happened.

Now to some extent this claim is true—we don't have any outside reference to these people. However, the article fails to mention what we do have. What we have here is a detailed account that looks and sounds ancient. For example...

- The writing style preserves indications that it is reliant on very old verse forms.
- The language contains some unique or very rare words. For example, the word for 'trained men' (verse 14) is used only here in the Bible, but is found in 18–19th Century BC Egyptian inscriptions and 15th Century BC cuneiform inscriptions in Israel.

- Although we do not know the names from other sources, they are the sorts of names that are regularly found at that time in those places.
- The author writes as though his readers don't know of some of the places he is talking about, since the world has changed from the events described. For example, in verse 3 he talks of 'the Valley of Siddim, (the Salt Sea)'.
- The list of defeated people, and the inventory of cities, bears all the hallmarks of having been based on a chronicle of great antiquity.
- The journey followed by the five kings coincides with the Kings Highway, the international caravan route, and speaks of highly developed areas where people live in cities. Archaeological surveys have shown this to be the case between the 21st and 19th centuries BC. Furthermore, these same surveys have shown that there was a complete and sudden interruption to such settled life as the result of some catastrophic invasion that systematically wiped out everything in its path. It is not unreasonable to find in Genesis an authentic echo of this invasion.

The point is that Genesis 14 has many ancient features that point to great antiquity, and while we do not have outside evidence for its historicity, the internal evidence is far stronger than any evidence against it. Such is true of much of the patriarchal narratives.

Melchizedek

Most of us have heard more about the enigmatic Melchizedek from the New Testament book of Hebrews (which also relies on a reference to him in Psalm 110:4) than from here. The writer of Hebrews urges us to notice the following points:

1. Melchizedek **blessed** Abraham, not vice versa (Hebrews 7:1).
2. Abraham **gave tithes** to Melchizedek, not vice versa (Hebrews 7:2).

3. 'Melchizedek' means **'king of righteousness'** and 'king of Salem' means 'king of **peace**' (Hebrews 7:2).
4. Melchizedek was **without father or mother, without genealogy, without beginning of days or end of life, but made to resemble the son of God** (Hebrews 7:3).
5. Melchizedek remains **a priest forever** (Hebrews 7:3).

Because the writer of Hebrews believed that Scripture is God-breathed, he believed that what was included was there because God wanted it included, and what was left out was left out because God wanted it left out. The general trend in Genesis so far has been that we are normally told of the genealogy, birth, and death of every important figure. Not so here. This man simply appears then vanishes, and the writer of Hebrews thinks this is because the Holy Spirit wanted to say something. The Holy Spirit wanted to point towards the sorts of things that the future king-priest would have:

- He too would be greater than Abraham.
- He too would be a priest.
- He too would be a king.

As Abram faces Melchizedek, he does so as the father of the great officeholders in Israel. Although it is strange to our modern ears, Moses, Aaron, David, and Elijah were there 'in his loins' (that is, they were present in prospect). So, when Abram paid tithes to Melchizedek, he was declaring on behalf of everyone who followed him that Melchizedek's office was superior to all of those which followed. Hence, if Israelites gave great honour to the Israelite priests of their day, then any priest according to the order of Melchizedek should be given more honour. What's more, if there is a priest according to the order of Melchizedek, why cling to a second rate priest?

The writer of Hebrews then makes the point that his argument is confirmed by Psalm 110. After all, between Genesis 14 and Psalm 110 there was a line of priests in place who were all descended from Aaron. These priests oversaw the whole sacrificial system. However, there was obviously something wrong with this system—it was weak and useless

(Hebrews 7:18–19). This was made obvious when a priest arose who was similar to Melchizedek.

Psalm 110 looks forward to one who would be just like this, and God promised that this one would be a priest forever according to the order of Melchizedek. If such a priest has arrived (as Jesus has), then perfection is present and perfection has arrived. That means the imperfect, the weak, and the useless are no longer needed. After all, who needs priests who continually die and who offer up bulls and goats as sacrifices, when you can have a priest who never dies and who offers up his own blood?

Abraham had something special out in the desert—he wandered the land of Canaan, intimately tied to his God, and as he did so he was relatively free of religious institutions. For all sorts of good reasons, religious rituals developed at a later stage in the history of Israel. There were priests and sacrifices and blood and temples. These things became a source of great security for the people of God, and a huge focus of attention. The problem is that these things were not the reality, but merely shadows of reality.

The writer of the Epistle to the Hebrews wants us to know that reality is about Jesus acting as our priest, shedding his blood on our behalf, sitting at the right hand of God and interceding on our behalf. If we have him, then we need no others. Moreover, to pin our hopes and our religion on anything else is no longer to trust in Jesus.

We need to understand this. After all, many of us as Christians long for the sort of security that we see in the Old Testament. Since the third century AD we have tried to reintroduce it into our churches. We copy Old Testament worship and structures, and often think about our faith in Old Testament categories. We want to divide God's people into priests and laity, and have high priests, and buildings where there are special holy areas, and so on. But we are not Old Testament people. We are Christians.

We have a great High Priest who has fulfilled all these shadow things and has given us reality. To go back to shadows when you've seen reality is very foolish, and casts doubts on the efficacy and importance of the reality. Jesus has offered the perfect sacrifice and brought us into the very presence of God himself. In him we have direct access to the God of all the earth.

10

The covenant with Abram

In the world after Genesis 3, there is a question of ultimate significance for every human. The question in desperate need of an answer is, 'How can a person be put right with God again?' Without an answer to this question, we are left to fend for ourselves in a world that is set against God and under his judgment. In Paul's words, those who are without God are without hope in the world (Ephesians 2:12).

By all accounts this is not a question that is uppermost in Abram's mind in Genesis 15. Nevertheless, in this chapter God chooses not only to answer the question Abram actually asks, but also another more important question. God's answer undergirds the truly Christian response to the issue of human sinfulness in the face of a just God. In many ways, it is this answer that makes biblical faith distinctive.

WAITING FOR THE PROMISES

After this, the word of the LORD came to Abram in a vision:

'Do not be afraid, Abram. I am your shield, your very great reward.'

But Abram said, 'O Sovereign LORD, what can you give me since I remain childless and the one who will inherit my estate is Eliezer of Damascus?' And Abram said, 'You have given me no children; so a servant in my household will be my heir.'

Then the word of the Lord came to him: 'This man will not be your heir, but a son coming from

your own body will be your heir.' **He took him**
outside and said, 'Look up at the heavens and count
the stars—if indeed you can count them.' **Then he**
said to him, 'So shall your offspring be.'

Abram believed the Lord, and he credited it to
him as righteousness.

(Genesis 15:1–6)

God promises (15:1)

In Genesis 12:1–3 God gave Abram three great promises that
would shape his life and the life of his children. God
promised Abram:

- Land ('Go to the land I will show you'—12:1).
- Children ('I will make you into a great nation'—12:2).
- Blessing ('I will bless you ... and you will be a blessing'
  —12:2).

We saw in Genesis 12:10–20 that Abram does not always
trust God's ability or disposition to come up with the goods.
Nevertheless, God continues to bless him even in his
disobedience.

Although Abram won the battle against the foreign
overlords in Genesis 14, the battle itself must have indicated
how fragile his hold was on the land, on the future, and even
on life itself. Abram lived in a world of great ones, and beside
them he must have looked very small. As had happened
before in the face of great ones and great problems
(12:10–20), Abram appears to be afraid (15:1). It is to this fear
that the word of the Lord comes in a vision in Genesis 15:1.

God makes promises again. This time he promises that
Abram will not need to fear because God is his shield and
very great reward. Both words have military overtones,
recalling the events of the previous chapter. God will meet
Abram's fear by being his rewarder and protector. With God
on his side, Abram should have nothing to fear. His tenure
on the land is guaranteed by God and not dependent upon
his own ability. The content of the rest of the chapter will
reinforce this.

Abram protests (15:2–3)

It appears from the next few verses that Abram is not as impressed as he should be. In some very frank words he raises questions about God's word, by questioning the promises given earlier. Despite God's promise of children he continues childless. His only heir is an adopted slave boy. In other words, he has not even begun on the journey towards being a great nation.

The frankness of the first sentences turns into bluntness in the second. Abram makes the point that, 'You have given me no children...'. The implication is clear—God has promised but he has not lived up to his word.

God responds (15:4–5)

God's response is twofold. First, he gives Abram a word, 'This man will not be your heir; but a son coming from your own body will be your heir.' The tone of this declaration is categorical—God is sticking by his very first word on the subject, and will keep his word despite Abram's question.

Second, God addresses Abram's doubt and scepticism by giving him a sign. He takes Abram outside his tent and orders him to look into the sky and count the stars (the word 'look' suggests a good, long look). We need to remember that these are the night skies untainted by the dulling lights of western civilisation. Myriad upon myriad of stars could be seen, and while Abram stares into the sky God offers another word to go with the sign—'So shall your offspring be.'

The exercise is very important. After all, the very same God who made the stars in the first place is making this promise and sign. This is God, the star-maker. If he can make the stars and make them too numerous to count, then surely he can also make children for a childless couple.

Abram accepts (15:6)

The first half of verse 6 tells us that Abram believed the Lord. The Hebrew probably indicates not so much a one-off action but a repeated or continuing action. He had heard God's word and seen God's sign, and he decided that his life would be one of trust in the one who stood behind them. It is as though he had measured reality up until this point by what he could see and touch—his own increasing age and that of his wife. Now he would measure reality by something less tangible—the word of a known promise-giver.

It is the second half of verse 6 that is incredible. Normally when we talk about righteousness we mean moral conduct, such as in Ezekiel 18:5 ('Suppose there is a righteous man who does what is just and right...'). Righteousness is therefore often a way of talking about God-like behaviour. However, in the Bible 'righteousness' is not simply a moral term used to describe a virtue that can be thought of in abstract terms. It belongs to the world of relationships. Therefore a person can be thought of as 'righteous' when they act rightly in their relationships.

If we take this concept of righteousness and re-examine our passage, then we can see that in hearing the promise of God and believing it, Abram is adopting a proper relationship with God. This verse therefore declares that according to God's reckoning, a person rightly relates to him when they believe his promise.

Travelling through the years (Romans 4)

The revolutionary idea presented in Genesis 15 exercised huge influence on the thinking of early Christians. In many ways it can be considered **the** text by which the apostle Paul lived and breathed. It was crucial to his understanding of what it means to be a Christian. Paul spells this out in a couple of places—Galatians 2–4 and Romans 4. (James also reflected on Genesis 15:6, and we will examine his comments in a later chapter.)

Romans 4 is helpful in our current context because it takes us for a look behind the scenes in Genesis. Paul's point in Romans 4 goes something like this:

When Abraham does what he does in Genesis 15, he becomes a model of what it means to be a Christian. He is a model because he does what Christians do. That is:

- He listens to God.
- He takes God at his word.

Now while putting it that way makes it sound easy, we know from Genesis that it was far from that. After all, to do this Abram needed to make a decision between two opposing forces that were at work in him. On the one side, there was the force of his own physical being—he was old and his wife was old. When Abram looked at himself and his wife he couldn't help but be realistic—they were well past being parents. On the other side, there was the force of God's word, which promised that Abram and Sarai would be the parents of a nation. The heart of Abram's conflict was that physical reality said the word of God could never be realised.

What Abram did was weigh up these two forces, placing on one side of the scales what he saw with his eyes and touched with his hands, and on the other, what he heard from the God of all the earth. Having done this, he gave more weight to God's promise than his own physical reality, and accepted God's word as true.

It is obvious how Abram is a model Christian. We too have two forces at work in us. On the one side, there is the force of our sinful nature in the presence of God. God is holy and righteous and just and we are unholy, unrighteous, and unjust. On the other side, there is the force of God's word: that God has sent his Son, Jesus, into the world to deal with our sin and independence. The Christian is the one who hears this word of salvation, weighs it, and regards it as trustworthy. The great news announced by God in the New Testament is that, as with Abram, God counts this as righteousness for us too.

THE COVENANT WITH ABRAM (15:7–21)

He also said to him, 'I am the LORD, who brought you out of Ur of the Chaldeans to give you this land to take possession of it.'

But Abram said, 'O Sovereign LORD, how can I know that I will gain possession of it?'

So the LORD said to him, 'Bring me a heifer, a goat and a ram, each three years old, along with a dove and a young pigeon.'

Abram brought all these to him, cut them in two and arranged the halves opposite each other; the birds, however, he did not cut in half. Then birds of prey came down on the carcasses, but Abram drove them away.

As the sun was setting, Abram fell into a deep sleep, and a thick and dreadful darkness came over him. Then the LORD said to him, 'Know for certain that your descendants will be strangers in a country not their own, and they will be enslaved and mistreated four hundred years. But I will punish the nation they serve as slaves, and afterward they will come out with great possessions. You, however, will go to your fathers in peace and be buried at a good old age. In the fourth generation your descendants will come back here, for the sin of the Amorites has not yet reached its full measure.'

When the sun had set and darkness had fallen, a smoking firepot with a blazing torch appeared and passed between the pieces. On that day the Lord made a covenant with Abram and said, 'To your descendants I give this land, from the river of Egypt to the great river, the Euphrates—the land of the Kenites, Kenizzites, Kadmonites, Hittites, Perizzites, Rephaites, Amorites, Canaanites, Girgashites and Jebusites.'

(Genesis 15:7–21)

To modern ears this is one of the more bizarre stories of Genesis. It is late at night, animals and birds are slaughtered and cut in pieces and then, in the darkness, the word of God comes to Abram and is confirmed by fiery articles passing through the dismembered corpses. Nevertheless, this is one of a number of climactic events in the life of Abram, the first formal mention of a covenant between God and Abram.

The first thing to note is the similarity between the two halves of the chapter. Each time, there is a word from God, a focus on one part of the promise (children/nationhood in the first half, land in the second), some expression of doubt or scepticism by Abram, and the giving of a further word accompanied by a sign. Each half concludes with a reaffirmation of the covenant (by Abram in the first half and by God in the second half).

As for the details of what happens, any explanation has to be tentative since we are given no direct interpretation. Nevertheless, the prophecy about the future of Abram's descendants in Egypt (verses 12–14) does seem to set the context for the following verses. Perhaps the awesome and frightening experience surrounded by birds of prey and guided by fiery symbols echoes the harsh experience of Israel. There are hints of the slavery in Egypt, rescue in the Exodus, being led through the wilderness by a fiery pillar, harsh treatment by surrounding nations, and the final entrance into the Promised Land. As Abram was the model of faith, here he is the model of what it means to have God as his shield and very great reward.

Although this whole section appears to be a covenant ritual, it is verse 18 that specifically mentions the word 'covenant'. Although the word covenant has occurred before (the covenant with Noah in Genesis 6:18; 9:8–17), this is the first opportunity that we have had to examine what it means and what part it plays in Genesis.

It is clear from this passage that making a covenant with someone (the actual term in Hebrew is to 'cut' a covenant) does not create the relationship. Abram already had a relationship with God, and God had spelled out the promises that went with that relationship. What is happening here is that the covenant solemnises and confirms the relationship that already existed.

In cutting a covenant, God is assuring Abram that he will fulfil his promises, and guaranteeing that the covenant will continue. Both of the conversations with Abram indicate that such assurances come at an important time for Abram.

Thinking more broadly about covenants

Such observations help us understand the references to covenants back in Genesis 6 and 9. There is some debate as to the meaning of the first reference to covenant in the Bible in Genesis 6:18. However, it is clear that when Noah emerges out of the ark in Genesis 9, he does so as the representative of a new but fallen, humanity. The language God uses indicates that God is establishing a covenant with all creation through its representatives—Noah and his descendants (all humanity—verse 9), the creatures from the ark (verse 10), and the earth itself (verse 13).

Although this may seem somewhat abstract, the impact is profound. As created beings we are in a relationship with God by reason of his creation of us. We are not our own, but are formed by God for relationship with him (compare Acts 17:24–31). Try as we might to neglect this relationship or hope that it does not exist, it is there. No matter who we are, there is a pre-existing relationship with the God of all the earth that needs to be addressed.

It is this that provides one of the major points of contact between us as Christian people and the world to which we wish to proclaim the gospel. All humans are created people, made for right relationship with God. This relationship is currently far from 'right'. All humans have made themselves enemies of God through sin, and without God's redemption will continue in that state of enmity. The role of God's people is therefore to wake people to the existence of a relationship that exists between them and their Creator, and to call them back to it by announcing the redemption that is only available in and through Jesus Christ, the offspring of Abraham.

11

Waiting for God

No one likes waiting. Whether it be standing in a queue waiting to buy a train ticket as the train pulls in to the station, waiting to hear the results of a job interview, or waiting for a loved one to return home, waiting can be a difficult experience. The more important the awaited event, the more difficult the waiting becomes.

Abram has been waiting. It is now ten years or more since he left his family to follow the call of this new God (12:4; 16:3; 16:16). The years have rolled by—years of wandering around this new land wondering what God was going to do and when he was going to do it. As this ageing couple waited, the promise that loomed large and urgent for them was that of children. This chapter of Genesis tells us how they handled the waiting for God to fulfil this promise—the mistakes they made, and the things they learned. Their waiting and learning will in turn provide models for us to learn from, since we too often find ourselves believing in a God who seems unwilling to keep his promises, or at least unwilling to keep them when we want him to.

THE STORY

Trouble (16:1–6)

> Now Sarai, Abram's wife, had borne him no children. But she had an Egyptian maidservant named Hagar; so she said to Abram, 'The LORD has kept me from having children. Go, sleep with my maidservant; perhaps I can build a family through her.'

Abram agreed to what Sarai said. So after Abram had been living in Canaan ten years, Sarai his wife took her Egyptian maidservant Hagar and gave her to her husband to be his wife. He slept with Hagar, and she conceived.

When she knew she was pregnant, she began to despise her mistress. Then Sarai said to Abram, 'You are responsible for he wrong I am suffering. I put my servant in your arms, and now that she knows she is pregnant, she despises me. May the LORD judge between you and me.'

'Your servant is in your hands,' Abram said. 'Do with her whatever you think best.' Then Sarai mistreated Hagar; so she fled from her.

(Genesis 16:1–6)

The main elements of the story are introduced to us in these first six verses. We are told that Sarai is barren, and that she perceives this to be at the hand of God ('the Lord has kept me from having children'—verse 2). She has an Egyptian slave girl whose name is Hagar (perhaps one of the maidservants acquired during the sojourn in Egypt–12:16). In her frustration to have children, Sarai tells Abram to sleep with Hagar, explaining to Abram that the child that comes about from the union will be hers.

This whole episode sounds very strange to our modern ears. Nevertheless, we have a number of texts from the ancient world that describe people making these sorts of contracts. It may well have been that there was a cultural obligation for Sarai to act in this way. For example, ancient marriage contracts sometimes had a clause within them allowing the man to take action like this were his wife not able to bear children. Such arrangements allowed people to deal with a matter that to them was a devastating problem of immense significance.

Abram agrees to Sarai's proposition and, in effect, takes Hagar as a second wife. Hagar conceives and then begins to look with contempt upon her mistress (compare Proverbs

30:21–23). In the world in which these people lived, having children was a way of gaining importance and significance. It was the way a woman took her place in the world. Hagar has been able to do this where Sarai has not, and so perhaps she begins to think that even though she is only a surrogate wife and mother, Abram's attitude to her will inevitably change and he will look upon her with increasing favour.

When Sarai notices this contempt she blames Abram for what has happened ('you are responsible...'—verse 5). Abram in turn responds by refusing to get involved, telling her to do with the slave girl as she pleases. Sarai does indeed do as she pleases. In her jealousy and spite, she treats Hagar cruelly and Hagar flees. The product of Sarai's action and Abram's collusion is therefore domestic disharmony. The end result is the presence in the world of a second wife (note that Hagar is called Abram's wife in 16:3), and a child whose existence was not part of God's revealed intentions for Abram and his family. These two problems will be the source of endless strife and ongoing family and national disharmony for years to come. The precedent set here of family dysfunction will continue throughout Genesis, as we hear of the lives of the families who descend from Abram. Just as in Genesis 12:10–20, one of God's people has not been able to wait for God, and has felt constrained to take things into his own hands. Again, the result is disastrous.

None of the participants in this first section of the story comes out well. Sarai lacks faith in God's ability to bring about the promise, and then attempts to shift the blame to Abram. Abram is complicit in the action by refusing to take leadership and assuming false neutrality. Although Hagar is the victim of the story and often just a pawn that is 'taken' and 'given' (verse 3), she shows pride, if not contempt toward her mistress. Just as in Genesis 3, everyone in the story steps out of their proper place, with tragic consequences. As the Israelite slaves would later be forced to flee from the harsh oppression of Egyptians, so this Egyptian slave is forced to flee into the wilderness by the harsh oppression of Israelites.

Intervention (16:7–14)

> The angel of the LORD found Hagar near a spring in the desert; it was the spring that is beside the road to Shur. And he said, 'Hagar, servant of Sarai, where have you come from, and where are you going?'
>
> 'I'm running away from my mistress Sarai,' she answered.
>
> Then the angel of the LORD told her, 'Go back to your mistress and submit to her.' The angel added, 'I will so increase your descendants that they will be too numerous to count.'
>
> The angel of the LORD also said to her: 'You are now with child and you will have a son. You shall name him Ishmael, for the LORD has heard of your misery. He will be a wild donkey of a man; his hand will be against everyone and everyone's hand against him, and he will live in hostility toward all his brothers.' She gave this name to the LORD who spoke to her: 'You are the God who sees me,' for she said, 'I have now seen the one who sees me.' That is why the well was called Beer Lahai Roi; it is still there, between Kadesh and Bered.
>
> *(Genesis 16:7–14)*

As God comes to rescue the Israelite slaves in the Exodus, so now he comes to the aid of this Egyptian slave girl in the form of the angel of the Lord. The phrase 'the angel of the LORD' occurs in many places in the Bible, and a number of times in Genesis. Often these references lead us in two directions as to the identity of the angel. For example, when the angel of the Lord appears to Moses in Exodus 3:2, we are told that it was God himself who spoke from the bush (Exodus 3:4). In other words, the language used implies that God himself is present, and yet God is often spoken of in the third person. The solution appears to be that 'the angel of the LORD' refers to a visible manifestation (in human or other form) of the Lord that is indistinguishable from the

Lord himself. The angel of the Lord is therefore more a representation of God than a representative of God.

Despite engaging in intimate relations with Hagar, Abram refers to her only as 'your servant' or 'her', but the angel of the Lord addresses Hagar by name (and status— servant of Sarai). It is clear that the angel of the Lord knows who she is and where she is from. He asks her about her situation, and tells her to return and submit to Sarai. At the same time, great promises are offered, along with a prophecy about the future of the boy and his descendants. As Abram's offspring would be huge in number, so will the descendants of his son by Hagar. His name will be Ishmael ('God has heard of your misery'—verse 11), and he will be a wild and isolated man whose life will reflect the conflict from which he came.

Hagar is greatly comforted in her distress and names the God who spoke to her. He is El-roi—a God who sees. The location of the well that will be found at the spring of water (verse 7) where all of this happened will become known as 'Beer Lahai Roi'—the well of the living one who has seen me. (The Hebrew used in verse 13 is difficult, and might be better translated 'Have I really seen the back of him who sees me?'—compare Exodus 33:23.) What happens here is unique in the Old Testament. There is no record of any one else ever conferring on God a name as Hagar does.

Resolution (16:15–16)

So Hagar bore Abram a son, and Abram gave the name Ishmael to the son she had borne. Abram was eighty-six years old when Hagar bore him Ishmael.

(Genesis 16:15–16)

Hagar obeys God and returns to the tent of Abram and Sarai. She bears Abram a son and Abram names the child 'Ishmael'. That she bears the child in Abram's tent and that he is named by Abram indicates that he is fully reckoned as Abram's son. Nevertheless, the absence of Sarai's name and presence in these last two verses seems to indicate that her goal of reproducing for Abram has not been realised by her actions. Abram has a son, but Abram and Sarai do not yet have progeny. The promises await fulfilment.

TWO WAYS OF READING THE PASSAGE

As part of the Abraham story

Defective faith

One of the great commentators on Scripture, John Calvin, says that this story is about defective or faulty faith. Like Abram in Genesis 12:10-20, Abram and Sarai take things into their own hands and are not willing to let God work out the promises in his own time. This interpretation finds added weight when some of the key elements of the story are put side by side with the story of Adam and Eve.

	Genesis 3		**Genesis 16**
Verse 2	The woman said to	Verse 2	So she said to
Verse 17	you listened to your wife	Verse 2	Abram agreed to what Sarai said
Verse 6	she took some	Verse 3	Sarai ... took
Verse 6	she also gave some to her husband	Verse 3	and gave her to her husband

The words are almost identical. Sarai is repeating Eve's sin, doubting God's generosity and best intentions for her. In her doubt, she then encourages Abram to go along with her scheme, which he does. Abram, like Adam, listens and is responsible in his compliance. Abram refuses to exercise his headship, and Sarai exerts the sinful desire to rule over her husband. Together they fail to trust in God and obey him.

The results of defective faith

Such defective faith inevitably has results. As in Genesis 3 there is disharmony. However, there is much more than disharmony. By these actions the promise to Abram is jeopardised—Ishmael, the son not according to promise, is born and immediately there is the possibility of conflict, the possibility of two sons of Abram. As we find out in the later chapters of Genesis, this ends up being a far greater threat than could ever be imagined. Moreover, those people who we now know as belonging to Arab nations trace their history back to Ishmael. What happens here seems trifling, but the effects of Abram and Sarai's defective faith endure even to this day. Centuries and centuries of disharmony, opposition, quarrelling and tension have resulted. Abram and Sarai's small act of unfaithfulness has spread like oil on the water, with the result that even today lives are being lost and millions upon millions of dollars are being spent to make war and to strive for peace. All because two people could not wait for God but had to do it their own way.

Note: It's happened again! (Genesis 15 vs Genesis 16)

If we compare this story with that in Genesis 12 we can also begin to notice another pattern emerging. In Genesis 12 Abram is given a great gift by God, and yet as the chapter ends he is demonstrating his own sinfulness. Similarly, Noah's family are rescued in the flood but immediately demonstrate that their hearts are still set on evil. A similar contrast occurs in Genesis 15 and 16. In Chapter 15, Abram hears the great promises of God and believes them. God reckons it to him as righteousness and God establishes his covenant with Abram. Despite this, within one chapter he and his wife demonstrate that they are no different to Adam and Eve.

This pattern is repeated time and time again in the Old Testament. For example, in 2 Samuel 7 David receives great covenantal promises from God, and yet almost immediately we are told of his great sin in stealing the wife of another man and murdering him to get her (2 Samuel 11-12). It is as though God wants the writers of Scripture to remind us that, although humans receive great blessing from God, their nature is still that of Adam and therefore still desperately in need of transformation.

What about us?

We know the struggles of Abram so well. Faith in God is never easy. It calls for persistence. Moreover, failure to trust God has ramifications and often brings bad results. Such passages remind us that fullness of life is found when God's promise is grasped by faith. It means believing that God has our best interests in mind, and hanging on to that belief no matter what.

Surely this is one of the hardest things about being God's person: trusting his word that he has our best interests in mind and not attempting to make things happen on our own. There are things that are so precious to us in life that we find it extremely hard to resist making them happen. We can't wait for God to make it happen in his time. Nevertheless, this passage urges us to wait, and be like Abram in Chapter 15 rather than Chapter 16.

As Hagar's story

Verse 7: A crucial verse

There is, however, another perspective from which we can view this chapter. We can view it from Hagar's side. In such a reading, verse 7 is crucial. In this verse we are told that the angel of the Lord came to her. The major human parties in this story would have been happy to leave things as they were—they had worked out a plan and although it had some downsides it would have worked out okay. But God is not happy.

The point is that God hates disharmony. He created us for harmony with him, with each other, and with the environment in which he placed us. He loves peace, righteousness, and justice, and so when he sees this woman and knows she is being treated abominably by God's people, he responds and reopens the issue. God loves the poor, the downcast, the outcast, and the refugee. This is his nature, and therefore he can never be exclusively committed to Abram and Sarai.

God and outsiders

One of the strong messages of this passage is that God is the God of the whole earth. His dealings with Abram have always had all the earth in mind. He has never, and will never, be solely committed to those on the inside of the covenant with Abram.

We see this in the New Testament in the episode involving the Syro-Phoenician woman (Mark 7:24–30). Jesus is engaged in his ministry to the Jews when a Gentile woman comes to him and begs him to help her daughter. In language that seems harsh to us but which was clearly understood by the woman, Jesus responds by telling her that it is inappropriate to give to Gentiles what has been reserved for the people of God 'first'. She reads Jesus' response as being full of hope and continues to ask Jesus to help. He hears her point and gives her what she asks for. Jesus knew that God had called him to minister to the Jews first but he cannot resist this woman's logic. After all, God's final intention through him is the salvation of all the world.

It is inevitable, therefore, that once Jesus has died God pushes his people out. He sends them to Israel, to Greek-speaking Jews, to Samaritans, to Ethiopian eunuchs, and eventually to the Gentiles and to us. God's nature is always to go to the outcast and to those in need, and such is the situation of all humans for all humans are under sin.

This chapter therefore gives us two examples to follow. On the one hand, we have Abram and Sarai, who fail to trust in God. On the other hand, we have God himself who goes to the poor, the downcast, the outsider, the dispossessed, and the unlikely. Following God in caring for the poor could include the literal poor whom we should treat with care, compassion, and generosity, but also the spiritually poor—those who have not yet heard the gospel.

Attention to both tasks—social justice and evangelism—spring from the character of God himself, and when both are found together a potent combination is formed.

12

Covenant again

COVENANTS ANCIENT AND MODERN

The word 'covenant' is alien to most of us in the modern world. The concept, however, is very common. For example, the wedding service in the Anglican prayer book begins with the minister giving an explanation of the meaning of marriage. This is followed by a public announcement by the couple that they consent to the marriage, and they exchange promises or vows. Subsequently the best man produces a ring or two. What happens with the rings in terms of words and actions indicates that the rings are a symbol of the marriage of the man and the woman. It is not as though the rings make the relationship, but they signify that the relationship exists. After this, various other religious elements are brought into play (a reading of the Scriptures, proclamation of the word of God, prayers) before a formal legal proceeding in which the participants sign some documents in front of witnesses.

The elements of this service are similar to almost any wedding service. They are also very similar to elements of ancient covenant ceremonies. Other modern equivalents to these ancient forms are international peace treaties, and mortgage agreements between an individual and a bank. Such covenants are culturally established ways of formalising a relationship between two or more parties and laying out the requirements, undertakings, and obligations of that relationship.

When we looked at Genesis 15 we started talking about covenants, and particularly the covenant with Abram.

Genesis 17 picks up the whole idea of covenant and develops it further. However, if we are not to misunderstand

Genesis 17 we need to go back a bit and rehearse the background. Genesis 17 is not the full statement of the covenant between God and Abram—it belongs with the previous statements and builds on them.

THE COVENANT WITH ABRAM

Its basic outline

Even though the word 'covenant' is not mentioned in Genesis 12:1–3, it is clear that is where the relationship begins, and that the basic outline of that relationship is stated there. In these verses, God lists the promises and the benefits of the relationship. What is strange is that in some senses the covenant is one-sided or unilateral. Nothing in Abram earns him this covenant. It is wholly initiated by God, based on his generosity and contained in his promise.

The context of the covenant (15:1–6)

Genesis 15 contains two sections that help us understand more about the covenant. In the first section, verses 1–6, God promises Abram that he will fulfil the promises of Genesis 12. Abram responds in belief and God credits it to him as righteousness. It is as though God says, 'Abram, if you believe my promise then this is enough for a relationship to be established between us.'

These verses say the same sorts of things as we found in Chapter 12. Abram doesn't earn this relationship with God. On the contrary, he is given it. The covenant between God and Abram is a covenant of grace appropriated by faith. It is given completely by God's generosity and grace, and received by belief.

In the second section, verses 7–21, the covenant that is already in existence is somehow developed. This development reflects practices of covenant making that were sometimes used in the world of the Old Testament. The two parties would be gathered, some animals would be cut up and their parts laid out on the ground, and the parties would walk through the middle of them. Perhaps it was a graphic way of the parties saying to each other, 'I'm making a covenant with you and in that covenant I'm agreeing that I will act in a particular way. I also understand that you will reciprocate by acting in a particular way. These are the expectations we have of each other and if either of us doesn't fulfil these expectations and obligations then may the god I serve make us like these carcasses.' Jeremiah 34:18–20 appears to refer to such a process.

As you can see, making a covenant in those days was a fairly solemn and graphic thing. Sometimes it was done in the presence of a god who would bring punishment, while at other times it was enacted in the presence of some human great one who would bring punishment. The nonverbal communication was strong, and the process was called 'cutting a covenant.'

This background helps us understand the general idea of what is going on in Genesis 15, but not some of the specifics. For example, although the form, language, and paraphernalia of covenant making are present, only one party—God (represented by the fiery elements)—actually passes through the pieces. Again, it appears as though God is indicating that this covenant is a one-sided, unilateral covenant—initiated, established, and fulfilled by him.

Reaffirming the covenant (Genesis 17)

By the time we get to Genesis 17, the covenant looks impossible. Although God, who made the covenant, promised that Abram and Sarai would be a great nation, they are by now well beyond childbearing age. This chapter is about how God responds to this discrepancy. The themes of promise and that of demand are evident throughout the chapter.

God's promise

> When Abram was ninety-nine years old, the LORD appeared to him and said, 'I am God Almighty; walk before me and be blameless. I will confirm my covenant between me and you and will greatly increase your numbers.'
>
> Abram fell facedown, and God said to him, 'As for me, this is my covenant with you: You will be the father of many nations. No longer will you be called Abram; your name will be Abraham, for I have made you a father of many nations. I will make you very fruitful; I will make nations of you, and kings will come from you. I will establish my covenant as an everlasting covenant between me and you and your descendants after you for the generations to come, to be your God and the God of your descendants after you. The whole land of Canaan, where you are now an alien, I will give as an everlasting possession to you and your descendants after you; and I will be their God.'
>
> *(Genesis 17:1–8)*

Thirteen years have passed since the last episode. Abram is now 99 years old and still has no children from his marriage to Sarai. In the first two verses of Chapter 17, God comes to him again and confirms the covenant he had previously made with Abram, telling him that he will be great in number even though he presently has no children. As part of the confirmation, God gives Abram a name change that will reflect what he intends to do. From now on his name will no longer be 'Abram' (probably meaning 'the father [God] is exalted') but 'Abraham' (interpreted in 17:5 to mean 'a father of a multitude'). This name change is followed by a reiteration of the promises:

> 'I will make you very fruitful;
> 'I will make nations of you and kings will come from you.
> 'I will establish my covenant as an everlasting covenant...'

The repetition of 'I will...' makes these statements very powerful. God is telling Abraham that this contract that has been made is to be confirmed and upheld by him—it is a covenant of graciousness and generosity. Like the covenant with Noah, this covenant of grace will be everlasting (permanent/eternal). Again these verses pick up previous covenants (for example, 'fruitful'—Genesis 1:28; 9:1) and develop them even further. Abraham will not just become a great nation, but the father of a multitude of nations. Not only will he go into the land, but God will 'give' him the land as a permanent possession. Moreover, the ultimate covenant blessing—'I will be your God'—will belong to both Abraham and his descendants. God will be their God and they will be his people (compare Exodus 6:7; Leviticus 26:12).

In passing, it is important to notice the reference to kingship in verse 6. Israel's request for a king 'such as all the other nations have' in 1 Samuel 8:5 is seen by God as a denial of his kingship over Israel (2 Samuel 8:7). However, there are a number of passages in the Pentateuch, the first five books of the Bible, that point towards kingship (Genesis 35:11; 49:10; Numbers 24:17; Deuteronomy 17:14–20; 28:36). It seems that, although God may not have liked the model of kingship put forward by his people in 1 Samuel, his plan for his nation included kings from very early on.

God also said to Abraham, 'As for Sarai your wife, you are no longer to call her Sarai; her name will be Sarah. I will bless her and will surely give you a son by her. I will bless her so that she will be the mother of nations; kings of peoples will come from her.'

Abraham fell facedown; he laughed and said to himself, 'Will a son be born to a man a hundred years old? Will Sarah bear a child at the age of ninety?' And Abraham said to God, 'If only Ishmael might live under your blessing!'

Then God said, 'Yes, but your wife Sarah will bear you a son, and you will call him Isaac. I will establish my covenant with him as an everlasting

covenant for his descendants after him. And as for
Ishmael, I have heard you: I will surely bless him;
I will make him fruitful and will greatly increase
his numbers. He will be the father of twelve rulers,
and I will make him into a great nation. But my
covenant I will establish with Isaac, whom Sarah
will bear to you by this time next year.' When he
had finished speaking with Abraham, God went
up from him.

(Genesis 17:15–22)

Verses 15–21 develop the theme of God's gift. The name
change from Abram to Abraham is mirrored by a name
change for Sarai ('princess') who will be now known as 'Sarah'
(a dialectical variation on Sarai, the meaning of which is not
explained here). Again God offers promises that are full of
statements about what God will do as far as she is concerned:

> I will bless her
> I … will surely give you a son by her
> I will bless her
> She will be the mother of nations
> Kings of peoples will come from her.

Again, the impetus for the fulfilment of these promises will
come from God. Again we see that this covenant, this
relationship between God and this man, his wife, and all
their children, is initiated and fulfilled by God himself. It
does not rest on Abraham but on God.

God's demand

Then God said to Abraham, 'As for you, you must
keep my covenant, you and your descendants
after you for the generations to come. This is my
covenant with you and your descendants after you,
the covenant you are to keep: Every male among
you shall be circumcised. You are to undergo
circumcision, and it will be the sign of the

covenant between me and you. For the generations
to come every male among you who is eight days
old must be circumcised, including those born in
your household or bought with money from a
foreigner—those who are not your offspring.
Whether born in your household or bought with
your money, they must be circumcised. My
covenant in your flesh is to be an everlasting
covenant. Any uncircumcised male, who has not
been circumcised in the flesh, will be cut off from
his people; he has broken my covenant.'

(Genesis 17:9–14)

Clearly we have only looked at one aspect of these verses.
There is another element that comes out equally as strongly:
God's demand on Abraham. A shift in attitude and
behaviour is required of Abraham.

In verses 1 and 2 we are told that the Lord is God
Almighty, and that the covenant is initiated and established
by him. Nevertheless, the demand in the face of this gift is
that Abraham 'walk before me and be blameless'. 'Walking
before God' means to live life before God, to take every step
looking to God and in the company of God. It is about living
a life of devotion to God and of deep piety. It is about being
like Noah, who was blameless (Genesis 6:9).

A similar theme emerges in verses 9–14. God has made
the covenant, but his people are called upon to demonstrate
that they want to participate in that covenant. The means of
this demonstration is circumcision of all the males in
Abraham's household. Circumcision is therefore a bit like
the ring in the marriage ceremony we mentioned at the
beginning. It doesn't make the relationship. Rather, it
demonstrates that you want to be in the relationship and
that you've accepted the demands of that relationship.
Circumcision is a sign or symbol of the relationship (note
verse 11 where it is called 'the sign of the covenant').

In other words, God says, 'Keep my covenant' (17:9) and
then he goes on to tell them how to demonstrate that this is

their intention. They demonstrate their willingness to keep the covenant by causing all the males to be circumcised. Circumcision does not equal keeping the covenant. Circumcision equals a demonstration that you want to live in the covenant (or perhaps, that you want you and your family to live in covenant).

In verses 23–27 Abraham circumcises himself and all the males in his household. By performing this rather painful ritual he is telling God that he is committed to being in the covenant. It is his choice. He is saying that this is where he wants to be—in relationship with God—and that he will pay the cost to be in this relationship.

Again, the ring analogy might also help us understand verse 14, which talks about men who are not willing to be circumcised. Imagine the situation where a married man or woman goes to a mixed gathering alone. As this person is about to enter the gathering, he or she removes the wedding ring and slips it into a pocket or purse. The act demonstrates that the person concerned does not want to be considered married. Here it is imagined that a male who refuses to be circumcised does so because he doesn't want to be considered to be in a relationship with God. Such a person will be given his desire by God. The important thing to note, however, is that it is not God who does the breaking of the covenant. Though humans are unfaithful, God remains faithful, for to do otherwise would be to deny his own nature (2 Timothy 2:13). Moreover, breaking the covenant does not mean terminating the covenant, because only the superior party in the covenant can do this. To break the covenant is to bring about the curses for non-observance (compare Deuteronomy 28:15; Isaiah 24:5–6).

A NEW TESTAMENT PERSPECTIVE

If we are Christians then we too have a covenant, cut and established in Jesus. This covenant is a gift, totally initiated by God and maintained by him—a covenant of grace, entered into by faith. It also has a promise—that the work of Christ is sufficient to bring us into and keep us in relationship with God, and keep us safe from God's wrath on the last day. It is a promise that we will inherit a new heaven and a new earth in which righteousness dwells.

This covenant also has a demand—to walk before God and be blameless. In other words, we are to show that we are in relationship with God by joyfully keeping his laws. Note how John says we have fellowship with God because of the work of Christ (1 John 1:5-2:2) but we demonstrate this relationship in obedience (1 John 2:3-6).

This concept of gift and shift, or promise and demand, is of fundamental importance. We have seen here that keeping laws did not relate Abraham to God, but was an outward sign of an inward and spiritual thing that happened to him. So it is with us as Christians. Keeping laws does not relate us to God. Accepting Jesus, God's grace, and the covenant relate us to God. Keeping God's laws joyfully demonstrates that we know God and love him (compare 1 John 5:1-3).

13

Full marks, Abraham!

IN THE HEAT OF THE DAY

The LORD appeared to Abraham near the great trees of Mamre while he was sitting at the entrance to his tent in the heat of the day. Abraham looked up and saw three men standing nearby. When he saw them, he hurried from the entrance of his tent to meet them and bowed low to the ground.

He said, 'If I have found favour in your eyes, my lord, do not pass your servant by. Let a little water be brought, and then you may all wash your feet and rest under this tree. Let me get you something to eat, so you can be refreshed and then go on your way—now that you have come to your servant.'

'Very well,' they answered, 'do as you say.'

So Abraham hurried into the tent to Sarah. 'Quick,' he said, 'get three seahs of fine flour and knead it and bake some bread.'

Then he ran to the herd and selected a choice, tender calf and gave it to a servant, who hurried to prepare it. He then brought some curds and milk and the calf that had been prepared, and set these before them. While they ate, he stood near them under a tree. 'Where is your wife Sarah?' they asked him. 'There, in the tent,' he said. Then the LORD said, 'I will surely return to you about this time next year, and Sarah your wife will have a son.'

Now Sarah was listening at the entrance to the tent, which was behind him. Abraham and Sarah were already old and well advanced in years, and Sarah was past the age of childbearing. So Sarah laughed to herself as she thought, 'After I am worn out and my master is old, will I now have this pleasure?'

Then the LORD said to Abraham, 'Why did Sarah laugh and say, "Will I really have a child, now that I am old?" Is anything too hard for the LORD? I will return to you at the appointed time next year and Sarah will have a son.'

Sarah was afraid, so she lied and said, 'I did not laugh.'

But he said, 'Yes, you did laugh.'

(Genesis 18:1–15)

Abraham is an old man now. It is the middle of the day and Abraham looks up and sees three men. He has not heard them approach; they simply stood nearby (verse 2). Something special was obviously afoot and so Abraham moved quickly. Despite his age and the heat, he ran from the entrance of the tent and threw himself to the ground in obeisance (verse 2b).

It is apparent that Abraham somehow knows that these men are connected with his God and the promises, and so he stammers out a request to the leader and then urges the men to make themselves comfortable while he brings food.

The old man rushes around like an excited child. Sarah is roused and urged to cook for the visitors. Again Abraham runs, this time to his herds where he looks around quickly and sharply for the calf he'd been carefully preparing for some special occasion. He knows it will be good and tender, and so he directs his shepherds to kill it and prepare it. Finally a banquet fit for kings is brought to the guests. Abraham stands back in the shade of a tree while they enjoy the meal.

Undoubtedly Abraham wonders why they have come and what they will say. Finally, the words come: 'Where is your wife, Sarah?' Abraham tells them, 'She's there ... in the tent.'

The stranger doesn't ask anything more about Sarah. There is no invitation for her to come out, or a request for Abraham to go and get her. Nor is there a remark on the meal. Instead, the leader of the group baldly states, 'I will surely return to you about this time next year, and Sarah your wife will have a son.'

Sarah is standing inside the door of the tent, perhaps curiously eavesdropping. When she hears the words of the stranger she can't help herself. She stifles a laugh, maybe of incredulity, or even regret or bitterness. After all, she and Abraham are no teenagers. He is over 99 by now and she isn't far behind. Her body screams out that she is well past the time of childbearing. For both of them, it seems that laughter is a way of coping (compare Genesis 17:17).

It is then that the identity of the stranger becomes clear —it is the Lord himself. The questions come quick and fast —'Why did Sarah laugh and say, "Will I really have a child, now that I am old?" Is anything too hard for the LORD?' And to make sure that it sinks in, God again puts a time on the promise—next year.

By this stage Sarah's curiosity has drawn her out of the tent. She is in the presence of the four men, and embarrassed and afraid before this man who is actually the Lord of heaven and earth. She denies her laughter. The Lord looks her in the face and gently reminds her that she certainly did laugh.

And then the moment is gone. There is nothing left to say, and so silently and completely the strangers leave. Perhaps Sarah returned to the day's activities, tidying up the food and the place where they had sat in the shade. Perhaps she finally believed the child would come and the promise be fulfilled.

The story of Abraham and Sarah is not the only one like it in the Bible. Similar stories occur at other key points in the history of God's people. There is Hannah, the mother of Samuel, in 1 Samuel 1–2, and Zechariah and Elizabeth, the parents of John the Baptist, in Luke 1. Each story involves people who are in situations of need. More than that, each of them involves the struggle of believing in a God who doesn't always do what we think he should do, or what he has indicated he will do at the time we think he should do it.

In such situations, the great temptation is to think that God does not act because he is not able to act. These stories help, for they explain to us that God has his purposes and that he has his own time and his own time schedule. He is the God of the impossible (Genesis 18:14; Luke 1:37). He is in control and, as Genesis 18:14 puts it, he will act 'at the appointed time'.

ABRAHAM'S REWARD

The way the world functions

Most of us have a deep-seated sense that the world is a moral world, and functions under a law of reward and punishment. We might think, 'If I do positive actions, I'll be rewarded with positive results,' and/or, 'If I do negative actions, I'll be rewarded with negative results'. This rule saturates every aspect of our lives, and governs the way we approach many aspects of life.

This rule is so fundamental that we often use it in the way we think about God. Our thinking goes something like this:

If I am good, God will reward me.
If I am bad, God will punish me.

The Bible appears to endorse such a view. Examples of it occur in numerous passages within Scripture (for example, Leviticus 26; Romans 2:6–10). These issues are at the forefront of the following passage.

The story

The main points of the story of Sodom and Gomorrah are straightforward:

- Genesis 18:20 told us that God had heard of the corruption of Sodom.

- In Chapter 19 he goes to find out for himself through two of his messengers.
- The messengers arrive and are welcomed by Lot, who offers them hospitality.
- The men of the city hear that the visitors are in the city and come to Lot's house, seeking to rape the two men.
- Lot urges them not to act wickedly, and even suggests that they might rape his daughters instead.
- The men of Sodom refuse, and continue to assault Lot and his household.
- At this point the visitors strike the men of Sodom blind.
- They then urge Lot to flee with his family.
- In the end Lot escapes with his wife and daughters (although his wife is turned into salt, because she looks back although she was warned not to).
- God sends some sort of fierce fire on Sodom that causes it to be totally consumed.

A difficult issue

It can be difficult for us to get to the deeper meaning of a passage such as this, because we are sidetracked by the way women are treated. It is particularly difficult in this case, where the poor treatment is being handed out by a father to his own daughters. Although a full explanation is not possible here, there are a number of things that we should take into account:

There is no condemnation or praise given here for Lot's actions. The passage simply describes the events. Lot does not expose his daughters to any danger he himself is not willing to face.

The culture Lot lived in is very different to our own. In such a culture the entertainment of a guest was a sacred duty (compare Abraham in Genesis 18:1–15). The unwritten law of hospitality was more heartily and stringently kept than many written laws, and demanded that the person taking in the stranger provided food and water, respect and honour, and even protection at the cost of life. Practising hospitality was a mark of righteousness.

The people here are operating under a different set of cultural values than we do. We may not understand them or agree with them. Nevertheless, they existed and were conformed to.

Assessing the participants

One way of examining this passage is to look at the two groups of participants—Sodom and Lot. Genesis 18 tells us that God is going to examine Sodom. Genesis 19:13 tells us the result of that examination—God is going to destroy the city because the outcry against it is justified. The city is evil, therefore it is judged by God and destroyed (verses 24–25).

On the other side, Lot is assessed also. The similarity between his behaviour and that of Abraham in Genesis 18:1–15 is quite pronounced. Lot does what his uncle does— he finds the strangers and treats them with hospitality. His actions are seen to be righteous (compare 2 Peter 2:7 where he is called 'righteous') and so he receives salvation and rescue (verses 10–29).

If we look at this passage from the perspective of the law of reward and punishment, then everything seems to work out just as we would have expected. Sodom is evil and is destroyed in devastating judgment from God. Lot is good and is rescued and helped by God.

An alternative perspective

A hint of an alternative reading

There are some hints within the passage that point to another way of reading it. For example, in Genesis 19:19 the word 'kindness' appears. 'Kindness' here translates the first appearance of a word that is used throughout the Old Testament to describe God. The Hebrew word is hesed, and it means God's spontaneous, surprising, unexpected, and undeserved generosity or love. The way Lot sees it, what happens is an act of exceptional grace, not a reward for his righteousness. Although God was under no obligation to rescue, he did. He did this because it is his nature to act in hesed. (For a fuller explanation of this passage and the Old

Testament use of the word hesed, I recommend an article by F. I. Andersen, 'Yahweh, the Kind and Sensitive God' in God who is rich in mercy [Lancer, 1986]).

The story of Genesis 18:16–33

With this in mind let's now return to the preface to the story in the previous chapter. Again, the principal elements are clear:

- Abraham is visited by some strangers (verses 1–15).
- One of the strangers talks to Abraham about Sodom (the conversation makes clear that to talk to the stranger is to talk to God himself).
- Abraham enters into a vigorous discussion with God about the grounds on which Sodom might be spared. How many righteous people are needed to save the city from destruction?
- Eventually, God agrees to Abraham's request that if ten righteous people are found then the city will not be destroyed.

The context of the discussion between God and Abraham is set by verse 19. God has chosen Abraham to be the father of a nation which will 'keep the way of the Lord by doing what is right and just'. It is because of this that he involves Abraham in what is about to happen. The implication of this verse is that if Abraham is involved in the process, he might better understand God's righteousness and justice.

Who stands before whom?

The next verse of particular interest is verse 22. In the NIV translation of the Bible the verse reads:

The men turned away and went towards Sodom, but Abraham remained standing before the LORD.

(Genesis 18:22)

The NIV Bible notes in a footnote, however, that there is an alternative ancient Hebrew tradition where the last half of the sentence says, 'but the LORD remained standing before Abraham'.

This is a more difficult option, because usually when a person stands before another, they are subjecting themselves to the other person's direction and leadership. Like us, the scribes would probably have found the idea of God standing before Abraham somewhat irreverent and even unacceptable. So they may have 'corrected' the reading to what they thought was appropriate. Therefore the footnoted translation may possibly be more original. If so, what it signifies here is that God is placing his planned actions under Abraham's scrutiny and subjecting them to Abraham's questions.

The value of the righteous

Abraham's response is to fulfil his duty to do 'what is right and just' by asking about the rightness of what God is planning (note verse 25b: 'Will not the Judge of all the earth do right?'). He asks God whether it is indeed 'right' to sweep the righteous away with the wicked in judgment. The implied question is whether God values the righteous more than he seeks the destruction of the unrighteous.

The law of reward and punishment says that good and evil have equal value. Abraham wants to know if this is so. Will God destroy an entire city because of the presence of evil people in it or must God, if indeed he is really God, break through in grace and mercy and spare the city because of the presence of good people? It is important to notice what is going on here. Abraham is not asking God to rescue the innocent *from* the company *of* the wicked but *because of* the righteous.

The impact of this passage is that Abraham is acting as God's unexpected associate in matters theological. He is quizzing God as to his enactment of the law of reward and punishment, and suggesting that if God is indeed the righteous judge of all the earth then he should put more weight on righteousness. Those who are in right relationship with God should be able to affect the fate of the many wicked.

Abraham gets it right

As we saw earlier, on a first reading of Chapter 19 it appears as though God acted according to a strict interpretation of the law of reward and punishment. He saved the righteous and destroyed the wicked.

However, I think a closer reading of the passage reveals that Abraham's deep feeling about how God's justice and righteousness should function is indeed right. Genesis 19:29 reads:

So when God destroyed the cities of the plain, he remembered Abraham and he brought Lot out of the catastrophe that overthrew the cities where Lot had lived.

The real reason for Lot's rescue is not his own righteousness but God's remembering Abraham, the man who is righteous (Genesis 15:6). In other words, the righteousness of one person can affect others. God does indeed value righteousness. In fact, he valued it far more than Abraham could ever have hoped for.

This interpretation finds support in another part of the Old Testament where the events of these chapters are mentioned. In Hosea 11, God's relationship with Israel is likened to that of a father to a son. This father loved his child with a very deep love, but the child responded by going after other gods. In verses 5 and 6 God's judgment is announced. Then, in verse 8 God issues an anguished question: 'How can I give you up, Ephraim? How can I hand you over, Israel? How can I treat you like Admah? How can I make you like Zeboiim?' (the cities of Admah and Zeboiim were two of the cities that were destroyed with Sodom and Gomorrah, apparently for the same reason—Genesis 10:19; 14:2,8; Deuteronomy 29:23).

God cries out:

My heart is changed within me; all my compassion is aroused.
I will not carry out my fierce anger, nor will I turn and
devastate Ephraim. For I am God, and not man—the Holy
One among you. I will not come in wrath.

(Hosea 11:8b–9)

145

The word used for God's heart being changed within him is literally 'turned over', and is the same word that is used in Genesis 19:25 for the 'overthrow' of the cities and their inhabitants. The point is that Israel has sinned like Sodom and Gomorrah and deserves the punishment of Sodom and Gomorrah (Deuteronomy 29:22-28). Nevertheless, God takes the punishment in his own being, in order that he might not have to come in wrath.

We who have read the New Testament know how God did this. God presented Jesus as a sacrifice of atonement (Romans 3:25), allowing Jesus to take the punishment of others in their place.

Abraham's inclination as to what was right for the Judge of all the earth to do was on track. Abraham just didn't go far enough. The Cross of Jesus tells us that God loves the people of this world, who have chosen to be his enemies through their independence and rebellion. God seeks all possible ways to restore these enemies to relationship. In fact, his righteousness is that he allows the righteousness of the **one** to save **all** the wicked who put their trust in him (compare Romans 3:21-26; 5:15-17).

This is great news for us. The law of reward and punishment clearly places us under judgment. We, like Adam, have gone astray and deserve judgment. However, the Cross announces that the Judge of all the earth has found a way to be just, and also justify the wicked. God weighs our wickedness against Christ's righteousness, and he remembers Jesus and rescues those who put their faith in him.

A GREATER GLIMPSE OF GOD

These chapters offer us a great glimpse as to who God is and how he relates to us. First, they urge us to realise that our view of God is inadequate if we consider him to be some sort of cosmic accountant adding and subtracting good deeds. He is the God of grace and mercy as well as justice and truth (compare Exodus 34:5-7).

Second, our view of God is inadequate if we do not allow the possibility of the sort of righteousness we see in Genesis—a righteousness that is all about relationship. Such a relationship is entered into and maintained through faith rather than law keeping. In the context of such a relationship there is security, such that the people of God can interact dynamically with God as Abraham did. This leads to the final point.

Our view of God is inadequate if we do not view him personally. He is a God of relationships, who hears, responds, reacts, and even changes his mind about things (compare the constant references in Scripture to God relenting, or changing his mind—for example, Exodus 32:14). He often does this in interaction with his people who talk to him openly, knowing that they are secure in his love (1 John 4:18).

14

When the grace of God rules

In any age the world is a far from sympathetic place for the person of faith. As we have seen time and time again in Genesis, the world is full of evil and disobedience. On the other hand, God is active and therefore the world is also full of the grace and goodness of God. As a result, there are good things in the world and even good people.

The stories we look at in this chapter raise some of these issues in stark manner. We see people making choices in a world that calls them to diverse allegiances.

THE DAUGHTERS OF LOT (19:30–38)

As Lot flees the cities of the plain, he recognises that God has been gracious to him and requests that this grace be extended further, so that he might flee to Zoar, a nearby small city (19:18–22). However, for some reason Lot is afraid to stay in Zoar (perhaps the inhabitants are made of the same stuff as people from the other cities of the plain) and so he and his daughters flee and find shelter in a cave in the mountains. The daughters of Lot had been pledged in marriage, but their prospective husbands were destroyed in the conflagration (19:14–17). Lot's wife became a pillar of salt when she looked back (19:26).

Since childbearing was so important and there are no men around but their father, the daughters of Lot decide that they will have children by him. In order to accomplish this they get him drunk and then sleep with him. They conceive and bear two sons—Moab and Ammon. Each of these sons was to become a great nation known for corrupt religion and immorality.

There have been two lines of approach to interpreting this passage. One has been to see the daughters as good examples. After all, having children is part of the creation mandate (Genesis 1:28). Preserving the line is also important, and so women who think and act in extraordinary ways in order to produce children in Genesis are often looked upon with favour (for example, Hagar in Genesis 16 and Tamar in Genesis 38; compare Rebekah's actions in Genesis 27). Using this type of interpretation, the story of Lot's daughters is about God's blessing continuing to flow to those connected with Abraham.

The other approach is to view the daughters as ungodly examples. Perhaps the daughters had learned from the cities they had lived in, and adopted their practices. Clearly, Lot would have considered their actions as ungodly, otherwise they wouldn't have had to get him drunk to do it. Furthermore, the ungodliness of the nations that come from the boys is not surprising, because they are tainted by their parents' sin.

The second reading of the text seems the most natural. There are no indications within the text itself that the deeds of the daughters are commendable (as opposed to the case of Tamar in Genesis 38). Furthermore, a negative reading of their actions would fit with the pattern we have already noticed in Genesis, where an act of God's grace and salvation is followed by an act demonstrating human frailty. In this case, two women who have experienced salvation from God's anger and judgment fall back into the sins of the people who have just been judged.

ENCOUNTER WITH ABIMELECH (20:1–18)

Although Abraham had been called by God to leave the cities and become a nomadic pilgrim, and although he had been promised the protection of God, it is clear that he lived in fear (Genesis 15:1). In particular, he appears to be afflicted with an idea that some of the local rulers would be attracted to Sarah, want to marry her, and therefore kill him. His consequent agreement with Sarah is dangerous because it puts the fatherhood of Sarah's children under a cloud.

The structure of the story is quite revealing. After a brief introduction (verses 1–2), there are three sets of conversations:

- God contends with Abimelech (3–8).
- Abimelech contends with Abraham (9–13).
- Conciliation is reached between Abimelech and Abraham (14–18).

The first two sets of conversations have a similar structure:

God vs Abimelech	Abimelech vs Abraham
Accusation:	
• You have abducted a married woman!	• You have done things to me that should not be done! Why?
Defence:	
• Will you destroy an innocent nation? (compare 18:23).	• Abraham says that he thought there was no respect for God in the place.
• Abimelech says he had no way of knowing she was married. **Response/Acquittal:** • God recognises Abimelech's innocence (he had known it before and prevented him from sinning) and is willing to acquit. • Nevertheless, there is a condition for acquittal—giving Sarah back to Abraham. Not doing so will mean that he is no longer innocent and must face the consequences of his sin.	• Being a nomad made him insecure and so he needed a ploy (note the implied blame of God—'when God had me wander...'—compare Adam and Eve in Genesis 3).

An acquittal is strikingly absent from the second conversation, implying that there is really no defence. Abraham may be able to explain why he acted, but his defence demonstrates his guilt in contrast to Abimelech's innocence. Abimelech did fear God, where Abraham feared other things more than he feared God (a similar play on the word 'fear' can be found in the comparison between Jonah and the mariners in Jonah 1 where the Gentile mariners come out looking better than Jonah).

Nevertheless, from the final conversation it is clear that Abimelech considers only himself to blame. He even appears to accept Abraham's faulty excuse (in speaking to Sarah he calls Abraham 'your brother'). Abimelech therefore makes amends, not only giving Sarah back to her husband, but guaranteeing Abraham freedom of movement throughout the whole of his realm, and giving gifts that he was under no obligation to give. The sum of money given to Sarah is incredibly large, and is intended to justify her honour in the sight of all. To top it off, Abraham intercedes on behalf of Abimelech, and the king and his family are healed.

The prayer of Abraham at this point is filled with a deep irony. Here is a man we can presume has been praying for his own barren wife, without success, praying for a foreigner's barren wives with immediate success. It is clear from such an incident that what matters most in prayer is not so much the faith of the one who prays, but God's will and timing. Abraham's prayers for a son have not been left unanswered because God can't answer or because Abraham's prayers are faulty. Rather, they are not answered because the appointed time (18:14) has not yet come.

This story is primarily concerned with the question of guilt. Abraham is the guilty party and the Canaanite is innocent. Obviously the fear of God can even exist outside Israel (compare Melchizedek in Genesis 14), and not everyone outside Israel is an enemy. Moreover, not everyone in the world is like the inhabitants of Sodom and Gomorrah.

Second, the passage reminds us again that God's action toward those who belong to him goes far beyond what they deserve or can expect. Abraham is guilty, but his offence and his guilt do not hinder God's goodness.

151

Third, Abraham is still God's means of blessing the world, even in his sinfulness. Therefore he can still intercede for others and exercise a prophetic role in the world.

The story has implications for us. Because of God's act in Jesus we know beyond a shadow of a doubt that God is on our side (compare Romans 8:28–39). Nothing can prevent his goodness. Nevertheless, in the face of overwhelming power, we too often live in fear of the world or the future or insecurity. Often we take precautions to keep ourselves safe. Such precautions are sometimes sinful and restrain us from doing God's will. Sometimes these precautions even cause God and the gospel to be maligned. They also reflect a doubt in God's goodness toward us.

GOD LIVES UP TO HIS WORD (21:1–24)

The faithful God (21:1–5)
As God had promised, Sarah is finally pregnant. The first five verses of the chapter capture the significance of this state:

- The Lord was gracious ... as he had said,
- And the Lord did ... what he had promised.
- Sarah became pregnant ... at the very time God had promised him.
- Abraham circumcised him ... as God commanded him.

The constant repetition is striking: God has spoken ... and spoken ... and spoken ... and spoken. And now he has fulfilled his word.

Nevertheless, given that we have waited for so long the passage is quite strange in its brevity. There is no fanfare, but simply an announcement that God keeps his promise and a woman conceives and bears a son, all in fulfilment of the promise of God. Here is a potent story about the faithful God who speaks his word, waits for the appropriate moment, and then keeps his word. Such faithfulness is so certain that you can simply remark on it and then move on.

Responding to God's faithfulness (21:6–7)

Despite having heard of God's fulfilment, the story doesn't end here. It ends with laughter and joy. Here is a woman who has lived many years with an unfulfilled promise, and suffered severe affliction as a result. But she is also a woman whom God has remembered, and the only appropriate response to such demonstrated faithfulness is joy. The prophet Isaiah captures it well as he reflects on the story:

> 'Sing, O barren woman, you who never bore a child; burst into song, shout for joy, you who were never in labour; because more are the children of the desolate woman than of her who has a husband,' says the LORD. *(Isaiah 54:1)*

Psalm 126 expresses the people's joy as they rejoice in God's faithfulness in this way:

> When the LORD brought back the captives to Zion, we were like men who dreamed. Our mouths were filled with laughter, our tongues with songs of joy. Then it was said among the nations, 'The LORD has done great things for them.' The LORD has done great things for us, and we are filled with joy.
>
> Restore our fortunes, O LORD, like streams in the Negev. Those who sow in tears will reap with songs of joy. He who goes out weeping, carrying seed to sow, will return with songs of joy, carrying sheaves with him. *(Psalm 126)*

There is a great danger that we Christian people forget what it means to us for God to be faithful to his word. The appropriate human response to such great grace can only be joy, laughter, and a spontaneous explosion of sheer delight at God's faithfulness.

The electing God (21:8–21)

Ishmael's pedigree is clear—he is the oldest son of Abraham. Similarly, his nature is apparent—he is a bit of a loner, a wild man who apparently didn't get on well with many of his relatives. Nevertheless, he does seem to have been deeply loved by his father. We see that in this passage, when Sarah urges Abraham to send Hagar and Ishmael away. Abraham is very reluctant (in fact, the Hebrew of verse 11 indicates that he was angry and displeased).

These verses paint a strong picture of Ishmael's experience of God and the people of God. In verse 9 we are told that Ishmael is engaged in some activity with Isaac that appears to threaten Sarah (the Hebrew word used can have positive connotations as in the NRSV's 'playing', or negative connotations as in the NIV's 'mocking'). Whatever it is, it sparks a sense that Ishmael is a threat to Isaac (and therefore to herself?). Her response is to demand that Abraham expel Ishmael and his mother.

Abraham's anger at this division in his family is met by God, who urges Abraham to do what his wife has suggested. So it is that Ishmael and Hagar are sent out with all the provisions they can carry. Then, when the provisions run out and both mother and child are near starvation, God intervenes again to preserve their lives and their influence.

At one level, this story simply functions as an explanation as to how Abraham lost one son. However, at another level it is about God being faithful again—this time to his promise to Abraham, Hagar, and Ishmael.

There is even more here. Often when we read anything past Genesis 12 and the choice of Abraham and his descendants, there is a temptation to think that God does not care about everyone else. This story and many others scattered throughout the Old Testament tell us that God is the God of all the earth. His purpose is that **all** the earth know and love him. Moreover, he cares for the people of the world and hates to see them hurt or damaged.

On the other side, he is also the electing God. He calls this one particular man, Abraham, and says that he is especially concerned for him. Isaac is the son of God's choice, where Ishmael is not. We are not told why, but simply that this is the case. This issue is a complex one, and we shall take it up again when we come to Isaac's twin sons, Jacob and Esau.

THE GOD WHO HAS HIS MOMENTS (21:22–34)

Our final story in this section concerns Abraham and Abimelech again. We know Abimelech to be a God-fearer—this was apparent in Chapter 20 and is confirmed in Genesis 21:22–23. Even though Abimelech feared God, Abraham mistreated him by the deception about his wife, and Abimelech's family suffered as a result.

In this chapter the two men meet again. Abimelech knows that Abraham is going to do well because of God's blessing. He also knows Abraham's past conduct, and wants to make sure that there are no more false dealings (verse 23). For this reason he requests that Abraham return the same 'kindness' he has shown to Abraham. The word for 'kindness' here is the one that was used by Lot to describe God's grace to him in rescuing him from Sodom (19:19). It means undeserved, spontaneous love or generosity.

The tone of Abimelech's speech appears to be something along the lines of, 'Abraham, when we last met I treated you as you didn't deserve. I responded to your corrupt action with generosity and forgiveness. Well, I want you to do the same with me when the time comes.'

Abraham agrees. He then brings a particular grievance over a well to Abimelech. This time Abraham is the generous one—he gives some sheep simply for the right to be recognised as the one who dug the well and who therefore has a right to use it.

This passage presents us with an alternative to the scenario given in the first part of Chapter 20. Abraham is a person who has been promised the land, who doesn't own it, and yet who lives in it. As such, he is in danger. One response is to be afraid and act in a cowardly manner by lying and cheating. Another response is to wait for God to fulfil his word, and to act as God does toward the people of the land ('kindness' is one of the paramount words used to describe God in the Old Testament). Again we have a contrast like that in Chapters 12 and 13 (Abraham lied to Pharaoh about Sarah, then worked for peace and reconciliation with Lot). We also have a similar contrast in results—curse versus blessing.

15

Genuine faith

ABRAHAM'S STORY

With the carefulness of old age Abraham had nurtured a tamarisk tree from seed (21:33). He had watched it grow and become established and had watched his son grow along with it. In a world where the great promises of God only came at his appointed time, Isaac was a guarantee that all God's promises would be fulfilled. Though Abraham was not yet a great nation, and though he did not yet possess the land, he did have Isaac. However, all of this is about to come into question.

At some later time, God comes to Abraham again. We are not sure when. All we know is that Isaac is no longer a baby but a lad (22:12) who is able to carry a reasonable load of wood for his father (22:6). As at the beginning, God comes in his word. This time, however, it is not a word of encouragement, or promise, or blessing, or rebuke, but a word of command.

The command is clear and explicit—'Take your son, your only son, Isaac, whom you love, and go to the region of Moriah. Sacrifice him there as a burnt offering on one of the mountains I will tell you about.' Each word is emphasised and builds on the previous words—'Take ... your *son* ... your *only* son ... *whom you love*.' Each word must have come with great pain.

The tension inside Abraham during that day and night must have been incredible. Perhaps he did not sleep at all. It seems probable that he didn't speak to Sarah. Undoubtedly he privately went over things time and again in his mind. On the one hand, God's word of promise to Abraham was clear—'It is through Isaac that your offspring will be reckoned' (21:12). On the other hand, the word of command was equally clear—'Take your son ... sacrifice him there as a burnt offering.' Both were God's word and, although seemingly contradictory, Abraham apparently resolved to live with the contradiction.

His confusion and grief show themselves in the events of the next morning. Abraham keeps himself busy by taking on the tasks the servants normally do. However, he does them all out of order. First, he saddles the donkey. Second, he gathers a couple of servants and Isaac himself. Third, he cuts the wood that will consume his son.

Finally, they set out for the place of God's choice. With seventy kilometres to travel, they need to move at some pace. They make good time, and on the third day Abraham looks up and sees the place on the horizon (22:4). The little entourage stops, and Abraham instructs the servants to stay with the donkey while they go to worship. He makes clear that after they have done this 'we will come back to you'.

At one level, the words Abraham says to his servants are a lie. After all, if he keeps God's word there will be no return for Isaac. Perhaps these words are therefore an indication that on another level Abraham holds out hope. Such hope would not be surprising, since everything about the God he has come to know demonstrates that he keeps his word. His word was clear that it would be through Isaac that Abraham's descendants would come.

So it is that Abraham takes the wood and loads it on his son. He then grabs the knife he uses to slit the throats of animals and carve them up. Together he and his son walk up the hill—executioner and victim.

It seems as though Abraham could not speak and so they walk on in silence until the boy speaks. He knows there is something wrong and so, as God had broken into Abraham's life three days before, Isaac breaks into his father's silence. The conversation echoes the conversation with God—an abrupt call, followed by an acknowledgement followed by a conversation.

'Father.'

'Yes, my son?'

'The fire and the wood are here but where is the lamb for a burnt offering?'

Abraham knows what he has to do when he gets to the top of the mountain. However, there are signs here too that somewhere in his confusion he holds out hope. This ambiguity comes out in his response, 'God himself will provide a lamb for the burnt offering, my son.' The constant repetition of 'your son', 'my son' throughout this story emphasises the harshness and difficulty of what is happening.

Finally they arrive at their destination. Abraham quietly gathers the rocks for the altar, unloads the wood, placing it on the altar as he had done many times in the past. Then comes the moment for Isaac. As readers all we can do is imagine the confusion and trust in the son as he submits to being bound with the rope, and the fear in his eyes as he sees the knife and understands what is happening.

Quickly Abraham grabs the knife and raises it heavenward. Then, from heaven, comes a voice: 'Abraham! Abraham!'

'Here I am.'

'Do not lay a hand on the boy. Do not do anything to him. Now I know that you fear God, because you have not withheld from me your son, your only son.'

Abraham raises his eyes. He looks around. The sacrifice still must go on. He sees a large ram. Abraham wields the knife on the ropes around his son, grabs the animal and wields the knife again, undoubtedly relieved as he thinks of what might have been.

Then, together, as Abraham had said to the servants, they worship, as the smoke billows toward heaven and the God who provides. In his joy, Abraham names the place after the hope he had expressed as he walked up the hill—'The Lord will provide'. Future generations would remember this day and, as they saw their need of God and of forgiveness, they would look to this place and say, 'On the mountain of the Lord it will be provided'.

> The angel of the LORD called to Abraham from heaven a second time and said, 'I swear by myself, declares the LORD, that because you have done this and have not withheld your son, your only son, I will surely bless you and make your descendants as numerous as the stars in the sky and as the sand on the seashore. Your descendants will take possession of the cities of their enemies, and through your offspring all nations on earth will be blessed, because you have obeyed me.
>
> *(Genesis 22:15–18)*

At some point in all of this Abraham hears the voice of God again. The angel of the Lord calls to him with the warm word of promise and an oath. These are the last words we know Abraham heard God speak. They echo the very first words we know Abraham heard God speak. This time, they are even more lavish, and contain some items that make them particularly emphatic.

- This is the only place a divine oath occurs in the patriarchal stories, here emphasised with the words 'by myself'.
- It is one of only two times in the Pentateuch that the phrase 'declares the Lord' occurs (the other is Numbers 14:28).
- The phrase translated 'surely bless' is used only here in Genesis (although our English versions mask this somewhat by using similar phrases in such places as Genesis 17:16). The Hebrew meaning here is more emphatic and serves to heighten the promise being made.
- It is the first time that Abraham's descendants have been compared to 'the sand on the seashore'. (Previously God has promised to make his descendants numerous—17:2, or as countless as the stars—15:5).
- This is the first time Abraham has been promised that his descendants will 'take possession of the cities of their enemies' (thus meeting one of Abraham's biggest fears, expressed a number of times during his life).

- It is the first time God has promised that not only Abraham, but also his descendants, will be a source of blessing for the entire world.

While Abraham's faith is reckoned to him as righteousness (15:6), his obedience is a clear demonstration of that faith, and is acknowledged as such. Moreover, it earns God's assurance of great blessing: '*Because* ... you have not withheld your son, your only son (notice the repetition of 'your son' again—compare verse 2), I will surely bless you.' Up until now, the promises were grounded solely on the word of God. Now, they are also grounded in the obedience of Abraham.

WHAT DOES IT ALL MEAN?

The clue to the meaning of this story can be found in the very first verse of Chapter 22: 'Some time later God tested Abraham.'

One of our problems with the idea of testing is that we often view it negatively. We think that to test is to be deceptive—to sneak up on someone and trick them to see if they will fail. However, there is another way of talking about testing. For example, if we have a new drug, a new engine, a new theory, or if we have written a new software program, we test it. We test its mettle by putting it through unusually severe conditions in order to see if it is going to be dependable. Sometimes we even test ourselves in this manner—pushing ourselves to the limit in order to prove our capabilities, or to get to know our abilities and ourselves.

This is what God is doing to Abraham here. He tests Abraham in the same way that he put Adam to the test, by placing him in a situation where he had to trust God to provide and to have his best interests in mind. God puts Abraham in a situation where it is difficult to believe that these things are true, and asks Abraham to believe him and obey him.

Where Adam failed, Abraham succeeded. Abraham categorically demonstrated that he loved God with all his heart, soul, strength, and mind. He showed that he loved God more than he loved anything, and proved that he was not in a relationship with God for what he could get out of it. Rather, he was in relationship with God because he loved God.

THE STORY OF JESUS

But this is not all that needs to be said about this chapter. After all, this chapter is integral to the rest of the Bible and, in many ways, can't be fully understood without reference to the story of Jesus.

In Hebrews 11:17–19 the writer talks about this passage and says that Abraham received Isaac back 'as a type' (NASB) or that 'figuratively speaking' he received Isaac back from death (NIV). Abraham received Isaac back from the dead in a manner that prefigured the resurrection of Christ.

It is not surprising that the writer of Hebrews finds in Genesis 22 allusions to the events surrounding Jesus:

- The language of fathers and sons and the particular reference to 'only son' and 'the son whom you love' is strikingly similar to the language used of Jesus in relation to God the Father in the New Testament (compare Mark 1:11; 9:7).
- Mount Moriah is one of the hills on which Jerusalem and the temple are built (2 Chronicles 3:1).
- As they journey, Abraham promises his son that God will provide a lamb for the sacrifice. As it happens, God didn't provide a lamb but a ram. It is easy to see how Christian interpreters would look to Jesus as the lamb provided later.
- The time between the command that Abraham sacrifice his son and the rescue of the son was three days. The father received his son back from death on the third day.

The similarities are very striking. God has a beloved Son and he does not withhold his Son. That Son is fully cooperative. The difference is also striking—with Jesus there is no last minute rescue. Jesus truly dies as the sacrificial lamb in our place. In so doing, God demonstrates again that he is the God who provides. In the death of Jesus he provides for our deepest need—our need for forgiveness and salvation.

Various passages from the New Testament echo the language used in Genesis 22. For example, in John 1:29, John the Baptist sees Jesus walking toward him and declares to everyone who will hear, 'Look, the Lamb of God, who takes away the sin of the world!' In Romans 8:31-32, the apostle Paul counsels us in the face of all our fears saying, 'What, then, shall we say in response to this? If God is for us, who can be against us? He who did not spare his own Son, but gave him up for us all—how will he not also, along with him, graciously give us all things?'

Adam was wrong and Abraham was right. God is for us and he does have our good constantly in mind. We know this because of the Cross of Jesus. No matter what else God says to us or demands of us, no matter what else happens to us, God loves us. We know this beyond a shadow of a doubt, because he took his only Son, the Son of his love, and gave him up to death for us.

OUR STORY

The life and example of Abraham and the sacrifice of Christ are crucially important as we consider our own story and our own situation. They tell us how to live before God.

God cannot be divorced from his word. If we love God we will love his word and seek to obey it. Abraham did this. Sometimes that word from God was warm and encouraging, and at other times it was fierce and threatening. Sometimes he must have wanted to embrace God's word and sometimes he must have wanted to flee from it. However, in this story when he was put to the test and pushed to the extreme, he came up with the goods—he not only trusted God but also obeyed.

This is where the crunch comes to all of us who are Christian, for God tests us even today. He does not tempt us as Satan does, so that we might fail. Rather, God tests us so that we might succeed and that our faith might prove genuine. Such testing occurs when we face situations that reveal the quality of our faith and devotion. He tests us so that he, we, and everyone else can see what sort of stuff we are made of. By such means God strengthens our faith and matures our character, leading us into a fuller assurance of his love and kindness. In other words, God tests us for our good.

James 2:14–26 contains another New Testament reference to the events of Genesis 22, but to understand it, we need to remember some background. Genesis 15 told us that Abraham believed and God reckoned it to him as righteousness. Genesis 22 records the offering of Abraham's son, Isaac. The original context makes clear that the events of Genesis 22 demonstrate that the faith Abraham had back in Genesis 15 was genuine. This is what James means in James 2:22—Abraham's faith was 'made complete by what he did'. As the angel said to Abraham in Genesis 22, his actions showed beyond a shadow of a doubt that Abraham did indeed fear God.

The rest of the New Testament agrees. Doing good deeds does not save us or bring us into relationship with God. Good deeds, as in Genesis 22, demonstrate that we are saved and are indeed related to God.

The larger context of James helps us understand the sort of good deeds James is talking about. They are just about anything that arises during the course of life. James is clear that the genuineness of our faith is tested in both everyday life and in extreme situations. He gives some examples of when our faith is put to the test in the ordinary situations of life:

- A newcomer walks through the door of church (James 2:1–13).
- We see a poor person in front of us (James 2:15–16).
- We listen to or read the word of God (James 1:19–25).
- We speak to our neighbour (James 3).
- We choose to pay wages (James 5:1–6).
- We see something we'd desperately like to have (James 4:1–6).

- We handle our money or plan our business (James 4:13–16).

Testing also happens in the more extreme situations in life, such as when:

- We can't work out what God is doing (James 1:2–8).
- We are tempted not to persevere (James 1:12–16).
- We are ill to the point of death (James 5:13–20).
- We are desperately poor and can't make ends meet (James 1:9–11).

All such situations ultimately come from God, and are opportunities for him and us to see what we are made of and to check where our affections really lie. As we respond to circumstances, will God be able to say of us: 'Now I know that you fear me'. If not, then our faith is faith without deeds. It is as lifeless as a corpse.

16

The last days of Abraham

A DEATH AND A PURCHASE (23:1–20)

Sarah lived to be a hundred and twenty-seven
years old. She died at Kiriath Arba (that is,
Hebron) in the land of Canaan, and Abraham
went to mourn for Sarah and to weep over her.

Then Abraham rose from beside his dead wife
and spoke to the Hittites. He said, 'I am an alien
and a stranger among you. Sell me some property
for a burial site here so I can bury my dead.'

... So Ephron's field in Machpelah near
Mamre—both the field and the cave in it, and all
the trees within the borders of the field—was
deeded to Abraham as his property in the presence
of all the Hittites who had come to the gate of the
city. Afterward Abraham buried his wife Sarah in
the cave in the field of Machpelah near Mamre
(which is at Hebron) in the land of Canaan. So the
field and the cave in it were deeded to Abraham by
the Hittites as a burial site.

(Genesis 23:1–4, 17–20)

It has been nearly 37 years since we last heard of Sarah
(17:17,21; 21:1–7). Her presence, feelings, and thoughts were
absent from the record of events in Chapter 22 (just as those
of Isaac are absent here). Now, suddenly, she appears again,
if only in death, and we find Abraham on his own dealing
with an actual, rather than potential death.

At times in the story so far, Abraham has demonstrated
an apparent lack of concern for Sarah, such as the two times

he allowed her to be taken into a foreign ruler's harem. Nevertheless, as Abraham's affection for his two sons was deep, so it was for Sarah. True, he performs the conventional mourning practices required, but he goes much further. At significant expense and with considerable effort he proceeds to buy a burial plot in which to place his beloved wife. The place he chooses is in the vicinity of Mamre, which had some of the happiest associations for the couple.

Sarah is the first woman of importance after Eve in the book of Genesis. Women will come into more prominence in the second half of Genesis, but none of them will have their age recorded at death. None of them will have the stature or place of Sarah.

The stories here and in the next chapter are gems in the book of Genesis because of their snapshots into the lives of these ancient, Bedouin-like people as they go about some of the routine matters of life—in this case, the purchase of a piece of land.

The story itself is full of innuendo and oriental courtesy. One can't help feeling that each party comes into the transaction wanting a particular result. They leave having obtained that result while looking generous and without having caused offence. Each party talks about 'giving' but what is going on is a sale and transfer of deed.

Of particular interest is how the parties raise the question of price. Abraham offers to purchase, Ephron offers to give, but just happens to mention what he thinks his 'gift' is worth. Abraham takes this mention as a price for purchase and hands over the money (it seems probable that the price is very steep).

The references to Hittites, the land of Canaan, Abraham's alien status, and his need to buy land serve to remind us of the promises and their fulfilment. Near the end of his life, Abraham, who lives by the grace and gift of God, has not yet been given the fullness of the promises. The only land in his possession is a small plot he has had to buy. He may have the promise of children and blessing (24:1), but he is still a long way from being in possession of the land that has been promised. It is still the land of the Canaanites. At the same time, this plot of land near Mamre can also be viewed as a deposit or promise of things to come as far as the land is concerned. Perhaps this parcel of land is like Jeremiah's in Jeremiah 32:6–15, purchased in confidence that one day the people of God will fully occupy it. Here then, Abraham expresses the same sense of hope that will characterise the final days of a number of his descendants (compare Genesis 47:28–48:7; 50:24–25).

FINDING A WIFE (24:1–67)

Abraham was now old and well advanced in years, and the LORD had blessed him in every way. He said to the chief servant in his household, the one in charge of all that he had, 'Put your hand under my thigh. I want you to swear by the LORD, the God of heaven and the God of earth, that you will not get a wife for my son from the daughters of the Canaanites, among whom I am living, but will go to my country and my own relatives and get a wife for my son Isaac.'

The servant asked him, 'What if the woman is unwilling to come back with me to this land? Shall I then take your son back to the country you came from?'

'Make sure that you do not take my son back there,' Abraham said. 'The LORD, the God of heaven, who brought me out of my father's household and my native land and who spoke to me and promised me on oath, saying, "To your offspring I will give this land" – he will send his angel before you so that you can get a wife for my son from there. If the woman is unwilling to come back with you, then you will be released from this oath of mine. only do not take my son

back there.' So the servant put his hand under the thigh of his master Abraham and swore an oath to him concerning this matter.

(Genesis 24:1–9)

The commission (24:1–9)

No matter how cordial the relationships were with the inhabitants of Canaan in the previous chapter, they were not the stock from whom a marriage partner for Isaac would come (Genesis 24:3; compare 9:25–27; 15:19). Moreover, no matter how little of the land so far belonged to Abraham's family, it was their land by promise and no child of Abraham's should leave it (24:5–8).

Other things to note include the discussion with the servant and the process of oath swearing. First, the language and form here are very similar to that used of the calling of prophets in the Old Testament, complete with the characteristic objection from the one being called (compare Exodus 3, Isaiah 6) and the confirming sign. There is a very strong suggestion of formal commissioning and responsibility. The process of the oath reinforces this.

Second, in all likelihood the mention of 'thigh' is a euphemism for genitals (compare Genesis 46:26 and Exodus 1:5 where the term used in our English versions for 'descendants' in Hebrew is literally 'those who came from the thigh of ...'. The word for 'thigh' is the same as the one used here). There are two possibilities that immediately come to mind as to the significance of this act. Perhaps in holding Abraham's circumcised member there is a sense of solemnly promising to ensure perpetuity. Perhaps such an oath promised to an elderly man held connotations that the wrath of his progeny (the issue of his 'thigh') would have to be faced were the oath not carried out (note that a similarly elderly Jacob extracts an oath using the same means in Genesis 47:29).

Meeting Rebekah (24:10–27)

A number of times in the Old Testament, meetings with potential marriage partners happen at wells (compare Jacob and Rachel in Genesis 29; Moses and Zipporah in Exodus 2:16–21). This story, however, is crafted around a significant theme—God's grace. On arriving at the well, Abraham's servant prays to the God of Abraham asking for success. Specifically, he asks that God might show 'kindness' to his master Abraham. The word used here is the one that we have encountered before—*hesed*—meaning overflowing, surprising, and non-obligated generosity or love. The servant is here calling upon that aspect of God's nature that will be mentioned time and time again in the Old Testament. It is the characteristic of God that forms the basis of Israel's past and the surety of its future.

At the other end of this part of the story this word occurs again. In verse 27 the servant praises the Lord because he has shown 'kindness and faithfulness'. God has answered the prayer and acted according to his nature. Moreover, such action assures the servant (and the reader) that this woman is the one of God's choice.

Meeting Laban (24:28–61)

What is needed now is for God's 'kindness' to be matched by another kindness—this time from Laban and his family (notice the request in verse 49). Though the servant and the reader can depend on God to be 'kind', the human participants are not so predictable. Nevertheless, the speech of the servant and the language used in this verse are heavily loaded. Instead of simply asking if Laban and his family agree, the servant uses the same language he has used of God. The implication of the request is, 'Will you do as God has done?', or even, 'Will you go against God?'

It is no wonder that Laban and Bethuel respond by acknowledging what the servant and the reader already knew—this matter is from the Lord. Again, God is active in the hearts of the participants. He continues to show kindness to Abraham.

Finally, in verse 58, the climax to this section arrives. We have God's kindness, the family's response of kindness, now what will Rebekah do? As Abraham was told 'Go ...'

and he went, so she too says simply, 'I will go.' In response, the promises to Abraham by God are reiterated in the family's blessing to Rebekah—she will indeed be the one through whom the promise of a multitude of descendants to Abraham will come.

A transition (24:62–67)

The longest chapter so far in Genesis is just about to conclude. It has not been about the story of creation or the covenant with Abraham. It is about the creation ordinance of marriage. The servant reports to Isaac, telling him the whole story, the two meet and marry, and Isaac loves Rebekah.

The whole narrative has witnessed a significant transition. We began in Canaan with Abraham, the master of a servant seeking a wife for his son. There were two scenes in Mesopotamia—one with the servant and Rebekah and one with the servant and Laban. Now we return with the servant and Rebekah to a new master (note that in verses 1–12 the master is specifically named as Abraham, whereas the master is explicitly said to be Isaac in verse 65). This passage therefore operates at a number of significant levels. At one level it marks a transition from Abraham to Isaac, after which all that must follow is Abraham's death. At another it tells us of the continuity of God's kindness toward Abraham and his descendants. At another it functions as a sort of obituary (note the comments by the servant throughout the passage that speak about Abraham and Sarah and their relationship with God).

THE DEATH OF ABRAHAM (25:1–11)

Abraham took another wife, whose name was Keturah. She bore him Zimran, Jokshan, Medan, Midian, Ishbak and Shuah. Jokshan was the father

of Sheba and Dedan; the descendants of Dedan were the Asshurites, the Letushites and the Leummites. The sons of Midian were Ephah, Epher, Hanoch, Abida and Eldaah. All these were descendants of Keturah.

Abraham left everything he owned to Isaac. But while he was still living, he gave gifts to the sons of his concubines and sent them away from his son Isaac to the land of the east.

Altogether, Abraham lived a hundred and seventy-five years. Then Abraham breathed his last and died at a good old age, an old man and full of years; and he was gathered to his people. His sons Isaac and Ishmael buried him in the cave of Machpelah near Mamre, in the field of Ephron son of Zohar the Hittite, the field Abraham had bought from the Hittites. There Abraham was buried with his wife Sarah. After Abraham's death, God blessed his son Isaac, who then lived near Beer Lahai Roi.

(Genesis 25:1–11)

It is hard to determine whether Keturah was married to Abraham while Sarah was still alive. The placing of the story and the fact that Keturah is called Abraham's 'wife' would seem to imply that this happened in the 40 or so years between the death of Sarah and Abraham's own death. In this case, these verses illustrate the extreme blessedness of Abraham's old age.

An alternative perspective comes from the fact that in 1 Chronicles 1:32 Keturah is called Abraham's 'concubine'. This ascription could imply that Keturah existed in a similar relationship to Abraham as Hagar had (John Calvin proposed in his commentary that Abraham might have taken Keturah as a replacement for Hagar when forced to divorce Hagar). Such a reading is reflected in the marginal reading of the NIV—'Abraham *had taken* another wife'.

There is no way to be certain as to which alternative is correct. In either case, the point of these verses is that through Keturah Abraham fathered yet more nations apart from those descended from Isaac and Ishmael.

The comments in verse 6 about the giving of gifts to the sons of his concubines and sending them away may spring from the same motivation expressed in Chapter 24—a desire to distance Isaac and his descendants from the local people. Whatever the case, it appears as though these sons did not share the same depth of association with Abraham as did Isaac and Ishmael (only they are present for the burial).

Finally, we are told of the death of Abraham. If the age of his death is to be taken literally then the following figures record some of the key points in Abraham's life:

- Call of Abraham (75 years old—Genesis 12:4).
- Covenant of circumcision (Abraham is 99 and Sarah is 90—Genesis 17:24).
- Birth of Isaac (Abraham is 100—Genesis 21:5).
- Death of Sarah (Sarah is 127, which would make Abraham 137—Genesis 23:1).
- Marriage of Isaac and Rebekah (Isaac is 40, which would make Abraham 140—Genesis 25:20).
- Birth of Jacob and Esau (Isaac is 60, which would make Abraham 160—Genesis 25:26).
- Death of Abraham (Abraham is 175—Genesis 25:7).

A number of commentators have argued that the numbers should be read symbolically and that Abraham died while his servant was away looking for a wife (hence the transition from Abraham to Isaac as master in Chapter 24). Whatever the case, we have no record of Abraham meeting Rebekah or the grandchildren (although this doesn't mean it didn't happen).

The phrase 'full of years' implies satisfaction. Abraham's life has been full and rich and now the time has come for him to be gathered to his people (since this occurs before burial it may contain a hint of belief in some sort of continued existence after life). The brothers join in burying their father, and the writer then indicates where the future lies—with Isaac, whom God blessed as he had blessed Abraham.

REFLECTING ON THREE STORIES

Life's like that!

When we read these stories there is a character about them that is different from much of what we have read before. They are stories about life as it is—old age, courting, marriage, death. There is often no explicit mention of God, and sometimes there is not that much explicit theological teaching. Nevertheless, throughout all the stories, we know God is present. He is in the background as the one who gives promises and the one who, through such events, works them out. He is present and active.

The stories are good for us who also go about life doing the same things—working, relating, marrying, giving in marriage, having kids, burying, and dying. As we do, life is often filled with the mundane, and it is all too easy to think that God is absent. Nothing could be further from the truth. Our God is the God of all creation, and his eyes wander throughout the world to support those who are his (2 Chronicles 16:9). He looks, he cares, he loves, and he works out his purpose in the world.

So, what is the appropriate response to such a God? It is to do as the servant did—it is to know his character, depend on it, and trust him. We do this by reading his word, meeting with those who know him, and speaking to him in prayer. And as we do, God will be at work in these mundane aspects of our lives. At times our story will look no different to that of the world around us. Nevertheless, it is different. Our stories are part of God's story and he is in them—present, active, and at work.

Models for us?

Perhaps you have heard people tell these stories of God's people, and indicated that their actions are to be models for our actions. There is no doubt that the story in Genesis 24 is about God's guidance of a particular man. However, we need to ask whether such stories are there to provide models of how to live and relate to God.

We need to be very careful about thinking this way. After all, just as Abraham's conduct in lying about his wife or taking a concubine is not a model of how to treat your wife or how to live in your old age, so the search for a wife for Isaac is not a model of how to seek God's guidance. The stories here are descriptions, not prescriptions. That is, they describe what happened rather than prescribing what should happen in our situation. In this sense, these people and these events do not provide models for us.

This is not to say that we do not learn great things from the stories of these great people. These stories tell us of people attempting to live for God. They indicate how sin can distort and delay God's purposes, and how trust in God expresses itself in good deeds. They offer examples of how faith affects everyday life. In this sense, the stories of these great ones teach, rebuke, correct and train us in righteousness (2 Timothy 3:16).

Looking beyond the present

There is one striking thing that occurs in the life of Abraham that is captured in these passages, even though it is never explicitly spelled out. Abraham never saw the promises of God fulfilled in his own lifetime.

Think of the promises. Abraham was promised a land. Does he have it? No! What he does have is a cave that he bought with his own money. He has not yet been given the land. What about the promise of being a great nation or a father of nations? Abraham lived to see the birth of his son and his growth into adulthood, perhaps he saw him married, and there is a chance he even saw grandchildren (none of these are mentioned, although a literal reading of the dates involved makes him alive for these events). He did father a multitude of nations (the descendants of his other wives). Nevertheless, he is still a long way from nationhood. Lastly, Abraham has been blessed, but that blessing is mainly connected with his own personal situation. He is not yet a blessing to the nations.

Nevertheless, Abraham lived a life of trust in the promises of God. He kept trusting, believing, and clinging to God. It is in this way that he is an example of faith for us (Hebrews 11:13–16). Such examples, like the example of Jesus, should be a spur to us, goading us on. Such is the guidance of the writer of Hebrews as he concludes his reflection on the saints of old:

> Therefore, since we are surrounded by such a great cloud of witnesses, let us throw off everything that hinders and the sin that so easily entangles, and let us run with perseverance the race marked out for us. Let us fix our eyes on Jesus, the author and perfecter of our faith, who for the joy set before him endured the cross, scorning its shame, and sat down at the right hand of the throne of God. Consider him who endured such opposition from sinful men, so that you will not grow weary and lose heart.
>
> *(Hebrews 12:1–3)*

BEGINNINGS: Of Israel

Part 5

The story of Isaac
Genesis 25:19–37:1

17

Esau and Jacob

There are many things in the Scriptures that raise questions about God, and many things that cause discomfort or even pain and distress. In my own experience, there are matters about God and his way in the world that I keep coming back to, and for which I do not yet have a satisfactory explanation.

As I have met other people with difficulties that they have not been able to resolve, I have become aware of how differently we react to such things. I have met people who have ceased to believe in God because of these issues. I have also met people who have ceased to think and ask questions because of the fear of what they might find. I have found bitter people, tired people, blissfully ignorant people, and people who know the questions and consider the answers to be amazingly clear and simple.

In this chapter we are going to look at some of the difficult questions of faith. As we do so, I hope you'll stick with it. If you find yourself getting angry with what the Bible says then ask yourself why. If you think my analysis is wrong, then check it out with the Scriptures. Whatever you do, don't turn tail and run. Finding ourselves and our thinking under threat is the beginning of learning. It is an open door to an increased understanding of God.

INTRODUCING ESAU AND JACOB (25:12–34)

It is very important as we enter into a new phase of the book of Genesis that we don't treat it in isolation. The story of Esau and Jacob, although unique in its own right, can only be understood properly as part of the story of Abraham (which in turn is part of the story that started in Genesis 1–11). This means that when we look at Esau and Jacob we need to keep the promises to Abraham in mind. After all, they were promises to his children as well. Those promises were that Abraham would receive from the hand of God:

- a land;
- children (God will make him a great nation); and
- blessing (God will bless him and make him a blessing to all the nations of the world).

Remembering Ishmael (25:12–18)

There was, however, another promise made along the way that is important to remember. Abraham did not only have one son to whom God is committed and to whom God made promises. There was the oldest son, Ishmael, who is reintroduced here with the familiar statement that structures the book of Genesis: 'This is the account of ...'.

A striking element of the account is that it talks about Ishmael in identical terms to Isaac ('Abraham's son'— compare 25:19). The reference to the years of his life (verse 17) is unique outside the chosen line. Moreover, the twelve tribes that we know will come from Isaac's descendants are mirrored in the twelve princes that will come from Ishmael.

The account looks both backward and forward. It looks back to the promises given to Abraham and Hagar, and reminds the reader that no word of God's returns void. In so doing, it also looks forward, and causes the reader to wonder how God will fulfil his word to the one to whom even greater promises were directed.

Introductions (25:19–20)

This is the account of Abraham's son Isaac. Abraham became the father of Isaac, and Isaac was forty years old when he married Rebekah daughter of Bethuel the Aramean from Paddan Aram and sister of Laban the Aramean.

(Genesis 25:19–20)

Verse 19 is the heading for a new section—'This is the account of Abraham's son Isaac'. Where Ishmael's account was seven verses long, Isaac's will stretch until Chapter 35, even though much of the account will centre on the exploits of his sons rather than on him.

As the preceding verses reminded us of the promises to Abraham concerning Ishmael, so here we are reminded of Abraham and reintroduced to Rebekah (as well as Laban, who will feature significantly in the coming chapters). The reference to Rebekah reminds us of that happy, bustling, bright-eyed woman who goes out to meet Abraham's servant at the well. She offers generous hospitality, and eagerly leaves her family to travel a long distance to be the wife of a man she has never met. She is the one who, like Abraham, will 'go' and participate in God's great plans and purposes through Abraham and his descendants. The picture presented in Genesis 24 is that of a confident, hopeful, and expectant young woman.

Episode 1 (25:21–26)

Isaac prayed to the LORD on behalf of his wife, because she was barren. The LORD answered his prayer, and his wife Rebekah became pregnant. The babies jostled each other within her, and she said, 'Why is this happening to me?' So she went to inquire of the LORD.

The LORD said to her, 'Two nations are in your womb, and two peoples from within you will be separated; one people will be stronger than the other, and the older will serve the younger.'

When the time came for her to give birth, there were twin boys in her womb. The first to come out was red, and his whole body was like a hairy garment; so they named him Esau. After this, his brother came out, with his hand grasping Esau's heel; so he was named Jacob. Isaac was sixty years old when Rebekah gave birth to them.

(Genesis 25:21–26)

If we compare this account with the Abraham account we can see that these verses will function in the coming chapters in much the same way as Genesis 12:1–3 functions in the Abraham story. Much of what will follow has parallels with the Abraham story:

- 'This is the account of Terah' (11:27)
- 'This is the account of Abraham's son Isaac' (25:19)
- 'Terah became the father of ...' (11:27)
- 'Abraham became the father of...' (25:19)
- 'Abram ... married' (11:29)
- 'Isaac ... married' (25:20)
- 'Sarai was barren' (11:30)
- 'his wife ... was barren' (25:21)
- 'The LORD said...' (12:1)
- 'The LORD said...' (25:23)
- Predictions (12:1–3; 25:23)
- First fulfilment (12:4; 25:24–26)
- Age of patriarch (12:4; 25:26)
- Second fulfilment (12:5–9; 25:27–34)
- Wife/sister scene (12:10–20; 26:1–11)

Episode 1 tells us about a reality that is much harsher than expectations. Twenty years pass (25:20,26) and Rebekah is no longer a young woman. Like her mother-in-law before her, she is childless in a culture that has little esteem for a woman who can't bear children. Isaac responds in prayer, and his prayer is answered—Rebekah conceives.

The pregnancy, however, is far from straightforward. There is something strange going on (the NIV's 'jostled' is rather tame given that the Hebrew is more like 'smashed themselves inside her'). The agony of the pregnancy is such that it drives her to wishing she could die (again, the NIV doesn't capture the strength of feeling which literally says, 'If it is like this, why am I here?'). So, as Isaac entreated God in prayer, Rebekah inquires of God.

The message received back from God is clear:

- There are two children in her womb.
- Both will survive.

- Both will be the fathers of nations.
- However, their lives will continue to be as they are in the womb—characterised by division and tumult.
- And the older will serve the younger.

So it is that when the time comes, twins are born. As they struggled in the womb so they struggle to emerge into the world for, as the first is being born, the second has his hand firmly grasped around his heel, trying to haul him back or pull him out of the way. Each child is named in a way that reflects character. The term 'red' (NIV) is used of David in 1 Samuel 16:12; 17:42 (where the NIV translates it 'ruddy'). It probably describes the colour of Esau's hair rather than his skin. In Hebrew the word sounds similar to the name Edom, which will become Esau's other name. 'Like a hairy garment' is a word play on the word 'Seir', the geographical locality associated with Esau and his descendants (compare Genesis 36:8) and has loose consonantal associations with the name 'Esau' itself.

Wordplays are also found in the naming of the second child. The baby emerges clutching Esau's heel and so he is called 'Jacob'—'he clutches by the heel'. While the name 'Esau' is unknown outside the Bible, the longer form of Jacob — Jacobel—is a well known Amorite name that means 'May God protect/reward [him]'). Given the first association, the name Jacob is not a name with very positive connotations—he who takes by the heel, he who supplants, he who seeks to take the place of another. One child will have the nickname 'Red' and the other 'Heel'.

Episode 2 (25:27–28)

The boys grew up, and Esau became a skillful hunter, a man of the open country, while Jacob was a quiet man, staying among the tents. Isaac, who had a taste for wild game, loved Esau, but Rebekah loved Jacob.

(Genesis 25:27–28)

Having already read two accounts of younger sons having dominance over older sons because of God's choice (Abel over Cain, Isaac over Ishmael), we have some idea as to how things will develop. This is confirmed by the birth, and by the descriptions in the coming verses. Things are going to be exactly the way God promised.

In these verses the struggle is fleshed out for us. Esau is a rugged man, a man of the field, a hunter. He is a man's man—Dad's boy, who knows how to pander to Dad's tastes. Jacob is a different man altogether. He is a quiet man, who prefers to stay at home. He is Mum's boy.

The conflict set up in the womb is not just a thing of the genes or the personality of the men involved. It is a conflict perpetuated by the conduct of the parents, and aggravated by their complicity and encouragement. Here is a pile of gunpowder about to ignite.

Episode 3 (25:29–34)

> Once when Jacob was cooking some stew, Esau came in from the open country, famished. He said to Jacob, 'Quick, let me have some of that red stew! I'm famished!' (That is why he was also called Edom.)
>
> Jacob replied, 'First sell me your birthright.' 'Look, I am about to die,' Esau said. 'What good is the birthright to me?' But Jacob said, 'Swear to me first.' So he swore an oath to him, selling his birthright to Jacob.
>
> Then Jacob gave Esau some bread and some lentil stew. He ate and drank, and then got up and left. So Esau despised his birthright.
>
> *(Genesis 25:29–34)*

Ignition is not long in coming. Esau has been out in the field hunting game, apparently meets with little success and arrives home famished. He urges Jacob to give him some of the stew, perhaps knowing that brotherly affection dictated that Jacob should meet his need. Instead, Jacob engages in callous calculation (the three words in Hebrew are 'swear—to me—at once' and the impact is therefore curt and calculating).

He grabs his brother by the heel again and offers to buy his birthright for a plate of red lentil stew. This verse contains yet another play on words—the stew is red, matching the colour of Esau and the name by which he will later be known—Edom. Esau amazingly consents to Jacob's request.

Animosity was present in the womb. The parents watered it and now it is growing wild.

We don't know what the author thought of Jacob's actions, but we know what he thought of Esau's. It is caught in the pattern of words and in the author's written assessment. We are told that Esau 'ate, drank, stood up, and went away' and that he despised his birthright. Such a breaking in to the story to give a moral assessment of the action of one of the participants is rare in narrative literature, and is very poignant here. Esau has treated with flippancy something of immense worth.

A DIFFICULT CONCEPT

The function of these fifteen or so verses is introductory. They offer us glimpses into the dynamics of this family under the headship of Isaac. In some ways, they give us their future lives in a nutshell.

Verse 23 appears to be the central verse. It explains the whole Jacob/Esau story. In this verse God makes clear that things are not going to proceed according to natural expectation. The older child would usually be the dominant child and the one through whom the blessing flowed. However, as in the past, God is not going to follow normal expectations. Even while they are in the womb, God has chosen to do things back to front—the blessings and benefits that are the right of the older son will be transferred to the younger son.

Like the accounts of Cain and Abel and Ishmael and Isaac, this account confronts us with a difficult concept that lies at the core of biblical faith. We are told here what has been apparent since we first opened the pages of Genesis, that is, that God is a God who makes choices. He chooses or elects one person over another. He is the electing God.

Having said this, we need to note how the writer of Genesis presents God's choice in action. We see continually that God does not choose because of anything in the people he chooses. Jacob is not God's person because God foresaw that Jacob would turn to him, but because God chose him to be his person. This is the mystery of God's choice, of the doctrine of election.

The scandal of such a doctrine is easy to see, isn't it? All our moral and religious sensibilities cry out against it. Nevertheless, if we can take it on board for a moment and engage in some lateral thinking, we may be on the brink of learning some great facts about God. For example, the reader of the Bible cannot help but note that God almost invariably chooses the poor, the widow, the stranger, the alien, the sojourner, the last, the younger son, the sinner, the publican, the prostitute. In other words, he often chooses those who have nothing that they can hold up before God as deserving of his mercy. Every time God inverts things and chooses the poor person instead of the rich person, he tells us that salvation and justification are completely by grace. If salvation is by grace, then even we can be saved.

So, what will be the marks of the people who think of themselves as having been chosen by God? The first thing is that they won't have anything to boast about. They will be humble. Second, they will know that their only hope is in God. Therefore they will hope on the promises of God, continually coming to him in prayer. Isaac was like this. He knew that he was dependent on God to fulfil his promise, and so rather than doing what his father and mother had done in getting extra women in to produce children, Isaac prayed, asking God to give him and his wife what they needed.

Thinking about Esau

The letter to the Hebrews was apparently written to Jewish Christians who were tempted to avoid persecution by reverting to Judaism. Perhaps it had become too difficult being Christian, and the burden of election was overwhelming its blessing. In Hebrews 12, Esau is mentioned by way of example to such people. There are two choices for them. On the one hand, they can follow Christ and share the rejection he suffered at the hands of the world. On the other hand they could refuse Christ and all that came with belonging to him. The writer of the Epistle to the Hebrews echoes the sentiment of Genesis—he urges the readers and us not to be like Esau and sell out. Faced with the difficulty of being God's people in a world set against him, we must not give up the imperishable blessing of relationship with Christ for a mess of pottage, for a bowl of red lentil stew.

Our temptation may not be that of the people for whom Hebrews was originally written. Nevertheless, the temptation to drop our faith because of some temporary, although painful, difficulty is nevertheless just as real. In the face of such temptation we must look to Christ as the heroes of Hebrews 11 did, and not buy the red lentil stew. After all, it will pass through quickly and there will be nothing left.

LIKE FATHER, LIKE SON (26:1–33)

As Abraham had experienced a famine, so does Isaac. Where Abraham failed to trust God and headed off to Egypt, God prohibits Isaac (26:2). He then reiterates to Isaac the promises given to Abraham (note the reference to Abraham's obedience in verse 5, which echoes the 'because' in 22:16). The promises are, however, a development on the earlier ones. Isaac will not only be given the land—he will be given 'all these lands'. Not only will the promises be given to Abraham and his offspring, but also to Isaac and to all his offspring.

While Isaac does not follow Abraham in fleeing the land during famine, he does follow Abraham in lying about his wife. He is a man living as an alien in a land occupied by groups of people that look more impressive than he is, and he fears for his own safety. In his fear he lies. Again God protects the integrity of Abimelech and Abimelech promises protection for Isaac.

In the security of such protection, Isaac sows some seed (the first time we hear of a Hebrew patriarch engaging in agrarian activity), and has unprecedented success. Despite his lapse of faith and propriety, he is blessed by God and becomes rich and prosperous. The Philistines see it and become jealous, expelling him from their presence.

In their envy, the Philistines continue to argue with Isaac about his wells. Isaac puts up with it, moving from location to location until finally there is a well over which there are no arguments. As Abraham had sought peace with Lot at possible cost (Genesis 13), so Isaac seeks peace at cost. As God came to Abraham in the midst of his fears, urging him not to fear and promising protection (Genesis 15:1), so he does with Isaac (26:23–24).

Finally God grants him peace with his neighbours. The Philistine leader arrives and sues for peace, citing as his reasons the Lord's obvious presence with Isaac. Isaac glosses over the former mistreatment, and graciously grants the request for peace. It is sealed with a covenant, and that very day Isaac's servants strike water.

Relatively speaking, there is very little material on Isaac in the book of Genesis. Apart from this chapter, Isaac generally only gets bits and pieces of other people's stories, with the result that he appears as a somewhat colourless character in the book. He is a person whose life is so often determined by others. By Abraham and Sarah in his youth, and by his sons in his old age. In many ways this chapter summarises this aspect of his character. Abimelech and the Philistines are the initiators here, and Isaac is the one whose life is determined by outside forces. Even Isaac's relationship with God is less exciting than Abraham's.

However, such a negative assessment is unfair to this man of God, as can be seen from the story of the covenant with the Philistines. Although Isaac makes a mistake in the first part of this chapter, he goes on to act rightly. He refuses to respond to unfair treatment by retaliating, and does everything he can to work for peace. As a result, the Philistines come to realise that God is with him. Through his efforts, the promise that

Abraham would be blessed **and** that he would be a blessing to the nations is fulfilled.

In this way Isaac is a pattern for all the people of God. God's goal in his world is that all the nations see the people of God, and the presence of God with them, and come streaming to God because of them (Isaiah 2:1–4; Zechariah 8:20–23), wanting to share in what they have. In Genesis 12:10–20, we saw that through Abraham's actions he was a curse to Pharaoh. A similar result comes from his actions toward Abimelech in Chapter 20. In Chapter 26, Isaac begins badly like his father, but then gets it right, and the result is that he is a source of blessing to Abimelech.

Isaac may be a plain man and he is undoubtedly far from faultless (he fails in his home life and he fails by lying about his wife to Abimelech). Nevertheless, he is also a godly man of prayer (25:21) who learns from his mistakes. He is an ordinary man who trusts in his God and lives to see God's blessing (the sort of man pictured in Psalm 37).

Isaac is not the sort of person that you'd find a biography of in a Christian bookshop, is he? He is not one of the heroes and high achievers, the ones with high profile and significant influence. Nevertheless, he is a godly person and a person God loves. He is the sort of person that Jesus says will inherit the earth (Matthew 5:3–10). Let's not despise Isaac and his sort. After all, these are God's people, and through such people the nations will come streaming into the kingdom of God.

18

Jacob's deception

For some time now I have made a habit of reading a Psalm a day as part of my regular Bible reading. In this last week I read Psalm 25 and Psalm 26 on consecutive days. Both Psalms are ascribed to David, and yet I found myself wondering how the same man could say such strikingly contrasting things. In Psalm 25:7,11, David confesses to great sinfulness. In contrast, David calls himself 'blameless' in Psalm 26:11 (and verse 3—'I walk continually in your truth').

The same contrast is found in the history of David's life. In 2 Samuel 9–20 often we find a man who is immoral and scheming, a weak father and a vacillating king. Yet 2 Samuel 22:24 records David's claim that 'I have been blameless before him and have kept myself from sin'. Considering David's record of murder, theft, and adultery and Nathan's condemnation of him in 2 Samuel 11–12, it is amazing that the writer can include this psalm in the book.

Because of my view of Scripture I know both perspectives are true, and yet I wonder how they can be. How can David the sinner be David the saint?

These same issues have already been raised in the lives of Abraham and Sarah, but they will be raised even more starkly and with no ambiguity in the passages we look at in this chapter. The people we read about here are no plaster saints. They may be patriarchs and heroes of Scripture, but they are also sons and daughters of Adam. How can God work with such people?

THE STORY OF JACOB'S DECEPTION (26:34–28:9)

Esau's marriages (26:34–35)

When Esau was forty years old, he married Judith daughter of Beeri the Hittite, and also Basemath daughter of Elon the Hittite. They were a source of grief to Isaac and Rebekah.

(Genesis 26:34–35)

These verses set the context for our passage, explaining that Esau was about the same age as his father when he married, but that he was different from his father in a significant way. He doesn't follow his father in marrying from the same tribal grouping or even within the same race or faith. Rather, he marries women from the people of the land. We are not told the details, but the result is that the wives are not a suitable match, and are a source of grief in the extended family.

Such grief is not just restricted to this generation. Numbers 20 records how the Edomites refused to act as brothers towards the Israelites when they sought safe passage through Edomite lands as they journeyed toward Canaan. The book of Obadiah catalogues how the Edomites set themselves against the people of God with great ferocity and cruelty at the sacking of Jerusalem. The New Testament reminds us that it is Herod, an Idumean (one from Edomite stock), who is responsible for the vicious slaughter of the infants in an attempt at getting rid of God's Messiah (Matthew 2:16–18).

Isaac's old age (27:1–4)

When Isaac was old and his eyes were so weak that he could no longer see, he called for Esau his older son and said to him, 'My son.' 'Here I am,' he answered.

Isaac said, 'I am now an old man and don't know the day of my death. Now then, get your weapons—your quiver and bow—and go out to the open

country to hunt some wild game for me. Prepare me the kind of tasty food I like and bring it to me to eat, so that I may give you my blessing before I die.'

(Genesis 27:1–4)

Isaac is getting old and his eyesight is failing. He understands that the day of his death cannot be known but that it might be soon (in fact, he does not die until 35:29). The appropriate thing would be to gather the family and take steps to prepare them. However, what Isaac does is to call in his oldest and favourite son and instruct him to go out hunting and then to prepare a secret dinner for them both where he will bless him.

We cannot be sure as to why Isaac takes such secretive steps. It may be because he knows about the prophecy given to Rebekah about the children in her womb, and that God has promised that Jacob will be the greater. Perhaps he wants to preserve the blessing for his favourite son. Alternatively he may know that his wife would not be happy with his blessing Esau rather than Jacob. We already know him to be a quiet man who doesn't like conflict, and he may simply be choosing the easy way out.

Rebekah and Jacob (27:5–17)

Whatever the reason, the text clearly tells us that Rebekah hears. We know about her love for Jacob, and so we know she won't take this quietly (note how the passage calls Esau 'his' son and Jacob 'her' son—verses 5 and 6). As soon as Esau departs, she calls Jacob, explains what she has heard, and instructs him very strongly as to what he should do (this is the only time in the Old Testament that this Hebrew word 'command' is used of a woman commanding a man).

Jacob's response is one of caution. He doesn't object to the morality of the plan, but simply worries about its potential to go astray. He thinks the plan has holes in it, and that it runs the risk that he will be caught out, in which case the planned blessing will be turned into a curse.

Rebekah assures him it will be all right and that she will take the curse. She and Jacob must know that a curse is a curse, and that it cannot be transferred from person to person. Nevertheless, the false assurance is enough for Jacob and he goes about his mother's will.

Isaac and Jacob (27:18–29)

Taking the deceptive food and wearing the deceptive garb, Jacob goes in to his father. Isaac is wary and surprised, and Jacob responds with two further pieces of deception:

- He lies about his identity (27:19,24).
- He brings God into the story and lies about him as well (27:20). There is deep irony when Jacob says, 'The LORD **your** God gave me success'.

Apparently the disguise is sufficient for the task, but the voice is still suspicious. Isaac is cautious and continues to question his son, but eventually he gives in and blesses him. The blessing given is profound, and has strong echoes of the oracle given in 25:23:

- God will give him the blessings of the earth.
- He will give him rule over his brother.
- Those who curse him will be cursed and those who bless him will be blessed.

Given that the blessing was intended for Esau, it is rich in promise. Although it has echoes of the Abrahamic promises (compare 12:3), it is not as full as might have been expected. There are no references to descendants or the possession of the land. Nevertheless, it was the blessing of Isaac, and now Jacob has both birthright and blessing. Rebekah's mission is accomplished. As Sarah before her, she could not wait for God's promise to be fulfilled and so has sought to make it happen herself.

Isaac and Esau (27:30–40)

No sooner has the pronouncement of blessing finished than Esau walks in with some more good food. The blinded Isaac asks who he is and Esau tells him. The Hebrew text describes his panic in the most graphic way possible—Isaac trembles with a very great trembling. He is uncontrollably anguished, knowing that he has been tricked. He knows the culprits, and he knows that his favourite son has been duped yet again.

Esau's reaction is equally anguished—he screams in distress because his brother has done it again. His deceiving scoundrel of a brother has done what he always does and lived up to his name.

Finally, Esau speaks again to his father. His plea is pathetic in its simplicity, 'Haven't you reserved any blessing for me? ... Bless me too, my father!'(27:36,38).

As the wronged men speak together, they share in the grief and in the hurt caused by Jacob. However, there is no way out of the situation. Even though Isaac is eventually persuaded to offer some kind of blessing to Esau, it is hardly a blessing. The only positive thing it says is that one day the tyranny of Jacob will be broken and the nation of Esau will be free.

Esau and Jacob (27:41–45)

The struggle of the womb reaches fruition and Esau's hatred blossoms. He begins to hate Jacob with a very strong hatred and publicly declares his intentions: he will wait for his father's death and then be avenged.

As the story had begun with Rebekah's eavesdropping, so now she hears again what is planned. She issues instructions again to her compliant son—Jacob is to flee to her brother's house and stay there until his brother's hatred abates. In the Hebrew text, Rebekah tells Jacob that it will only be for a few days and then he will be able to come home again.

Rebekah knows the cost. Should Esau kill Jacob then she will end up without either of her sons—one will be dead and the other will be killed or forced into exile like Cain.

Rebekah and Isaac (27:46)

So it is that Rebekah talks with Isaac. She covers up the real reason for her discussion, and tells her husband that she is wearied by the Hittite wives of Esau (note the repeated reference to Esau's wives at the end of Chapter 26, here, and in 28:6–9). She thinks Jacob should have wives from the same background as herself and Isaac (not for cultural/religious reasons but out of self-interest).

Wrapping things up (28:1–9)

In words reminiscent of his father (24:1–4), Isaac issues instructions to Jacob. He is to return to Rebekah's family and find a wife from the daughters of Laban.

Jacob leaves. There is no record of farewells, but we do know that the few days anticipated by Rebekah turn into more than 21 years. Rebekah, who held such promise back in Chapter 24, never sees her favourite son again. She is left to live with Esau and the Canaanite women.

Esau soon sees what pain is being caused by his marriages, and attempts to alleviate it by finding some better wives. The oldest son of Isaac, but the one not chosen by God, marries one of the daughters of Ishmael, the oldest son of Abraham, the other one not chosen by God. It is a touch of very deep irony.

REFLECTING ON THE PARTICIPANTS

The significance of this story is reflected in an analysis of the participants. The narrator has left clues as to his own interpretation of these events.

Isaac

There are two things that stand out about Isaac in this story, particularly in comparison with Abraham. First, there is the fact of Esau's wives. We know that Abraham saw it as his duty to find a good wife for his son. Isaac does not do so, and his slackness in this regard causes aggravation in the household.

Second, there is the deathbed blessing proposed by Isaac. What he plans to do is highly irregular. In contrast, Abraham arranged matters within his family so that there would be a minimum amount of disharmony (25:5–6).

One can't help feeling that Isaac is not following the example of Abraham because he has some aversion to God's word expressed to Rebekah at the birth of the twins. In seeking to act on his own and not let God work things out, he has done what Adam did. The results are similar— disharmony and tension with his wife and even in relation to God and his plans.

Rebekah

What we know of Rebekah from earlier accounts is that she is beautiful, energetic, and decisive. Like Abraham, she is willing to leave family for the land of promise.

However, in this story, although she knows God's promise and the proper way to act, she clearly oversteps the boundaries of normal and acceptable moral behaviour. If Isaac acted like Adam, Rebekah acts like Eve and takes her husband's authority, exerting her own in contradistinction from him and against his wishes. Even though she has God's word and God's will on her side, she refuses to trust God to bring about his own purposes. Instead, she uses deceitful means to bring about God's will.

Esau

Even though Esau is the primary victim throughout the story he doesn't escape either. After all, he marries contrary to good sense, precedence, and possibly according to God's will. It is possible that in doing so he is deliberately rejecting family tradition. In any case, the end result is pain and trouble within the family.

Further, he doesn't object or question Isaac when Isaac attempts to hold a secret meeting in order to bless him. He goes along with his father's scheme to go against God's promise.

Jacob

Finally, there is Jacob. It is clear that he lines up with his mother and that together they enter into a heartless, exploitative, premeditated act of deception toward a father and husband, a brother and son. By any standards it is beyond the pale, and even if Jacob didn't plan the deed, he went along with it.

The Old Testament is clear at all points—children are to honour and obey their parents. Moreover, they should not break God's ordinance and give their mothers primacy of authority over their fathers.

As we noted, it is apparent from the story that Jacob's worry about the deception is not the morality of what they are doing but whether or not he is going to be found out. The implication is that he does indeed support his mother's aims. As the true deceiver, he is not worried about the act of deception, just whether the risky proposal is assured of success.

An author's assessment?

So far, we have simply noted things that are present in the narrative and made an assessment based on them. We have done this in the absence of any actual statement by the author as to how he views the participants (unlike 25:34 where the author does express his view). Nevertheless, as the story goes on, there seems to be an assessment implied in the way the author presents the stories of some of the participants.

For example, consider the ongoing life of Rebekah. As the result of this act she loses her son for the rest of her life, never seeing him again and never meeting her grandchildren by him. She ends up having to live the closing years of her life with Esau and the Canaanite wives that caused her such disgust and grief. Rebekah pays dearly for her sins.

As for Jacob, he has to flee from home to escape his brother's wrath. He ends up in the house of his uncle who, with strong echoes of this story, cruelly deceives him. On his marriage night his uncle takes advantage of the darkness (compare Isaac's bad eyesight) and substitutes an older sister for a younger one. Jacob gets a dose of his own medicine.

Jacob is also deceived by his children as he had deceived his own father. Like his mother he will spend his old age mourning his favourite son, taken from him by deception.

To cap it off, the author of Genesis compares Abraham, Isaac, and Jacob on their death beds. Abraham died at a good old age, and full of years. Isaac is gathered to his people, old and full of years. But Jacob has no such reference. The author simply tells us that Jacob drew up his feet into the bed, breathed his last, and was gathered to his people. In addition he records Jacob's own assessment of his life—'my years have been few and difficult'. Jacob's words are poignant. He is saying that his life story is one of unrelieved trials and tribulations. We the readers know that this has been the case since the day he decided he would cheat his brother and father.

Each of the characters in this story is descended from Adam and Eve. Each of them is frail and sinful.

A forgotten participant

Given all of this, it is important to note that we have forgotten one participant in the story—God. Behind this story sits the God of all the earth who has a purpose—that Abraham and his children are blessed and are a blessing, and that Jacob succeed Isaac just as Isaac succeeded Abraham.

We may not know why he has chosen to do things this way, but the preceding chapters have definitively told us that this is the way he wants things to go. We know this must be because he knows this is best.

This is where the difficulty comes, isn't it? After all, if this is his purpose, how can he bear to use such flawed people as Jacob, Esau, Isaac, and Rebekah? This is a point that is raised time and time again in Scripture. Scripture is adamant that humans are thoroughly sinful and rebellious. Scripture is also adamant that God works in and through such people in the world to accomplish his purpose. Somehow, God allows humans to do their own thing while at the same time working out his own purpose.

We have a great example of this principle in the New Testament. The centre of the New Testament story is the death of Jesus—an act of intense barbarity and cruelty instigated out of jealousy. It is the most immoral act ever performed in the history of the world. In this event creatures take their Creator and subject him to one of the most horrific forms of execution imaginable. Their action is irresponsible and reprehensible.

Nevertheless, in many ways we could say that there was never a moment in history where God was more in control. From the beginning of eternity God had planned this moment and worked toward it. He had orchestrated history for this moment.

The Cross is an event that is totally the result of sinful human wills. At the same time it is an event that is totally the result of the divine will. Peter captures both sides of this mystery of the doctrine of God's sovereignty in his Pentecost Day sermon when he says:

> This man was handed over to you by God's set purpose and foreknowledge; and you, with the help of wicked men, put him to death by nailing him to the cross.
>
> *(Acts 2:23)*

The mystery of God's sovereignty has huge ramifications for Christian faith. We can view the world from the human perspective or from God's perspective. From the human perspective the world looks totally out of control. It is a place where humans butcher others by the millions, where fighting and arguing are the norm, and where human will and desire are in full flight. From a human perspective, the world is full of people like Isaac, Rebekah, Jacob, Esau, and us.

However, there is another way to view the world—from God's perspective. God says that he created this world good, and that he has a good purpose for it. That good purpose is that it will be made anew into a place where only righteousness dwells. Moreover, he will even use sinful humans and their sinful wills to bring about this state.

Such a perspective is greatly comforting as we view the world around us. We may not understand how God can make his purposes out of such human sinfulness, but we can be assured that he can and is doing so.

As far as we are concerned at a personal level, there is further great comfort. Even if we are Christians, our daily lives have not nearly caught up with the status God has given us as justified in his sight through the death of his Son. Like David in Psalm 25, we are all too aware of our own sinfulness.

On the other side, we know that God chose us, that he expressed that love in the death of Christ on our behalf, and that he loves us even now. We know that his purpose is that we are made complete in Christ (compare Paul's prayer in 1 Thessalonians 5:23). We know that God will, in his faithfulness, bring about that purpose (compare John 10:28; Romans 8:28–39). Our future is tied up in his hands, and he is able to preserve us despite the mistakes we make and despite the fact that we are tainted with the brush of Adam and Abraham and Isaac and Jacob.

Such an assurance does not excuse us from sin or free us to act sinfully. Nor does it free us from the consequences of sin. Nevertheless, it does assure us that God loves us, and that his grace alone assures our future. Such an assurance frees us to act rightly in response to God's grace and in hope of God's future grace toward us.

19

Struggling with God (i)

When Jacob sneaks into the presence of his father, dressed in the garments of deceit and carrying lamb dressed up as wild game, the conversation that follows is full of lies. In one of those lies Jacob says to Isaac, 'The Lord your God gave me success'. The transition from Jacob the deceiver who controls his own destiny, to the Jacob who calls himself the servant of this God, is the story of struggle and difficulty. So far we have met willing participants in God's purposes, who have chosen at times to do things their own way. Here we meet one whose whole direction in life seems self-focused. How will God deal with this man through whom the promises flow?

As we watch Jacob struggle with God and bargain with him, we learn a lot about what not to do. Nevertheless, we also see much that echoes with our own existence and that of the people of God throughout history.

You will notice in this chapter that we are moving at an increased pace. If we started in first gear with Genesis 1–3 and moved into second gear after Chapter 4, we are now in overdrive. This is possible because of the foundations we have laid. It is also necessary because the impact of these chapters is found much more in the big picture than in the fine detail.

Because we are looking at big slabs of material, there will undoubtedly be a temptation to skip reading the Scriptures themselves. Don't do it! Remember that this commentary is designed to give a framework for your understanding of the Bible, not to take its place.

MEETING WITH THE GOD OF ABRAHAM AND ISAAC (28:10–22)

> Jacob left Beersheba and set out for Haran. When he reached a certain place, he stopped for the night because the sun had set. Taking one of the stones there, he put it under his head and lay down to sleep. He had a dream in which he saw a stairway resting on the earth, with its top reaching to heaven, and the angels of God were ascending and descending on it. There above it stood the LORD, and he said: 'I am the LORD, the God of your father Abraham and the God of Isaac. I will give you and your descendants the land on which you are lying. Your descendants will be like the dust of the earth, and you will spread out to the west and to the east, to the north and to the south. All peoples on earth will be blessed through you and your offspring. I am with you and will watch over you wherever you go, and I will bring you back to this land. I will not leave you until I have done what I have promised you.'
>
> *(Genesis 28:10–15)*

A fearful dream

Centre stage is now occupied by Jacob, the quiet, tent-loving homeboy. Alone, he is fleeing for his life because of his deceit and the anger of his brother. Perhaps he is frightened or even depressed (in Genesis 35:3 Jacob calls this the 'day of my distress'). The evening begins to press in on him, and Jacob grabs some stones and puts them under his head as a makeshift pillow (or perhaps around his head as protection).

The dream he has is very graphic, and consists of a ramp or stairway leading to heaven, with angels ascending and descending on it. In his dreams he looks more closely and notices the Lord himself standing at the top of it, and he hears him speaking promises.

The first promises are the same as those given to Abraham and Isaac, and cover issues of land, children, and blessing.

The second promises speak to Jacob in particular, and

seem designed to meet his particular needs and disposition.

First, God speaks words of assurance: 'I am with you'. The staircase itself, intimately connecting Jacob and God, would have confirmed this in a visible form. If we are right in thinking that Jacob felt alone and frightened, then these words parallel the words given by God to Abraham and Isaac, who also experienced fear in the Promised Land (although probably over different issues—compare Genesis 15:1; 26:7). Jacob need not be frightened. Even though he is a fugitive, God has not abandoned him.

Second, God tells Jacob that he will 'keep' him (NIV has 'watch over you'). The ascending and descending angels are at Jacob's disposal. Later in his life, Jacob probably refers to this when he talks about 'the Angel who has delivered me from all harm' (48:16).

Last, God assures the homeboy that he will bring him home. God will not leave him abandoned and displaced, but will return him to where he belongs.

As far as we can tell, this is Jacob's first personal encounter with the God of his parents. He is scared and overwhelmed, and confesses that he had not realised that God was in this place. However, having met God he responds appropriately by setting up a sacred pillar and naming the place ('Bethel' – 'the house of God'). Finally, he makes a vow that echoes and responds to each of the three personal promises given by God.

This event created the obvious possibility for a new orientation for Jacob. It is also obvious that any transition to being completely free of his old nature is still some distance away. The vow is still very much conditional (notice the 'if' in verse 20). The final transition will take some time yet.

Some larger biblical reflections

Psalm 23

When Jacob fleshes out the three promises given to him by God, he talks in terms of God:

- being with him;
- watching over him on the journey he is taking, by giving him food to eat and clothes to wear; and

- returning him safely to his father's house (28:20–22).

There is a striking parallel between God's promises and Jacob's reinterpretation of them, and Psalm 23—

- Verses 1–3 talk of God being a shepherd who guards, cares for, and watches over his sheep (compare Genesis 48:15 where Jacob talks of God as the one who has been his shepherd all his life).
- Verse 4 talks of God being 'with' the Psalmist and that therefore there is no need to fear.
- Verse 5 talks of God supplying David's material needs.
- Verse 6 talks about God's goodness and love following David and causing him to dwell in the house of the Lord forever (bringing David back to where he belongs —to the presence of God).

The promises given to Jacob are not just promises directed to Jacob. They may have practical and immediate reference to him in his particular situation, but they are also a summary of the best promises of God, directed toward the deepest yearnings of the people of God. Moreover, they are words that the New Testament picks up and gives back to us in Christ.

- Jesus is called Immanuel, 'God with us' (Matthew 1:23), and we are told that he will always be with us, even to the very end of the age (Matthew 28:20).
- Jesus tells us that he will protect us, and that no-one will snatch us out of his hand or separate us from him or his Father (John 10:27–29).
- Jesus tells us that we should not worry about food and clothing, because if God can clothe the grass of the field he can give us all that we need (Matthew 6:25–34).
- Jesus promises that he has gone to prepare a place for us, and that he will bring us to be where we belong— with him (John 14:1–3).

Most of these promises are made by Jesus in the context of responding to our fears. The overwhelming impact of them is therefore that God is for us and will keep us. His perfect love for us should cast out all fear. He will fulfil his promise to us just as he did to Jacob.

A true Israelite

John 1:43–51 describes an event from the early days of the public ministry of Jesus. In verse 43 Jesus finds Philip and urges Philip to follow him. Philip in turn finds Nathanael, and tells him that he has found God's promised one. Nathanael is sceptical but agrees to come along with Philip and have a closer look.

When Jesus sees Nathanael coming toward him he says, 'Here is a true Israelite, in whom there is nothing false.' There are a number of associations with the Jacob story here. First, the Greek word translated as 'nothing false' is the same one used for 'deceit' in the Greek translation of the Jacob story. Second, the term 'Israelite' reminds us that Jacob the deceiver was renamed the much more positive name of 'Israel' by God in Genesis 32:22–32. Jesus is probably saying that here is an 'Israel', not a 'Jacob'.

As a result of the ensuing conversation Nathanael comes to realise that Jesus is indeed the Son of God, the King of Israel. At this point Jesus answers him by saying:

> 'You believe because I told you I saw you under the fig tree. You shall see greater things than that.' He then added, 'I tell you the truth, you shall see heaven open, and the angels of God ascending and descending on the Son of Man.'
>
> *(John 1:50–51)*

Jesus is obviously drawing on the story of Jacob. At Bethel, God revealed himself to Jacob, and the angels descended to earth and spoke to humans (as well as God speaking directly to Jacob). What Jesus is saying is that God is doing this again—he is making a new Bethel, a new house of God, a new place of revelation. In the ministry of Jesus, God will tear open heaven again and come to earth, and this time not on Jacob but on Jesus. Jesus is the new house of God and place of divine revelation. He is the place where God speaks to humanity and where permanent contact with God and heaven is made.

RUNAWAY PROSPERITY (29:1–30:24)

Then Jacob continued on his journey and came to the land of the eastern peoples. There he saw a well in the field, with three flocks of sheep lying near it because the flocks were watered from that well. The stone over the mouth of the well was large. When all the flocks were gathered there, the shepherds would roll the stone away from the well's mouth and water the sheep. Then they would return the stone to its place over the mouth of the well.

Jacob asked the shepherds, 'My brothers, where are you from?' 'We're from Haran,' they replied. He said to them, 'Do you know Laban, Nahor's grandson?' 'Yes, we know him,' they answered. Then Jacob asked them, 'Is he well?' 'Yes, he is,' they said, 'and here comes his daughter Rachel with the sheep.'

'Look,' he said, 'the sun is still high; it is not time for the flocks to be gathered. Water the sheep and take them back to pasture.'

'We can't,' they replied, 'until all the flocks are gathered and the stone has been rolled away from the mouth of the well. Then we will water the sheep.'

While he was still talking with them, Rachel came with her father's sheep, for she was a shepherdess. When Jacob saw Rachel daughter of Laban, his mother's brother, and Laban's sheep, he went over and rolled the stone away from the mouth of the well and watered his uncle's sheep. Then Jacob kissed Rachel and began to weep aloud. He had told Rachel that he was a relative of her father and a son of Rebekah. So she ran and told her father.

As soon as Laban heard the news about Jacob, his sister's son, he hurried to meet him. He embraced him and kissed him and brought him to his home, and there Jacob told him all these things. Then Laban said to him, 'You are my own flesh and blood.'

(Genesis 29:1–14a)

The setting for the story

The promises, both those to Abraham and particularly those to Jacob, frame the stories that are to come. Will God indeed bless Jacob, give him the land and children? Will he be with him, watch over him, and bring him back? Will God resolve the issues with each of these promises? How can God give children to a man with no wife? How can God watch over a man who is determined to watch over himself? How can God bring Jacob home when an angry brother awaits him?

Everything according to plan? (29:1–14)

At first glance everything seems to go according to plan. Jacob finds the right well, the right family, and God's providential guidance is apparent. God is truly with Jacob as promised.

However, a comparison with Genesis 24 and the choosing of Isaac's wife demonstrates that there are still some very significant issues unresolved.

GENESIS 24	GENESIS 29:1–14
Isaac is represented by a servant who has the evident blessing of Abraham.	Jacob is on his own, making his own way.
The servant is obviously a man of faith.	Jacob's faith is not mentioned in this passage. In the previous passage he bargains with God.
Rebekah is a person of evident character.	Jacob, not Rachel is highlighted.
Laban goes out to meet the servant, and is greeted with gifts and wealth.	Laban goes out to meet Jacob, and is met by a man without independent means of support.
The future bride comes out and marriage is mentioned quickly.	The future bride comes out but there is no mention of marriage.

Things are not nearly as smooth as they were with the servant and Isaac back in Genesis 24. God is with Jacob. but there is still no sign of descendants, or of a return to the land. Jacob is a man with promises but without means. He is also at the mercy of a man who takes advantage of others for his own good. There are still many obstacles to be overcome.

Marriage (29:15–30)

> Then Jacob said to Laban, 'Give me my wife. My time is completed, and I want to lie with her.'
>
> So Laban brought together all the people of the place and gave a feast. But when evening came, he took his daughter Leah and gave her to Jacob, and Jacob lay with her. And Laban gave his servant girl Zilpah to his daughter as her maidservant.
>
> When morning came, there was Leah! So Jacob said to Laban, 'What is this you have done to me? I served you for Rachel, didn't I? Why have you deceived me?'
>
> Laban replied, 'It is not our custom here to give the younger daughter in marriage before the older one. Finish this daughter's bridal week; then we will give you the younger one also, in return for another seven years of work.'
>
> *(Genesis 29:21–27)*

At one level, there is a distinct improvement in this episode. In the previous episode God had guided and kept watch over Jacob. In this episode he gains two wives and is therefore well on the way to having descendants. However, his return home (which was going to be in a few days) is now a long way away.

The story tells us a lot about God's dealings with people. It is obvious that Laban sees Jacob's interest in Rachel but also sees that he has no resources. When he asks what Jacob's wages should be, he undoubtedly knows what the response will be and grasps the avenue for exploitation. He is a man of cunning, a more than equal match for another man of cunning.

As we noted earlier, the associations between this passage and Genesis 27 are rich. There are two daughters, one younger and one older. Jacob is in the position of Isaac—his favourite is the younger one. Like Isaac, he is tricked in the darkness and by subterfuge. There is an inversion of rights, and the whole incident results in friction within the household. Laban has done a Jacob to Jacob, and through it God has judged his person (compare Amos 3:2; Hebrews 12:5-6, quoting Proverbs 3:11-12). Nevertheless, while Jacob's sin is exposed and judged, and while Laban is God's instrument for punishment, the end result is two wives who will bear Jacob the twelve tribes of Israel.

Children! (29:31–30:24)

> **Then God remembered Rachel; he listened to her and opened her womb. She became pregnant and gave birth to a son and said, 'God has taken away my disgrace.' She named him Joseph, and said, 'May the LORD add to me another son.**   '
>
> *(Genesis 30:22–24)*

As with Sarah and Rebekah, the main issue here is Rachel's barrenness and how she comes to bear a child. Nevertheless, in passing we are told again of God's love and care for the disadvantaged, dispossessed, and unloved, represented by Leah. In all, Leah bears seven children—one for each of the years that Jacob laboured for his second wife.

Rachel's barrenness also results in rivalry and tricks involving maids (30:3-13) and fertility or aphrodisiac drugs (30:14). Names of children are given that bear hints of gloating. Here is a family fathered by a lying trickster and mothered by far from perfect women. The result is strife and ungodly competition. Nevertheless, God is at work and twelve patriarchs are born. Again, divine grace triumphs over human sinfulness.

The climax of the passage is found in Genesis 30:22–24. In verse 22 we are told that 'God remembered Rachel'. The phrase 'God remembered' occurred in Genesis 8:1 when God remembered Noah and caused the flood to abate and in 19:29 when he remembered Abraham and rescued Lot from the holocaust of Sodom and Gomorrah (compare Exodus

2:24). God's remembering is not just recalling something. It has the connotations of his springing into action, of acting on behalf of the one remembered. The point is that no amount of trickery or deception or human antics will give Rachel or the people of God a future. Their hope and future lies with God and his remembering.

So it is with us. When we are helpless and weak, then we are strong (compare 2 Corinthians 12:7–10). Then we are ready for God and ripe for him to remember us. At such a point God can be God for us.

20

Struggling with God (ii)

TIME TO GO HOME (30:25–31:55)

Jacob had pitched his tent in the hill country of Gilead when Laban overtook him, and Laban and his relatives camped there too. Then Laban said to Jacob, 'What have you done? You've deceived me, and you've carried off my daughters like captives in war. Why did you run off secretly and deceive me? Why didn't you tell me, so I could send you away with joy and singing to the music of tambourines and harps? You didn't even let me kiss my grandchildren and my daughters good-bye. You have done a foolish thing. I have the power to harm you; but last night the God of your father said to me, "Be careful not to say anything to Jacob, either good or bad." Now you have gone off because you longed to return to your father's house. But why did you steal my gods?'

Jacob answered Laban, 'I was afraid, because I thought you would take your daughters away from me by force. But if you find anyone who has your gods, he shall not live. In the presence of our relatives, see for yourself whether there is anything of yours here with me; and if so, take it.' Now Jacob did not know that Rachel had stolen the gods.

So Laban went into Jacob's tent and into Leah's tent and into the tent of the two maidservants, but he found nothing. After he came out of Leah's tent, he entered Rachel's tent. Now Rachel had taken the household gods and put them inside her camel's

saddle and was sitting on them. Laban searched through everything in the tent but found nothing.

Rachel said to her father, 'Don't be angry, my lord, that I cannot stand up in your presence; I'm having my period.' So he searched but could not find the household gods.

(Genesis 31:25–35)

In the previous episode, the promise of blessing and descendants was met, in addition to the other promises. Finally, Rachel bears a child. Jacob has the descendant he wanted and all that remains is to return home.

As Abimelech saw that God blessed Isaac and therefore wished to continue association with Isaac, so Laban perceives that he has been blessed by Jacob's presence and seeks its continuance. Jacob proposes an arrangement with Laban, who agrees to it. While we don't know how the details about sheep mating in certain circumstances works, it is apparent that God is behind its success (31:10–13) and that it works because God decides to use it (31:9). Over a six year period, Jacob becomes a man of substance and wealth. Moreover, as Jacob's deceit met with God's judgment, so does Laban's—the wealth he had plotted to gain from Jacob becomes Jacob's, as his daughters had become Jacob's wives. To cap it off, deceit again flowers from Jacob as he decides to leave without telling Laban (31:20–21).

In the incident that follows from verse 22, there is one item that is of particular interest—the story of Rachel and the household gods. In Genesis 28:10–15, we heard the God of all the earth give some undertakings. He would fulfil the promises to Abraham and he would be with Jacob, watch over him, and bring him home. In Genesis 31, Jacob knows that everything he has is from God and that God has kept and is keeping his word (31:42). This is a picture of a real and living God in action.

In contrast, we have the false gods that Rachel steals from among her father's household gods (31:19). False gods need to be carried around by humans, protected, and brought home by human agents. The picture of a menstrual Rachel protecting the gods is particularly derogatory (31:35). Such ridicule by Israelites of the emptiness of false gods occurs time and time again throughout the Old Testament (compare Isaiah 44:9–20).

The picture of Rachel having left the home of idolatry to ally herself with the fortunes of the God of Abraham, Isaac, and Jacob, but still clinging to the household gods, is also striking. Perhaps we have here an echo of another similar event, when the Israelites experience God's rescue in the Exodus only to turn around and make a molten calf out of their earrings. Like Rachel, it seems as though the children of Israel were never quite ready to trust God alone. They always wanted to take false gods along for the ride (compare the prophecies of Hosea and Amos or almost any other Old Testament prophet!).

In some ways, the story of Rachel therefore stands as a parable for the people of God, who have always wanted to hide some household gods in the corners of their Christian existence. According to the New Testament, we are those who have turned away from idols to serve the new and living God and to wait for his Son from heaven (1 Thessalonians 1:9–10). Despite this there is always the temptation to return to our old ways, and therefore the warning to keep ourselves from idols (1 John 5:21).

An idol is something that we must have, that we cannot do without. Such things deny that God alone is our God. There is no place for them with the people of God, no matter what form they take.

MEETING WITH THE GOD OF JACOB (32:1–32)

Jacob also went on his way, and the angels of God met him. When Jacob saw them, he said, 'This is the camp of God!' So he named that place Mahanaim.

Jacob sent messengers ahead of him to his brother Esau in the land of Seir, the country of

Edom. He instructed them: 'This is what you are to say to my master Esau: "Your servant Jacob says, I have been staying with Laban and have remained there till now. I have cattle and donkeys, sheep and goats, menservants and maidservants. Now I am sending this message to my lord, that I may find favour in your eyes." '

When the messengers returned to Jacob, they said, 'We went to your brother Esau, and now he is coming to meet you, and four hundred men are with him.'

In great fear and distress Jacob divided the people who were with him into two groups, and the flocks and herds and camels as well. He thought, 'If Esau comes and attacks one group, the group that is left may escape.'

(Genesis 32:1–8)

After 20 years away, Jacob has two wives, 12 children, and abundant possessions. God has kept his promises to him, his father, and his grandfather concerning blessing and children. He has kept his promise to Jacob about being with him and watching over him. All that remains is the promise of land and a return home. These promises will be the focus in Genesis 32 and 33.

As we read this chapter, it is important to remember with whom we are dealing—Jacob—the heel, the deceiver, the supplanter. He is a man with a personal and spiritual problem that God has obviously begun to deal with, but which still needs a final resolution.

Verse 3 sets the context for the passage. Here we are told of Seir and Edom, and therefore reminded of Esau, the brother Jacob cheated and defrauded. Messengers are sent and in verse 6 they return.

We are not told what Esau has said, but we are told what he has done in response to the message—he is on his way, accompanied by 400 men. Although afraid and distressed, Jacob decides to press on, but divides his company in two, reasoning that if Esau should attack then there would be a chance that one company of people will survive and be able to escape. Then Jacob turns to pray:

'I am unworthy of all the kindness and faithfulness you have shown your servant. I had only my staff when I crossed this Jordan, but now I have become two groups. Save me, I pray, from the hand of my brother Esau, for I am afraid he will come and attack me, and also the mothers with their children. But you have said, "I will surely make you prosper and will make your descendants like the sand of the sea, which cannot be counted."'

(Genesis 32:10–12)

In this prayer we see some changes in Jacob. He calls upon the God of his fathers, reminds God of his promises, and tells him that he expects that he will keep his promises. However, in these requests is also recognition of his low place. He recognises that he has been the recipient of grace, that he is unworthy of God's blessing, and that he wants to continue to live this way ('save me...'). Within half a dozen lines, the man who has never called himself the servant of anyone, human or divine, calls himself both the servant of Esau (verse 4) and of God.

One can't help feeling that Jacob is at a turning point in his life. He realises that only God can sort out the situation, and that amid all the tangles and confusion of his life, ultimately it is God with whom he deals. This is the focus of verses 24–30. Although there is much that is obscure in this account of the wrestling match, there are various pointers toward a possible solution. They include:

- The river Jabbok is mentioned a number of times as a boundary at the time of the Israelite occupation of East Jordan. To cross the Jabbok is therefore to cross into the first territory of the Promised Land (compare Numbers 21:24; Deuteronomy 2:37; 3:16; Joshua 12:2; Judges 11:13,22). Whatever is going on, it seems that all Jacob's family and possessions can enter the land of promise, but not he. Something must happen before such an entry is possible.

- The reference to God's face in verse 30 points forward to Jacob's subsequent encounter with Esau in 33:10, where he says that to see Esau's face is like 'seeing the face of God'. In that context, Jacob met Esau expecting harm only to find favour and graciousness. Similarly, Jacob expected here that to see God face to face meant death, only to find that by God's favour his life was spared. What happens here is an act of grace.

- An important part of the story hangs on a term that has already been significant in Jacob's story—'blessing'. As Jacob struggled to get a blessing from his father, so he struggles here to get a blessing from God. As he succeeded then, so now. However, although the blessing is what Jacob is after, it is probably not the primary thing that God wants to convey at this moment. The primary thing conveyed by God is a change of name and all that it means.

- It is hard to know who is meant when God says that Jacob has struggled with God and with men and overcome. Since the latter part of the sentence (struggled with God and overcome) seems to be interpreted within the passage in verse 30, this is probably the best place to start. Jacob has wrestled God, seen his face, and survived—something that is theoretically impossible. This helps us interpret the first part of the sentence (struggled with men and overcome). The two men with whom Jacob has wrestled in his life are Esau and Laban. He survived the confrontation with Laban because of God's intervention, and God's statement seems to imply that Jacob's prayer concerning Esau will be or has been answered as well. This statement therefore encapsulates Jacob's past, present, and future, all of which rest on God's mercy to him. This interpretation would explain Jacob's confidence in the next chapter as he steps out to meet Esau.

- Changes of name, particularly for adults, are very significant in the Bible, especially for a man whose name has such negative connotations. The new name, 'Israel', etymologically means 'God strives/struggles' although it is interpreted here to mean 'the one who strives/struggles with God'. Given the description of what happened, perhaps the ambiguity is intentional.

Many commentators consider that the events of this night amount to some sort of 'conversion' of Jacob away from his self-made nature to an increased dependence upon God. It seems, however, that a submission to God and a determination to trust his future to God had already happened earlier in the chapter (hence the prayer and the references to himself as 'servant' in relation to God and Esau). Moreover, there are no hints of a fundamental change in Jacob's nature through the conflict at Jabbok.

Nevertheless, as we shall see, it is clear from Chapter 33 that something has changed because of the overnight meeting. At the Jabbok, God came to Jacob, acknowledged that Jacob's approach to life was characterised by conflict, and yet assured him that his future would be shaped by God's mercy, as his past had been (compare 32:9–12). This assurance is sealed by a name change. The name 'Israel' therefore functions as a promise of survival, from the God who has entered into conflict with this man and who will continue that conflict with his descendants who will cross this very same river many years later. As with Abraham, the name change is a promise of grace and commitment from God.

With such a promise of survival, Jacob is free to reject his old way of doing things. He will not always do so, but in the coming two chapters there are real indications that he can and will do so in a way that he has not been able to before.

So it is that with the new day this man of conflict and struggle emerges with two marks. He bears a new name, which captures his existence as a man of conflict and trouble, but also of survival and promise by the mercy of God. He also walks with a limp, a constant sign that in the long run he is subject to God not himself. With a new understanding of

217

himself in relation to God, he can be confident in entering God's promised land and facing his brother.

MEETING ESAU (33:1–20)

Jacob looked up and there was Esau, coming with his four hundred men; so he divided the children among Leah, Rachel and the two maidservants. He put the maidservants and their children in front, Leah and her children next, and Rachel and Joseph in the rear. He himself went on ahead and bowed down to the ground seven times as he approached his brother.

But Esau ran to meet Jacob and embraced him; he threw his arms around his neck and kissed him. And they wept. Then Esau looked up and saw the women and children. 'Who are these with you?' he asked.

Jacob answered, 'They are the children God has graciously given your servant.'

Then the maidservants and their children approached and bowed down. Next, Leah and her children came and bowed down. Last of all came Joseph and Rachel, and they too bowed down.

Esau asked, 'What do you mean by all these droves I met?'

'To find favour in your eyes, my lord,' he said.

But Esau said, 'I already have plenty, my brother. Keep what you have for yourself.'

'No, please!' said Jacob. 'If I have found favour in your eyes, accept this gift from me. For to see your face is like seeing the face of God, now that you have received me favourably. Please accept the present that was brought to you, for God has been gracious to me and I have all I need.' And because Jacob insisted, Esau accepted it.

(Genesis 33:1–11)

There is a new-found boldness in Jacob as he steps out on the other side of the river. This is demonstrated in his no longer cowering behind Mum (Chapter 27) or his wives or children (32:16). Instead, he goes on ahead of his family. Upon meeting Esau he bows seven times, completely subjecting himself to his brother. It is clear that his attitude is that of repentance and seeking for reconciliation.

This is confirmed by verse 11, which literally reads: 'Please take my blessing which I brought for you.' The innuendo could not be missed—he stole the blessing from Esau and is seeking to return it. Truly there is a new attitude here, a new man.

However, it appears as though Jacob is not the only one who has changed. Last time we met Esau he was waiting for his father to die so that he could take revenge. Jacob's death was very much in the forefront of his mind. However, here Esau races toward Jacob, throws his arms around him, and kisses him. Together they weep. Esau tries his hardest to reject the gifts, but eventually accepts them and invites Jacob to come and live with him.

Here too is a man totally changed. The impact of verse 10 is that the full and free forgiveness he displays toward his brother is a model of God's love. This is part of the impact of Jacob's words in verse 10: 'To see your face is like seeing the face of God.' In the face of Esau, Jacob finds forgiveness, acceptance, and love.

There is a striking similarity between the elements of this scene and those of the lost son in Luke 15:11–32. There we find a Father greatly wronged by a disobedient and obstinate son. Despite this wrong, the Father puts aside all propriety, picks up his skirts and runs out to meet his son before throwing his arms around him, kissing him, and bringing him home. Seeing the face of Esau here is indeed like seeing the face of God.

In any case, these two changed men face reality. The subsequent verses seem to imply some lingering suspicion and lack of trust. They amicably part company, and Jacob settles back into the land that God swore to give him. The final promise is fulfilled—he has come home.

21

Struggling with God (iii)

As you read the story of this chapter, a whole host of emotions and reactions will undoubtedly accost you. Nevertheless, once the general plot is extracted, we will find that it is very familiar. It is the plot of so many of our books and modern movies. We will find a victim who is abused and mistreated. We will find scoundrels, and heroes who vanquish them. We will find violence and revenge.

We will also find ourselves wondering who is at fault and which people are the heroes. My hope is that we will also find a way to bring such stories to bear on the great issues of faith, and how we should react to events in our world.

THE RAPE OF DINAH (34:1–31)

The rape (34:1–4)
The story of Chapter 34 is fairly straightforward. Jacob arrives at the city of Shechem in Canaan, camps within sight of the city, and buys a plot of land from the sons of a man called Hamor. Even though the land was his theologically, Jacob did the right thing and thereby worked at forming good relations with the local people (33:18–20).

Dinah, the daughter of Leah goes out to visit the women of the land. The Hebrew graphically tells the story of what happened—Shechem, Hamor's most important son, saw her, took her, and raped her. However, after the event his heart turned from lust to love, and he sought to make the appropriate restitution and to marry her.

The men talk (34:5–19)

Back at the Israelite camp, Jacob hears but decides to do nothing, perhaps waiting to consult with his sons. Before this can happen, Hamor arrives with Shechem.

In the meantime, Jacob's sons arrive home and become indignant and angry. They perceive that an outrage has been committed (they probably see it primarily as an outrage against Jacob).

In the ensuing conversation, Hamor comes forward, skips over the rape, offering no explanation, and gets straight to the point: Shechem has fallen in love with Jacob's daughter and wants Jacob to give her to him in marriage. He explains that the situation shouldn't be viewed too negatively, as it may provide an opportunity for negotiation and cooperation. This and other similar marriages could cement their relationships, and be to their mutual advantage in terms of land ownership and trade opportunities.

Shechem then speaks. Unlike his father's speech, Shechem's speech is coloured by what has happened with Dinah, and he casts himself upon the goodwill of Jacob and his sons. He is willing to pay any price the brothers demand (in later Israelite law the man who rapes a woman must marry her and make a marriage present of not more than 50 shekels).

The fathers then disappear from the discussion and the sons take over. Jacob's sons pass over the mention of money and gifts and engage in deceit by talking about tribal identity and how it is tied up with circumcision. They point out that before any further discussion can proceed the issue of circumcision needs to be resolved. With the impediment of uncircumcision removed, the sorts of things suggested by the Hivites become feasible. Without its removal, the sons of Jacob will have no option but to take their sister, Jacob's daughter, and go.

Shechem and Hamor report back (34:20–24)

Verse 24 tells us that the words of Shechem and Hamor seem good to the other inhabitants when reported to them. It is of note that they dress up the proposal in a prettier parcel than the one in which they had received it, and only mention the issue of circumcision late in the discussion. Once it is mentioned they quickly move on again to talk of property, livestock, and animals. The Hivites take the bait and every male is circumcised.

The rape of the Shechemites (34:25–31)

On the third day, when the pain of circumcision is excruciating, two of the blood brothers of Dinah leave the camp and advance upon the city. The men of the city can hardly move because of the pain and so it is easy for Levi and Simeon to cut their way through the men, killing every last one of them. Finally they arrive at the house of Hamor and Shechem where apparently Dinah has been all along. They kill the men, take Dinah, and then, together with the other sons of Jacob, systematically pillage the city, taking their flocks, their herds, their donkeys and everything that is theirs. As Shechem had seized Dinah, so the brothers seize the women of Shechem and make them their prey.

The act committed here is an act of treachery unparalleled by any Israelites in biblical history. Biblical law gives no warrant for such a terrible act of vengeance. It is 'overkill'—the sort of ethnic violence that in our day we have seen so much of and been revolted by.

When they return home drenched with blood and laden with booty, it is apparent that Jacob has been totally unaware of the deceit. He confronts Levi and Simeon over the trouble and ruin they have brought on him and the family.

The rebuke washes over the boys. Shechem tampered with them and theirs, and he has paid for his mistake. So these boys will regard and treat anyone who treats their sister like a whore.

Now although this is the end of the chapter the story doesn't finish here. Chapter 35 tells us the conclusion. God speaks again to Jacob, urging him to leave Shechem. Jacob therefore cleanses his family of idolatry, and together they set out for Bethel. The nations surrounding them don't act in reprisal, because God causes a great terror to fall upon them.

Interpreting the story

The number of interpretations offered for this story are as diverse as they are for any rape. Some commentators reckon that Dinah was somehow complicit in her own rape by going out to visit the people of the land when she should have stayed at home. Others reckon that Jacob is the scoundrel because he didn't react when the daughter of his unloved wife was raped. Hence, when Levi and Simeon talk about someone treating their sister like a whore, they are really talking about Jacob, who was willing to sell her for peace. Some commentators therefore consider that the real heroes are Simeon and Levi in that they alone act on Dinah's behalf. Others say that although Shechem was undoubtedly guilty of crime, he and his father turn out to be the good guys in the story.

Some clues for reading the story

As with all literature, the framing of the story tells us something about how the author intended us to interpret it. Chapters 32 and 33 tell us that Jacob is concerned to get his relationship with God and with his brother sorted out. He has come to a place where he is willing to trust God and his promises. He knows the land belongs to the Canaanites at this stage, and this is why be buys land in Chapter 33. In Chapter 35 we see Jacob focusing on God again. In other words, the immediate context urges us to look at Jacob favourably at this point.

Moreover, the story of Jacob's life has been one of deceit—deceiving and being deceived. However, we have seen him grapple with this in the past chapter or two, and it seems to be a way of life he is trying to leave behind.

In this context, it is striking that the author chooses to use the word 'deceit' for what the boys do to the Hivites in verse 13. The overall impression therefore is that it is the boys who are the bad guys in this story, not Jacob.

A further clue for interpreting this story comes from the larger context of the Patriarchal stories. Up until this point, the assessment of the Canaanites has been almost uniformly positive. We need to be wary of assuming that because they are Canaanites, they must be scoundrels.

The last clue in Genesis as to the correct interpretation of this incident is given by Jacob himself in Genesis 49:5–7. By including this assessment, the writer of Genesis doesn't leave any room for thinking that the good guys are Simeon and Levi. They are men of anger and violence, and such are not required or desired in the assembly of Israel.

Finally, the rest of the Bible confirms all of these clues. The Bible tells us that the tribe of Simeon doesn't survive as a tribe. It is absorbed into other groupings and dispersed as Jacob said it would be. The tribe of Levi becomes the powerful priestly tribe, but they are never given land of their own, which is not surprising because their ancestor demonstrated that they had no right to own a portion of the land of Canaan. He showed no ability to live with the demands of owning that land.

A rereading of the story

Hence, while we may have sympathy with Simeon and Levi, they are not the heroes here. If that is the case, then how should we read this story?

First, let's consider Dinah. Dinah is the daughter of Leah, which means she is the daughter of the unloved wife of Jacob.

Second, rape is rape in any society and this passage doesn't try to water it down or condone it. What Shechem did is inexcusable. Nevertheless, because God knows the sinful nature of men he puts laws in place so that women who are dishonoured by rape can have their honour restored. In biblical culture this is accomplished by forcing the rapist to marry the woman, and to publicly acknowledge his sin by paying a price to the family. The rapist is never allowed to divorce this woman. Shechem offers such reparation. The overall presentation of him is of a man deeply in love and who, having committed an awful sin, seeks to do as much as can be done in the world of his time.

Third, the scoundrels in this passage are obviously Jacob's sons. We know this by the narrator's use of the word 'deceit', which has a negative tone in its context. Moreover, we know this because of the distance he puts between the boys' actions and those of Jacob.

Fourth, Jacob is presented in this passage as careful and prudent. He is a man of peace who is back in the land of promise, and attempting to live without deceit and violence any more. Perhaps he could have shown a bit more emotion regarding his daughter, and perhaps he could have done something stronger. However, the situation was extremely delicate, his hold on the land tenuous, and his family as a whole vulnerable. He needs to be careful and slow.

Jacob's hot-headed sons tire of him, and deceive as he had deceived. They supplant him as he had supplanted his brother and as his mother had supplanted her husband. The results are disastrous, just as they were for him—pain, hatred, mistrust, and disharmony.

The main point of the story is therefore clear. God has given his people great and glorious promises, but these promises are very difficult to realise. On the one hand there are Canaanites in the land and they are the dominant people. As such, they appear as an insurmountable obstacle to the fulfilment of the promises. Nevertheless, they are not the greatest obstacle. The greatest barrier to the promises is the Israelites themselves, for they too are descendants of Adam and Jacob—sinful, deceitful, and cruel.

This passage is poignant in its question. How can God's purposes be fulfilled? Human sinfulness is never going to go away, so how will Israel ever receive all the promises?

The answer is the same one we have encountered again and again as we have read Genesis: Israel's only hope is God and his grace. Perhaps this is why verses 1–5 in Genesis 35 are there, to tell us that Israel's only hope is God and his intervention. If this is so, then the only response is to trust him and throw away all idols to worship him.

Some observations about women and men

It is salutary to put together the information regarding Dinah in this story. She is the daughter of the not-so-favoured wife of Jacob. The violation of Dinah is referred to in several places. She is seized and raped in verse 2, defiled in verses 5, 13 and 27, suffers a disgraceful thing in verse 7, is taken with violence by her brothers in verse 26, and treated like a whore in verse 31. Her voice and interests are never heard in the whole story and the people doing the acting are all men.

The only person who treats Dinah with any sort of respect is, curiously, a man, Shechem. Yes, he rapes her and therefore abuses her like the other men in the story. Nevertheless, the many-faceted love he subsequently has for her is in sharp contrast to what happens elsewhere. In fact, it is Shechem who finally goes to such extreme lengths (eventually giving his life) in order to arrange for marriage with her.

Even so, Dinah still has no voice of her own. She is a person whose identity is determined by men, by who they are and by whom they think she is.

One of the problems for us is that although the world of Genesis 34 seems quite primitive to the men among us who read it, I suspect that the women who read it know that the picture presented there is one which is all too true even today. We still live in a world where men, men's rights, and men's honour control the lives and existences of so many women. We are still a long way away from living how God intended in Genesis 2.

The politics of violence

But there is more in this story. As I mentioned at the beginning, this is a well known plot that the smooth, muscle-bound men of our movies parade before us time and time again. In such movies, there is inevitably a victim who is abused or abducted or somehow mistreated. The perpetrators are distant and malevolent. Then the heroes— men of principle and strength—are drawn in and come to the rescue. Sure, they are violent and kill many more people than the evil ones. Sure, they are cruel, but the sins of the oppressors justify such violence and revenge. Violence and revenge are all right in these contexts.

Sometimes the plot is slightly different from this. In this alternative plot someone is oppressed or mistreated but the oppressors have chosen the wrong man to oppress. Before long the oppressed becomes the oppressor. Again he is violent and cruel but it's all fair—after all, he had been grossly wronged. Surely over the top violence is okay when violence has been used? Surely it's okay to answer violence with violence, and appropriate to respond in equal, if not more aggressive violence?

These are the morals of Jacob's boys, the morals of our movies, and the morals of our age. It is an age where men are so often concerned about rights and honour and revenge, an age of the sword.

What can Christians say about this age and about the ethics of Jacob's boys?

At this point we must return to the Cross of Jesus Christ. On that cross we see God abused and defiled. His rights as God are stolen by his creation. And in response, this God sues for peace. He holds his peace and turns his anger upon himself, returning hatred with love. In love for his enemies, the one in the position of power uses his power to serve and be a ransom for many.

Surely it must be the Cross that determines our attitude to these two great issues of our age—the issue of women and men, and the issue of violence and revenge. We must stop following the ethics of Jacob's boys.

RETURN TO BETHEL (35:1–29)

When Jacob first left his family, he met God in a dream (28:10–17). In response to that revelation, Jacob had promised that if God should do as he had promised then he would be Jacob's God (28:21). The word of God in 35:1 reminds Jacob of this vow.

Jacob's response is to call upon the family to purify themselves (perhaps from blood and perhaps from intercourse if rapes had occurred in Chapter 34) and change their clothes. They were to yield up their foreign gods and earrings, which may have been booty from the Canaanite city. Jacob continues the process of making God not only his God but also the God of his family. At Bethel there is a re-enactment and restatement of much of what has occurred, and God continues to enrich the promises already given.

The spiritual high of Bethel is followed by tragedy as Rachel dies. In Genesis 30:1 she had said to Jacob, 'Give me children, or I'll die!' In Genesis 30:24 she prays for another son. Here she dies giving birth to that son—the gift of children finally killing her. On her deathbed she names the child Ben-Oni or 'son of my trouble', while Jacob renames him Benjamin, 'son of my right hand'. As things work out, the first name seems more apt.

The incest committed by Reuben in verse 22 is probably not primarily a sexual matter, but one to do with ascendancy. It is probably a takeover bid, a claim to his father's estate. Jacob hears of what has happened but again keeps his peace at this time, although on his deathbed Jacob cites this event as the reason for Reuben not getting the rights of firstborn.

In verses 23–26, the sons are listed according to their mothers rather than in chronological order, simply highlighting the tensions within the family and preparing us for the Joseph narrative to follow.

Finally, Jacob reaches his father's house. Rebekah is apparently dead, and Isaac is not far behind. As if to mark their reconciliation Esau and Jacob join together in burying their father, and are listed by the author in order of birth.

THE GENEALOGY OF ESAU (36:1–43)

Throughout Genesis we have been introduced to God's elect, and those who were not elect but who lived beside them. Abraham is matched with Lot, Isaac with Ishmael, and Jacob with Esau. Again, we have here the genealogy of one of those who was not God's elect, thus reinforcing what has been apparent from the first page of Genesis and which was reinforced in the Abrahamic promises (Abraham will be a blessing to all peoples—12:3). God's goal is the incorporation of all people and nations into the blessings of relationship with God.

This is confirmed when God rescues his people out of Egypt and brings them together at the foot of Mt Sinai to receive the law. Although it looks as though God is going to set them apart as his special people with no focus but themselves, the giving of the law is prefaced by the phrase 'though the whole earth is mine, you will be...'. In other words, even in giving the law and setting aside Israel as his own treasured possession, God's focus is still on the whole world.

Perhaps this is why, among the ten 'this is the account of...' statements scattered throughout Genesis there is no 'this is the account of Abraham...'. Abraham is not just the father of one family but the father of a multitude of nations (Revelation 7:9). Abraham's genealogy consists of all those who bless themselves because of Abraham.

BEGINNINGS: Of Israel

Part 6

The story of Jacob
Genesis 37:2–50:26

Sold into Egypt

A BRIEF INTRODUCTION TO THE JOSEPH NARRATIVE

A special part of the Bible

With the words 'This is the account of Jacob' (37:2) we enter into a very special part of the Bible. The story that follows has always fascinated readers. It is special for a number of reasons.

First, it is a story we modern people identify with easily. It is a story of a spoiled brat in a family torn apart by strife. Although the central character brings trouble upon himself, he is nevertheless badly treated and encounters great difficulty. Through such difficulty he develops into a mature and competent leader, who ultimately repays his family with care and compassion. It is therefore a feel good story about a bad boy made good.

Second, it is a story full of psychological insight.

Third, it is one of the closest things we have in the Bible to that familiar form of literature, the novel. This story is not unlike a novel in its development, insight, and character development. Another example in Scripture is that of David in 2 Samuel 9–20.

Fourth, it is full of intrigue, deception, reconciliation, and warmth. It has all the elements of a good story.

Its purpose

However, the Joseph narrative is not just a good story. It performs a particular function within the book of Genesis, and is not primarily included for entertainment.

First, the story provides an important link between the Hebrew patriarchs and Egypt. It explains how these people who originally lived in Chaldea and then roamed Canaan eventually found themselves away from the land God had promised them. This sets the scene for God's great deliverance in the Exodus.

Second, the account continues the story of the promises given to Abraham. The promises of land, children, and blessing undergo some significant development within these chapters. For example, on the positive side:

- the family grows significantly;
- their name becomes great (Joseph rises to a position of prominence);
- Joseph is blessed;
- Israel is blessed; and
- the nations are blessed through Joseph.

However, among these positive things there is a real setback. The people of God find themselves in Egypt, hence the need for the Exodus—the principal event of the next book of the Bible.

Third, the story develops its own ideas and theology, some of which we have already touched on in previous stories. For example, we will encounter:

- God's providence, or hidden power that works in, through, and despite humans;
- human frailty that is so evident in favouritism, sibling rivalry, hatred and murder.

Since this story comes under the heading of 'the account of Jacob', it may be helpful to refresh our minds in relation to the people in it. It will be important to understand this as we see the story unfold.

The Children of Jacob (aka 'Israel')

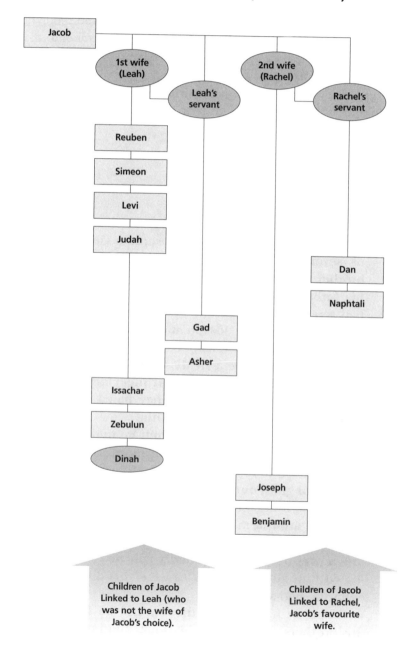

Focus

At first glance, the focus of these chapters seems to be Joseph. After all, he is the chief player, the one on whom the spotlight falls. However, we have already read the introduction to the story—this is the account of Jacob. In other words, this is not the story of the son of Jacob but of Jacob himself. It is therefore the story of his whole family. It may centre on Joseph, but only because he is so often the member of the family who is active.

GENESIS 37

The story

This is the account of Jacob. Joseph, a young man of seventeen, was tending the flocks with his brothers, the sons of Bilhah and the sons of Zilpah, his father's wives, and he brought their father a bad report about them.

Now Israel loved Joseph more than any of his other sons, because he had been born to him in his old age; and he made a richly ornamented robe for him. When his brothers saw that their father loved him more than any of them, they hated him and could not speak a kind word to him.

Joseph had a dream, and when he told it to his brothers, they hated him all the more. He said to them, 'Listen to this dream I had: We were binding sheaves of grain out in the field when suddenly my sheaf rose and stood upright, while your sheaves gathered around mine and bowed down to it.'

His brothers said to him, 'Do you intend to reign over us? Will you actually rule us?' And they hated him all the more because of his dream and what he had said.

Then he had another dream, and he told it to his brothers. 'Listen,' he said, 'I had another dream,

and this time the sun and moon and eleven stars
were bowing down to me.'

When he told his father as well as his brothers,
his father rebuked him and said, 'What is this
dream you had? Will your mother and I and your
brothers actually come and bow down to the
ground before you?' His brothers were jealous of
him, but his father kept the matter in mind.

(Genesis 37:2–11)

Joseph is now seventeen years old. Jacob has put him under
the oversight of the sons of the lowest order members of the
family—the sons of Bilhah and Zilpah, the maids of Rachel
and Leah. Together we have the two extremes of Jacob's
family—the sons of the maids, and the favourite son of the
favourite wife. In verse 2 we are told that Joseph brings a 'bad
report'. Although the words used here do not necessarily
mean that the report was untrue, the word for 'report' does
not have good connotations elsewhere in scripture (e.g.
Numbers 14:36; translated 'slander' in Proverbs 18:10 and 'bad
reputation' in Proverbs 25:10) and the addition of 'bad' may
indicate that Joseph was not telling the truth. However, even
if the story is not untrue, Joseph's conduct would
undoubtedly have inflamed the already incipient hatred of
Joseph (compare verse 4). Even the clothes Joseph wore non-
verbally declared Jacob's favouritism. Joseph had a special
tunic (how it is special is not clear from the Hebrew words
used to describe it).

It is clear that with such a family arrangement, trouble
could not be far away. In order to emphasise this, the writer
tells us twice of Jacob's love for his son (verses 3 and 4) and
three times of the sons' hatred of Joseph (verses 4, 5, and 8).

If Jacob's disposition and actions and Joseph's tale-telling
were not enough, Joseph also had a dream which he paraded
before his brothers. The sheaves of corn clearly represented
Joseph's relationship to his family, and they didn't need any
exotic dream manual for interpretation. It reflected the
destiny his father had for him as well as Joseph's own attitude

in life—he was, and would be, the dominant son. The dream simply gave some sort of divine imprimatur to this calling.

The second dream was even more exorbitant in its scope because not only the brothers, but also his parents, were bowing down before him. Even Jacob finds such arrogance a bit overwhelming and rebukes Joseph while at the same time keeping these things in mind.

We know from previous narratives that the parents and grandparents of these boys harboured favouritism, giving special place to special people and favouring certain children over others. Their love for certain individuals inevitably gave the sense of hatred in comparison. Similar attitudes begin to emerge in the children of such parents and before long hatred is rife.

In verses 12–36, the long, simmering hatred finds another well earned focus, and boils over in a way that will rupture Jacob's family for at least another twenty years. The brothers are shepherding near Shechem where they murdered a whole village. For some reason, Joseph is not with them but Jacob decides that he should go to them and bring back news (given Shechem's proximity, perhaps Jacob is particularly wary). Joseph arrives in Shechem but gets lost. For three verses the narrator has him wandering around the wilderness, and during this time we have opportunity to wonder how hatred and jealousy will find some output.

The presence of Shechem in the narrative and the delay of these three verses serve to heighten the tension. What is going to happen? Will the young man be all right?

It is very likely and quite ironic that the distinctive tunic is the cause for the brothers recognising his arrival while he is still at some distance from them. In any case, they have ample time to conspire to kill him.

The hatred for Joseph is so deep that the text doesn't record any euphemisms in their description of what they intend to do. They only want one result—death. Fortunately, the oldest brother, Reuben, overhears all of this. He has already angered his father once by sleeping with the handmaid of Rachel. Perhaps he dares not risk that anger again, or perhaps he sees the damage his action caused in the past. No matter what the reason, he takes responsibility and attempts to rescue the boy. His strategy appears to be to persuade them not to kill but simply to leave him in the desert from where he can rescue him later.

The plan is carried out effectively. Reuben disappears from the scene, and the brothers callously eat while their brother lies in the pit (Genesis 42:21 tells us that he was distressed and pleaded for his life at this point). At about this time they see a group of travellers moving along one of the main trade routes through Canaan. Judah proposes a plan to sell him as a slave, figuring that this will avoid the danger of bloodguilt while also offering some financial gain. This would also allow a small concession to their own feelings of guilt about their treatment of their brother, their own flesh and blood. Joseph is sold for twenty shekels, which was the going price for male slaves between five and twenty years old at this time. Since a shepherd in those days might expect to earn eight shekels a year, the sale of Joseph would represent a handy bonus for the boys of Jacob.

At this juncture Reuben reappears to rescue Joseph, to find he is no longer in the pit. He is distraught at the turn of affairs, but with his brothers forms a plan to cover their tracks and avoid false hope on the part of their father—they slaughter a goat and soak Joseph's tunic in the blood. When they hand the evidence to Jacob and he recognises it, we find some very poignant ironies caught within the text.

- The word used here to describe Jacob's recognition of Joseph's robe is the very same word used of Isaac's failure to recognise the disguised Jacob back in Genesis 27:23.
- The skin of a goat was the means of deceit Jacob used with his father, just as his own sons deceive him with the blood of a goat here.

Once again, the sins of Jacob's youth have come home to roost. Jacob falls to mourning. Normally, public grief lasted a week for a parent. Sometimes it spanned a month in the case of a figure of national importance. However, Jacob talks of mourning for the rest of his life. As David's mourning for his favourite son, Absalom, would be over the top (2 Samuel 18:24–19:8), so too is that of Jacob for his favourite. Moreover, the reader knows that the mourning is not necessary because Joseph isn't dead. He is at that moment beginning a new life in Egypt.

Understanding what is going on

The story here is a unit in its own right, separated from the rest of the Joseph narrative by the somewhat isolated and distinct story that features in Genesis 38. It forms a bridge between what has gone before and what comes after. On the one hand, it demonstrates the inevitable culmination of the family strife that has gone before. On the other, it explains what is going to happen in the future, and what assurances we can have about that future.

While we see here a family where relationships are deeply fractured and dysfunction is the normal pattern of affairs, we know from the preceding story that God is in control of the events surrounding this family. He has formed this family and he provides the meaning for its existence. He has couched his future plans and our future in the shape of this family. It is hard for us to see that future coming to anything. After all, there are no apparent candidates for God's activity. There are no Noahs here, but simply people like us.

Having read all of Genesis, however, we know that we are dealing with a God who looks at chaos and darkness and speaks to form light and order. For this reason, this family without human hope is a family with real hope.

SOME SIDEWAYS REFLECTING

There is a modern trend to explain who we are by where we have come from. We are what we are because of what has happened to us. Because our parents or someone else did this or that, we are this way or that way.

It is clear from this and many other passages in the Bible that there is a great deal of truth to this. For example, Jacob is a deceiver and one who shows favouritism. He leaves his mark upon his children as his parents left their mark upon him. In a sense, it is not surprising that his children resort to deception, lies, theft, and murder. The sins of the fathers are visited upon the children to the third and fourth generations (compare Exodus 20:5).

However, it would be a mistake to think this was the whole story. It is clear throughout Scripture that we are not simply the products of those who have preceded us. There are two other factors to take into account.

First, we are responsible human beings. We shape our own destiny. Our sin is our sin, our reactions are our reactions, and our conduct is our conduct. The Israelites had a proverb that said one generation inevitably bore the consequences of a previous generation's sin: 'The fathers eat sour grapes, and the children's teeth are set on edge' (Ezekiel 18:2; compare Jeremiah 31:29). This proverb is quoted in Ezekiel because God is declaring it to be false. Each person must bear the burden for his or her own conduct (Ezekiel 18).

Second, we must not forget that we are also objects of God's mercy. Our lives are not simply shaped by our past. In fact, the most formative influence on our lives is God's purpose for us, his good will for us. He alone is our future and our hope.

In the light of Scripture, it is inappropriate when we face a problem to look for a resolution to that problem in our personal past. Rather, the Christian way ahead would seem to be to go back to external history, where God in the flesh died in our place. This event forms our identity far more than any other event. More than anything else we are children of God and brothers and sisters of Christ—forgiven, reconciled, accepted, and responsible.

What God requires of us is that we act in our present as children of this God. We cannot change our past, and while it may be helpful to understand it, this must never be where the focus of attention is for the Christian. The focus of our attention must be on who Christ was for me in the past, and therefore on who I am going to be in the present, and what God will make of me in Christ in the future.

The Bible is clear. If we do not care for our brother or sister, if we do not love our neighbour as ourselves, then there is no one to blame but ourselves. However, the Bible also makes clear that with the Spirit of Christ at work in me, such love can be possible. Transformation can happen, no matter what my past has been.

We can see this happen in the Joseph story. Joseph is a spoiled brat. He suffers great adversity at the hands of his brothers. Nevertheless, he learns to be God's person, and God uses him for his purpose. For Joseph to look back would simply breed revenge and bitterness and, as we shall see, he refuses to do this.

23

The ones to whom God looks

There are many events from my childhood that I remember graphically. Some of them I wish I could forget. One in particular still causes me to flinch in embarrassment. I was in my teens and my father and I had discovered fishing. We decided that a small dinghy with outboard motor might help us reach our quarry better. We headed down to the river to take the new purchase for a spin.

I was an adolescent with a well-established sense of competition with my father. In my view he had no idea how things ought to be done and I had every idea. By hook or by crook, I was going to be the first one to pull the cord on that brand new motor, get it started, and head out into the river.

So it was that I scrambled for prominence, bustling around my father, making sure the boat was in the water and the outboard motor placed where it should be. My father was also so keen to keep me at bay that neither of us noticed that the screws holding the motor in place had not been tightened. I can't remember who got to pull the cord on the motor but I can remember what happened. The motor burst into life, jumped straight off the back of the boat, and sank in three or more metres of water. I can also remember people on the shore watching as we dived to retrieve the motor, tie ropes on it, and drag it to shore. For some reason, that motor never quite functioned to its full potential.

Each of us can tell stories of our youth—stories that are etched in our minds for one reason or another. Many of those stories also record things that were so formative in our learning that our adult lives are indebted to their influence. In my case, I now check things over and over again. I am cautious with new equipment, and I don't like people watching me try out something new!

The story we look at here is one of a man learning. As with much learning, it seems that the process was difficult and humbling.

THE STORY

Judah marries a Canaanite (38:1–5)

At that time, Judah left his brothers and went down to stay with a man of Adullam named Hirah. There Judah met the daughter of a Canaanite man named Shua. He married her and lay with her; she became pregnant and gave birth to a son, who was named Er. She conceived again and gave birth to a son and named him onan. She gave birth to still another son and named him Shelah. It was at Kezib that she gave birth to him.

(Genesis 38:1–5)

Verse 1 makes clear that these events occur at about the same time as Joseph is sold into slavery. Judah, the fourth eldest son of Jacob, marries a Canaanite woman. They have three children in fairly quick succession—Er, Onan, and Shelah.

Tamar marries Judah's sons (38:6–11)

Judah got a wife for Er, his firstborn, and her name was Tamar. But Er, Judah's firstborn, was wicked in the LORD's sight; so the LORD put him to death.

Then Judah said to onan, 'Lie with your brother's wife and fulfill your duty to her as a brother-in-law to produce offspring for your brother.' But onan knew that the offspring would not be his; so

whenever he lay with his brother's wife, he spilled his semen on the ground to keep from producing offspring for his brother. What he did was wicked in the Lord's sight; so he put him to death also.

Judah then said to his daughter-in-law Tamar, 'Live as a widow in your father's house until my son Shelah grows up.' For he thought, 'He may die too, just like his brothers.' So Tamar went to live in her father's house.

(Genesis 38:6–11)

Verse 6 introduces us to Tamar. Again, although we are not specifically told about her background, she appears to be Canaanite. Further, we are not told exactly what Er did wrong except that it was wicked in God's eyes and that God therefore put him to death.

Many Ancient Near Eastern people practised the rite of requiring a brother to produce children for a dead brother. The progeny of such a union would be given the name of the dead man and regarded as his children. Such a practice was particularly important in the case of firstborn sons.

Many readers of Genesis (particularly Jewish readers) read the text knowing that Judah will be the key tribe in Israel, and the tribe through which the kings promised to Abraham and Isaac will come. However, in this passage the line of Judah appears to reach a dead end—Er is dead, Onan refuses to cooperate with God's purposes and therefore joins his brother, and Judah becomes fearful for the safety of his third son and withholds him from Tamar.

Tamar traps Judah (38:12–19)

After a long time Judah's wife, the daughter of Shua, died. When Judah had recovered from his grief, he went up to Timnah, to the men who were shearing his sheep, and his friend Hirah the Adullamite went with him.

When Tamar was told, 'Your father-in-law is on his way to Timnah to shear his sheep,' she took off her widow's clothes, covered herself with a veil to disguise herself, and then sat down at the entrance to Enaim, which is on the road to Timnah. For she saw that, though Shelah had now grown up, she had not been given to him as his wife.

When Judah saw her, he thought she was a prostitute, for she had covered her face. Not realizing that she was his daughter-in-law, he went over to her by the roadside and said, 'Come now, let me sleep with you.'

'And what will you give me to sleep with you?' she asked.

'I'll send you a young goat from my flock,' he said.

'Will you give me something as a pledge until you send
it?' she asked.

He said, 'What pledge should I give you?'

'Your seal and its cord, and the staff in your hand,' she answered. So he gave them to her and slept with her, and she became pregnant by him. After she left, she took off her veil and put on her widow's clothes again.

(Genesis 38:12–19)

In the society in which Tamar lives, she has no legal comeback to what has happened to her and so she begins to think about how she might produce children by another means. An opportunity presents itself when shearing time comes. Sheep shearing was a lively festival in the Ancient Near East, and a time when wine was consumed quite freely (this may explain why Judah does not recognise Tamar).

The pledges given to Tamar are quite significant—a seal (signet) and its cord, and a staff. These are the ancient world's equivalent of credit cards—they offer security, identity, and authority. The proposed payment of a goat is also significant.

Three generations of deceit have now occurred, each involving an item of identity and a goat. Jacob deceives Isaac wearing a goat skin. Judah deceives Jacob by dipping Joseph's tunic in the blood of a goat. Now Tamar deceives Judah, and the deceit involves his items of identity plus a goat.

Tamar is vindicated (38:20–26)

> **Meanwhile Judah sent the young goat by his friend the Adullamite in order to get his pledge back from the woman, but he did not find her. He asked the men who lived there, 'Where is the shrine prostitute who was beside the road at Enaim?'**
>
> **'There hasn't been any shrine prostitute here,' they said.**
>
> **So he went back to Judah and said, 'I didn't find her. Besides, the men who lived there said, "There hasn't been any shrine prostitute here." '**
>
> **Then Judah said, 'Let her keep what she has, or we will become a laughingstock. After all, I did send her this young goat, but you didn't find her.'**
>
> **About three months later Judah was told, 'Your daughter-in-law Tamar is guilty of prostitution, and as a result she is now pregnant.'**
>
> **Judah said, 'Bring her out and have her burned to death!'**
>
> **As she was being brought out, she sent a message to her father-in-law. 'I am pregnant by the man who owns these,' she said. And she added, 'See if you recognize whose seal and cord and staff these are.'**
>
> **Judah recognized them and said, 'She is more righteous than I, since I wouldn't give her to my son Shelah.' And he did not sleep with her again.**
>
> *(Genesis 38:20–26)*

Since Tamar is technically still betrothed and has become pregnant to someone outside the family, she is guilty of adultery and therefore should be sentenced to death.

Nevertheless, the threatened burning to death is a very extreme punishment by most ancient standards. Under this judgment, Tamar draws out her trump card—the tokens of Judah's identity.

Judah's response to Tamar is of particular note: 'She is more righteous than I'. Other passages in scripture that use similar language help us understand what is being meant here (e.g. 1 Samuel 24:17; 1 Kings 2:32; Jeremiah 3:11; Habakkuk 1:13). This phrase does not necessarily mean that Tamar is righteous where Judah is not. In referring to Shelah and his own failure to make him available to Tamar, he is indicating that Tamar was more faithful to God's purposes in producing children than he had been.

Twins are born to Judah and tamar (38:27–30)

When the time came for her to give birth, there were twin boys in her womb. As she was giving birth, one of them put out his hand; so the midwife took a scarlet thread and tied it on his wrist and said, 'This one came out first.' But when he drew back his hand, his brother came out, and she said, 'So this is how you have broken out!' And he was named Perez. Then his brother, who had the scarlet thread on his wrist, came out and he was given the name Zerah.

(Genesis 38:27–30)

As with Jacob and Esau, the twins that are born are fiercely competitive. Again the older takes second place. Again, the first is last and the last first. And the New Testament will pick this up and tell us that God's principle is that the first will be last and the last first.

A story which at first glance appeared marginal now becomes very significant. Tamar is determined to have descendants for Judah even if he is not. The descendants she procures will be Jesse and David and eventually Jesus, the Saviour of the world. Tamar's actions are specifically mentioned in the genealogy of Jesus in Matthew 1.

WHAT'S IT ALL ABOUT?

The main purpose of the story appears to be the birth of progeny to Judah, and therefore the potential fulfilment of the promises given to Abraham and Isaac about kings coming from their line (Genesis 17:6,16; 35:11). However, there are a number of other important elements that feature in the story.

The Canaanites

Throughout Genesis the issue of children has been important. Onan dies because he will not procreate as God has commanded (Genesis 1:28; 9:7). His aversion to producing children has far-reaching implications for his brother, father, grandfather, and so on all the way back to Abraham. In this way Onan has great disregard for the purposes of God (as does Judah).

The same could not be said for Tamar. She may not know the full impact of what she is doing. She may simply be doing what women of her culture do—that is, seek to have children at all costs. Nevertheless, she is doing what no one else seems willing to do—propagate descendants of Abraham. What's more, she is doing these actions as a foreigner.

Here is a Canaanite, an outsider to the people of God, emerging from the story as the heroine. Whether she is carrying out her actions inadvertently or deliberately is not clear, but the effect is the same. She effectively aligns herself with God and his purposes, and, in her, God's promise that all the families of the earth will find blessing in Abraham is fulfilled.

What is righteousness?

The passage also offers a very interesting perspective on righteousness and builds on what we already noticed in Genesis 15:6. Our view of righteousness often has to do with rules. The righteous person is the one who can tick off the boxes beside God's laws. However, this is not the definition given here. Here the righteous one is the one who acts in accord with God's plan and purposes. Judah is not righteous, because he does not act in such a way as to cause God's plans to be fulfilled. What is more, he knows what he is doing.

Tamar, on the other hand, is righteous because she acts in such a way as to cause God's plans to be fulfilled. This is not to say that she is commended for **how** she went about this. Nevertheless, she has a righteous disposition toward the promises and purposes of God, and is determined to see them brought about.

Change in Judah

Judah is the fourth son of Jacob and his mother is Leah, Jacob's less favoured wife. Judah is presently in line for succession, because each of the brothers ahead of him has lost the right of succession because of unrighteous actions. (Levi and Simeon perpetrated a massacre against the Canaanites over the rape of Dinah; Reuben slept with his father's concubine.)

Up until this point, Judah has been on track to lose his position as well. After all, Judah is the one who suggested selling Joseph into slavery for financial gain in Chapter 37. Moreover, he has not exactly been a model figure in this chapter. The cumulative picture is of a quick-tempered man, who seems to care for little outside his own interests. He is coarse and rough (there is no mention of him mourning for any of his sons, and he summarily orders the harshest of treatments for his daughter-in-law).

Nevertheless, this story demonstrates some development in Judah. Judah observes Tamar's risk taking and commitment to the plans and purposes of God, and admits that she comes out of the situation better than he does. By all counts, it appears that this Canaanite woman has taught him a thing or two.

Perhaps this is at least part of the reason things are so strikingly different when we meet Judah in Genesis 44. There Joseph has trapped his brothers by hiding his silver cup in a sack of grain, and is threatening to take Benjamin as his slave in punishment for the alleged theft. Judah speaks out, acknowledges the guilt of his family, and faces up to the consequences of that guilt. When Joseph continues to push about taking Benjamin, it is Judah who again steps in. He takes Joseph aside, and in a long speech explains that his father's life is intimately bound up with the life of Benjamin. Were Benjamin not to return home then Jacob would die of grief. In conclusion Judah asks that he might stay in the place of Benjamin.

Judah knows that legally Benjamin should pay for the sin he has supposedly committed in stealing the cup, but he also knows the effect this would have on his father. Hence, where once he deceived his father and had little regard for his father's reaction, now he puts his own future on the line for the sake of his father. He acts righteously, with proper concern for relationships. It is evident that he is a changed man from the one we met in Chapter 37.

It fits well with the Joseph narrative to regard the events of Chapter 38 as contributing to this process of change. The main point of the Joseph story is that God is sovereign and in control of all the circumstances of life—both good and evil—and that he uses all of them in his plan and purpose for his people. Moreover, that plan and purpose is intimately bound up with the development of individuals, and so he works in their lives and circumstances to form and shape them.

Hence, although there has been no specific mention of God in Chapters 37 and 38, it appears that he has been at work—preserving Joseph, giving children to Judah, and teaching and training Judah through a shrewd, risk-taking Canaanite woman.

The God who is at work in these stories has not changed over the centuries. He is still sovereign and he works in our world too—in the situations that we are in and the people with whom we interact. And in each of these situations and encounters he is challenging us. Will we learn? Will we change? Will we be people who act rightly as God's people?

In this way it is possible to see all of life as the medium of God's activity. He is not just active when we read our Bible and pray. He is also active when we live in our world. Hence, when we wake up tomorrow we don't wake up to a day without God. Tomorrow is God's day, for he made it, formed it, and works in it. What's more, he wants you to enter tomorrow determined to be his person in it, and to let Christ be formed in you as you allow his word to interact with your situation.

24

Joseph in Egypt

SCENE 1: POTIPHAR'S HOUSE (39:1–20)

Now Joseph had been taken down to Egypt. Potiphar, an Egyptian who was one of Pharaoh's officials, the captain of the guard, bought him from the Ishmaelites who had taken him there.

The LORD was with Joseph and he prospered, and he lived in the house of his Egyptian master. When his master saw that the LORD was with him and that the LORD gave him success in everything he did, Joseph found favour in his eyes and became his attendant. Potiphar put him in charge of his household, and he entrusted to his care everything he owned. From the time he put him in charge of his household and of all that he owned, the LORD blessed the household of the Egyptian because of Joseph. The blessing of the LORD was on everything Potiphar had, both in the house and in the field. So he left in Joseph's care everything he had; with Joseph in charge, he did not concern himself with anything except the food he ate.

(Genesis 39:1–6a)

Setting the context (39:1)

After the interlude of Chapter 38 we return to the main story of Joseph. Genesis 39 reminds us that Joseph had been taken to Egypt and sold as a slave to Potiphar, the captain of the guard (compare 37:36).

Prosperity (39:2–6)

Having set the context, the writer tells us that the Lord was with Joseph just as he was with his father. The result was that Joseph prospered and succeeded in the house of Potiphar, as Jacob had succeeded in the house of Laban.

The first sign of Joseph's success is that he is taken into the house of Potiphar rather than being a slave in the field. Sure enough, just as with Jacob, everything Joseph touches turns to gold, and Joseph is promoted so that he has charge of the whole household. As God had promised Abraham that he would bless him and his descendants and cause them to be a blessing, so Joseph is blessed and made to be a blessing to Potiphar. Eventually Potiphar entrusts everything into Joseph's hand except the food he eats.

Enticement (39:7–10)

However, God's blessing of Joseph is not just an asset but also a problem. He is blessed not only in his management but also in his looks—he is stunningly attractive ('well-built and handsome'), a fact that does not escape the notice of Potiphar's wife. Her desire issues in a direct request: 'Come to bed with me!'

Joseph refuses her advances, offering three reasons:

1. To lie with Potiphar's wife would be an abuse of the great trust placed in him by Potiphar.
2. To lie with Potiphar's wife is an offence against Potiphar.
3. To lie with Potiphar's wife is a great sin against God.

The first two points were common morality in the ancient world, and any moral person would be able to assent. The third reason indicates that morality is also God-given. Adultery would be a great offence against the God who made Joseph, and who made him to live rightly with God and his neighbour.

Potiphar's wife continues to insist and Joseph continues to refuse.

Disgrace (39:11–20)

Finally her patience wears out. They are alone in the house. She traps him and grabs hold of his garment. Again she insists and Joseph flees. With no hope of her desire being realised, the woman's desire turns to retaliation and revenge.

Potiphar's wife gathers the servants and carefully crafts her speech to them. First, she blames her husband—he was the one who brought this one into the house. Second, she appeals to incipient racism and jealousy—he brought in 'a Hebrew'. Third, she identifies herself with the servants rather than with her husband—he brought in a Hebrew to insult 'us'.

After setting this background she tells her fabricated story, adding the lie about screaming so that she can clear herself of any suspicion. Finally Potiphar returns home and she proceeds to denounce Joseph to her husband.

There are some differences between what happened, what she said to the household, and what she now says to her husband. First, she is more respectful and circumspect than she had been with the members of the household. She still calls him the Hebrew. She still blames her husband, but only for bringing him into the house, not that he had brought him in to insult her (although it is subtle enough to leave the question open as to whether or not he might have had this in mind). Instead of saying that Joseph left the garment in her hand, she says that he left it beside her, thus implying that he had disrobed quite voluntarily as a preliminary to rape.

The denunciation has the desired effect. Potiphar is furious and Joseph is put into the prison where prisoners from the royal court were put.

It should be noted that the punishment is somewhat unexpected, since the usual punishment for rapists would probably have been death and undoubtedly so in the case of a foreign slave. We are not told why this less severe punishment was exacted, although a few possibilities suggest themselves:

- Joseph protested and cast doubt in Potiphar's mind.
- This woman had a history that might have cast doubt in Potiphar's mind.

- Potiphar could not bear to execute such a handsome and able man.

In any case, it seems as though there was some ongoing connection between Potiphar and Joseph, because we are told that Potiphar was the captain of the guard of the prison.

SCENE 2: PRISON (39:21–40:23)

But while Joseph was there in the prison, the Lord was with him; he showed him kindness and granted him favour in the eyes of the prison warden. So the warden put Joseph in charge of all those held in the prison, and he was made responsible for all that was done there. The warden paid no attention to anything under Joseph's care, because the Lord was with Joseph and gave him success in whatever he did.

(Genesis 39:20b–23)

God's blessing (39:21–23)

In prison, God continues to be with Joseph. According to verse 21, the Lord showed him 'kindness' (hesed—God's surprising, unexpected and overflowing love). Again God's blessing is apparent in material ways. The chief jailer commits all the other prisoners into Joseph's care and everything Joseph does prospers. So life goes on under God's blessing even in Egypt, despite difficult circumstances.

Butlers, bakers, and dreams again (40:1–23)

Some time later, Pharaoh finds offence in some of his workers. The chief cupbearer, who was often a confidant and favourite of the king, offends Pharaoh, as does the chief baker, who often functioned as a royal table scribe. These are important people, but they nevertheless end up in jail and under Joseph's care, where they begin to dream.

Dreams were particularly important in the ancient world as one of the significant means whereby the gods would break into human affairs and make their wills known. For this reason, dreams were things to worry about.

The cupbearer's dream is all about threes:

- a vine with three branches;
- three actions of the vine—budding, blossoming, ripening;
- three actions of the cupbearer—taking, pressing, placing.

The interpretation is also straightforward—Pharaoh will restore the cupbearer. The cupbearer understandably rejoices, and Joseph urges him to put in a good word for him when the dream is fulfilled.

The chief baker has been looking on and obviously likes what he sees and hears, and so he too brings his dream. The forecast for him, however, is not so good—he will end up dead, impaled and eaten by the birds. Sure enough on the third day things happen just as Joseph had foreseen in his interpretation. However, the cupbearer did not remember Joseph. Since we have often heard of God remembering people in seemingly helpless situations, this may be an indication that God will soon remember.

SCENE 3: PHARAOH'S COURT (41:1–57)

When two full years had passed, Pharaoh had a dream: He was standing by the Nile, when out of the river there came up seven cows, sleek and fat, and they grazed among the reeds. After them, seven other cows, ugly and gaunt, came up out of the Nile and stood beside those on the riverbank. And the cows that were ugly and gaunt ate up the seven sleek, fat cows. Then Pharaoh woke up.

He fell asleep again and had a second dream: Seven heads of grain, healthy and good, were growing on a single stalk. After them, seven other

heads of grain sprouted—thin and scorched by the east wind. The thin heads of grain swallowed up the seven healthy, full heads. Then Pharaoh woke up; it had been a dream.

In the morning his mind was troubled, so he sent for all the magicians and wise men of Egypt. Pharaoh told them his dreams, but no one could interpret them for him.

(Genesis 41:1–8)

Dreams again (41:1–7)

Two years pass and Joseph is still in prison. This time it is Pharaoh who dreams. The content of the dreams is quite straightforward:

- Seven sleek and fat cows succeeded by seven thin and ugly cows who swallow up the fat ones.
- Seven plump and good ears of grain succeeded by seven thin and diseased ears that swallow up the plump ones.

Looking for an interpretation (41:8–13)

Because Pharaoh knows the dreams are important, he looks for interpreters but none of his paid dream interpreters can deliver the goods. Finally the chief cupbearer regains his memory and tells Pharaoh of the young Hebrew in the prison.

Joseph and Pharaoh (41:14–46)

The chapter reaches its climax. Pharaoh rapidly sends for Joseph. We are told of Joseph's preparation, and of his acknowledgement that interpretation can only come from God (and, by implication, not the dream manuals of magicians).

Pharaoh recounts the dreams with some differences from the content described at the beginning of the chapter. It appears as though the ugly cows have played on Pharaoh's mind, because in this telling they are obviously threatening.

Joseph speaks again, reiterating his claim that God is the source of the interpretation. The interpretation has four points:

- Both dreams amount to the same thing.
- The seven cows or ears of grain represent seven years.
- Seven years of famine will follow seven years of plenty.
- The duplication of the dream indicates that it will be promptly and certainly fulfilled.

Having given the interpretation, Joseph offers some friendly and uninvited advice, urging Pharaoh to find a wise and discerning man to oversee the land. During the years of plenty they should gather food and store it up, so they will have something to fall back on in the years of famine.

Pharaoh appreciates the advice and appoints the obviously wise and discerning Joseph. After all, he is clearly a man in whom the Spirit of God dwells. And so it is that Joseph becomes second in charge in Egypt, with all the fringe benefits that go with the job.

Fulfilment (41:47–57)

Sure enough, the dreams are fulfilled. During the seven years of plenty Joseph uses his power well, and does what is good for the people. He is a wise and discerning leader. During this time he also marries and has two sons.

When the days of famine set in, again Joseph leads well. As God had promised, he is a source of blessing for those among whom he lives. In fact, he is a source of blessing for the entire known world as they all come to this wise leader to buy grain. And before long even his brothers and his fathers hear of the presence of grain in Egypt, and the scene is set for the next stage in the drama.

WHAT DOES IT ALL MEAN?

An overview of the three scenes

Although the stories are quite complicated, there is an underlying structure that helps us understand what the author hoped to convey. In particular, there are some striking similarities and differences in the structure of the three scenes: Joseph in Potiphar's house, Joseph in the prison, and Joseph before Pharaoh.

First of all, there are some parallels between scenes 1 and 2:

- They begin in the same way. We are told that God is with Joseph, leading us to expect God's blessing, which does indeed follow.
- In each of the scenes, God blesses Joseph and he succeeds.
- In each of the scenes God blesses other people through Joseph. Potiphar does well and the chief jailer ends up with a well-functioning jail.
- However, each of the two scenes ends unhappily. In Scene 1, Joseph ends up in jail while in Scene 2 he remains in jail despite successfully interpreting the dream of the cupbearer.

Scene 3 is somewhat different. It has an ominous start since there is no mention of God's blessing. The implication is therefore that Joseph is on his own now—God is no longer blessing. However, then the surprise comes in that Joseph rises instead of falling. We wait for his fall but it never arrives. Instead, he just grows and grows in stature and status until he is not just in charge of a minor functionary's house or an Egyptian prison, but all of Egypt. He is placed next in authority to Pharaoh, who recognises that the Spirit of God is in him.

The dangers of assimilation

There have been other things that have happened almost unnoticeably in the story. In the early parts of the story, Joseph is obviously a Jew. People notice it and call him 'a Hebrew'. However, at the end of the story he is looking more and more like an Egyptian and in danger of being assimilated. His outer garb is Egyptian, his name is Egyptian, he has mastered the Egyptian language, he has an Egyptian wife who is the daughter of a sun-worshipping priest and he has children whose names may indicate bitterness towards his own people and a desire to forget his Israelite past.

Joseph apparently still holds on to his religion, but there are hints that Joseph is in real danger of becoming an Egyptian. It is at this very point that his brothers arrive. Hence, these few chapters have set the scene for their arrival.

The two dream scenario

There is yet another theme that runs through this chapter. Since we first started dealing with Joseph we have been hearing about dreams that come in pairs. First, Joseph himself dreams two dreams in which he dreams of his brothers and his parents bowing down before him. Second, the cupbearer and the baker have a dream each. Third, Pharaoh himself has a pair of dreams.

Given this, it is interesting to note what Joseph tells Pharaoh when he interprets his dreams for him in Genesis 41:32—'The reason the dream was given to Pharaoh in two forms is that the matter has been firmly decided by God, and God will do it soon.'

What Joseph is saying is that when dreams are doubled God is saying that the future is fixed—it will surely happen. More than that, when dreams are doubled God is saying that he will shortly bring it about.

He too had dreamed similar double dreams, which means that his dreams about his brothers and his parents are fixed by God. They will surely happen and they will happen shortly.

The point can't have been missed by Joseph. He knows his own dreams. He knows what they mean and that they are true. Moreover, he knows they are fixed by God. However, close on 20 years have passed and the fulfilment of the dreams looks a long way away. Then, just at the point when he is tempted to become an Egyptian, God comes to him again in the circumstances of his life and reminds him that things are fixed by him and will shortly happen.

It is important to notice, though, that the twenty years has not been wasted on Joseph. Twenty years ago he was a spoiled, brash, arrogant brat who apparently had time only for himself and his own ego. He was no one's friend, a teenager who chattered endlessly and was a pain and a curse to those who knew him. But not now.

Twenty years of hardship have turned a boy into a man. Twenty years of misfortune have made him grasp his faith as his own and he is now an intelligent, wise, God-fearing man without peer in Egypt. The years of waiting have forged him into God's man, waiting and ready for God's time.

SOME OBSERVATIONS FOR US

It is this issue that is of particular relevance for us. We too are people who wait for God's promised and fixed future for us as individuals, and for us as members of all humanity and all creation. We wait for Christ to return, and for a new heaven and a new earth and a place where there are no tears, or pain, or illness, or loneliness, or heartache, or broken relationships, or persecution, or evil. The time we wait for will be a time when the devil will be done away with, and when our sinful bodies will be replaced by new bodies that no longer turn us away from our creator. We wait for Christ from heaven.

God has told us that this future is fixed and is sure. Moreover, he has told us that it will happen shortly. So what should we do as we wait? What sort of people should we be?

Paul gives us an indication in 1 Corinthians 15. He tells his hearers that the resurrection will occur and death and sin will be done away with at the end of time. Then he closes with this exhortation:

> Therefore, my dear brothers, stand firm. Let nothing move
> you. Always give yourselves fully to the work of the Lord,
> because you know that your labour in the Lord is not in vain.
> *(1 Corinthians 15:58)*

If we know the end and it is fixed, then our focus should not be on our present suffering or pain but on the future. Moreover, we should be preparing for it. Paul picks this up in Titus 2:11–13.

For the grace of God that brings salvation has appeared to all men. It teaches us to say 'No' to ungodliness and worldly passions, and to live self controlled, upright, and godly lives in this present age, while we wait for the blessed hope—the glorious appearing of our great God and Saviour, Jesus Christ.

But perhaps the final comment should be given to Peter in 2 Peter 3:8–14.

But do not forget this one thing, dear friends: With the Lord a day is like a thousand years, and a thousand years are like a day. The Lord is not slow in keeping his promise, as some understand slowness. He is patient with you, not wanting anyone to perish, but everyone to come to repentance.

But the day of the Lord will come like a thief. The heavens will disappear with a roar; the elements will be destroyed by fire, and the earth and everything in it will be laid bare.

Since everything will be destroyed in this way, what kind of people ought you to be? You ought to live holy and godly lives as you look forward to the day of God and speed its coming. That day will bring about the destruction of the heavens by fire, and the elements will melt in the heat. But in keeping with his promise we are looking forward to a new heaven and a new earth, the home of righteousness.

So then, dear friends, since you are looking forward to this, make every effort to be found spotless, blameless and at peace with him.

25

Reunion and reconciliation

The Joseph story is magnificent in its narrative art and diverse in its interest. We could probably spend a book on it alone, but instead we will now cover the next few chapters of Genesis in a broad sweep. In this chapter, we will:

- outline an overview of the story;
- give a 'big picture' perspective on the story—what it is about and why it is here; and
- make some observations on key ideas and themes within the story and how these are of relevance to us.

As I have said before, it is very important that you read the story for yourself. However, here I urge you to do so not just because it is important, but because if you don't you will miss out on a very special treat. This is one of the masterpieces of literary art in the Old Testament as well as a source of great spiritual joy and encouragement.

STORY 1 (42:1–38)

The context for this story has been set by Genesis 37–41. Joseph is in Egypt because of his arrogance and his brothers' cruelty. There is a famine throughout the ancient world and God in his providence has given Egypt warning of this famine. He has also given Egypt Joseph, an able manager who has been able to ensure that the country is well prepared and equipped for the difficulties the famine will bring. These are the events of Genesis 42:

- Jacob sends all his sons (except Benjamin) to Egypt to buy grain.
- The brothers arrive in Egypt.
- They have an audience with Joseph where Joseph recognises them (though they don't recognise him) and accuses them of being spies.
- Joseph imprisons the brothers.
- They have a second audience with Joseph where he says that he will let them go only if they leave one brother (Simeon) with him and bring back Benjamin with them.
- The brothers depart Egypt.
- They report to Jacob what has happened and Jacob is extremely reluctant to let them return with Benjamin.

STORY 2 (43:1–45:28)

The famine has now become very severe and Jacob's family has need of further grain. This story follows a similar pattern to the previous one and can again be summarised in seven points:

- Jacob sends all his sons (including Benjamin) to Egypt to buy grain.
- The brothers arrive in Egypt.
- They have an audience with Joseph where Joseph entertains them in a grand manner before sending them off with grain (and a planted silver goblet in Benjamin's sack).
- Joseph captures the brothers and accuses them of theft (of the goblet).
- They have a second audience with Joseph where he says that he will let them go but keep the thief (Benjamin) as his slave. In response Judah offers to take Benjamin's place. Joseph breaks down and discloses who he is.
- The brothers depart Egypt to bring back their father to Egypt to survive the famine.
- They report to Jacob what has happened and Jacob is overjoyed at the news of Joseph.

STORY 3 (46:1–47:31)

The structure of Story 3 is slightly different to the first two:

- God sends Jacob (plus the whole family) to Egypt, assuring him that the promises will not be put in jeopardy by this move.
- The whole family journeys to Egypt.
- Joseph has an audience with Jacob where Joseph tells Jacob and the brothers how to approach Pharaoh.
- Pharaoh has an audience with Jacob where Jacob blesses Pharaoh and Pharaoh agrees that the family can settle in Egypt.
- Joseph is a cause of blessing to his family and the whole world, through his crisis management during the famine.
- Jacob requests that he be brought out of Egypt after his death. Joseph agrees.

OBSERVATIONS AND APPLICATIONS

The doctrine of God's sovereignty

The clue to interpreting this story can be found in two speeches, one in Genesis 45 and the other in Genesis 50.

In Chapter 45 Joseph has just disclosed his identity to his brothers. Then he says this:

'I am your brother Joseph, the one you sold into Egypt! And now, do not be distressed and do not be angry with yourselves for selling me here, because it was to save lives that God sent me ahead of you. For two years now there has been famine in the land, and for the next five years there will not be ploughing and reaping. But God sent me ahead of you to preserve for you a remnant on earth and to save your lives by a great deliverance.

'So then, it was not you who sent me here, but God. He made me father to Pharaoh, lord of his entire household and ruler of all Egypt. Now hurry back to my father and say to him, "This is

**what your son Joseph says: God has made me lord
of all Egypt. Come down to me; don't delay." '**

(Genesis 45:4b–9)

The second defining speech occurs in Chapter 50, after Jacob
has died and the brothers fear that with their father out of the
way Joseph will seek to right the wrongs committed against
him. They figure that he has really been holding a grudge
and waiting for the opportunity to express it. Their response
is to go to Joseph, seek his forgiveness, and make themselves
his slaves (50:15–18).

Joseph responds in the following way:

**'Don't be afraid. Am I in the place of God? You
intended to harm me, but God intended it for good
to accomplish what is now being done, the saving of
many lives. So then, don't be afraid. I will provide
for you and your children.' And he reassured them
and spoke kindly to them.**

(Genesis 50:19b–21)

The references to God in both speeches by Joseph are very
significant. Joseph is saying very clearly that God had a
purpose for his people—that they be preserved and the line of
Abraham be continued (compare the same theme presented
in the interlude of Genesis 38, the story of Tamar). In order
for this to happen, God's people needed to be in Egypt for a
time, and in order for the Israelites to come to Egypt and
remain alive God needed Joseph to be there ahead of them.
Joseph is categorical—God is behind all that has happened.

At the same time the narrator, the brothers, and Joseph,
do not hide the fact that the sons of Jacob were wrong in
what they did. They sinned and acted culpably and wrongly.
They needed to repent of what they had done.

In many ways this story captures so much that we have
heard time and time again in the story of the Hebrew
patriarchs. God is sovereign and has a purpose for his world
and his people, but those people are made of the same stuff
as their forefather, Adam. However, despite the sinfulness of

humans, God will work out his purposes. Nothing can stop him, not even human sinfulness.

The comfort offered by this is immense. In the first place, it offers great comfort to us when we feel as though we live in a world that is out of control. So often it appears as though God is absent, just as he seemed absent for large sections of the story of Joseph. However, the Joseph story tells us such impressions are a lie. God is always present, always overseeing human affairs, always involved, and always pushing toward his purpose of bringing the whole world to submit to the lordship of his Son, Jesus Christ (Ephesians 1:3–10).

However, God's sovereignty over human affairs is a comfort in another, very personal way. Each of us knows what we are like, and as we read through the story of Abraham, of Isaac, of Jacob, and of his sons, there is much we can identify with.

We can identify with their desire to worship the God of all the earth and to have him as the centre of existence.

We can also identify with their humanity and frailty—we don't always trust God and we often act in sin and rebellion.

But if we know and love Jesus, we can also identify with their position as people who are the objects of God's favour. Because of this, we can be assured that God's sovereignty will have similar effects with us. God will work on us and gradually bring us to his purpose—that we be formed in the likeness of Christ.

Such a process will invariably be slow and at times painful. It will undoubtedly be incomplete at the time of our death.

But it will be done because this is God's purpose for us, and God always accomplishes his purpose.

The third comfort in this doctrine comes from the fact that God uses people who are just like us. Whether we are like Abraham, or Sarah, Isaac or Rebekah, Jacob or Rachel, Leah, Judah, Tamar, or Joseph, God can use us. Imperfect as they were, God used them and so, imperfect as I am, God can use me. The comfort and joy here is immense, for if God could use only perfect people, then he wouldn't use us. On the other hand, if he has room for imperfect, sinful, but repentant people, then he undoubtedly has room for us.

A good life?

Since the story is headed 'the account of Jacob' it is helpful to spend some time thinking about Jacob himself. Many of us tend to think life was okay for these Old Testament saints. Everything worked out for them in the long run—God was with them and life was full for them. But is this so?

Let's consider Jacob's life for a moment and look at his own assessment, when he speaks to Pharaoh:

And Jacob said to Pharaoh, 'The years of my pilgrimage are a hundred and thirty. My years have been few and difficult, and they do not equal the years of the pilgrimage of my fathers.'

(Genesis 47:9)

The translation of this verse is a bit soft. Jacob's literal words, with his emphasis, are:

'Fewness and badness have been the years of my life.'

Some of us may think that this is a bit rich from a man of 130 years of age but, as he points out, he is just a youngster compared to his forefathers. Moreover, they have not only been few, they have also been hard.

When you think about it, it isn't hard to agree with Jacob. After all, drawing on John Calvin's comments in his *Institutes of the Christian Religion:*

- This is the man who experienced a troubled boyhood with a distant father who preferred his older brother.
- He is the boy who was instructed by his mother to defraud his brother and trick his father.
- He obeyed her and the consequences were that he was forced to flee from his family, never to see his mother again.
- He spent many years in hard and cruel servitude at Laban's house. In his own words, by day the cruel Palestinian sun consumed him and at night the cold of the desert pressed in on him, and he forced himself to stay awake to protect the herds from being attacked.

- At the end of seven years he was tricked by Laban and cheated of his wife.
- In the end he spent a total of twenty years being tricked and unjustly afflicted by his father-in-law.
- All the time this was going on his own family was being torn apart by hatred, quarrelling, and rivalry among his wives.
- Even his relationship with God was fraught with conflict and struggle, as is conveyed by the name he was given by God—'Israel'.
- Finally he arrived home only to lose his favourite wife in childbirth.
- In the meantime his daughter was seized and raped and his sons engaged in revenge, only to make Jacob and his family hated by all the inhabitants of the land.
- His eldest son took Jacob's wife and raped her.
- His sons plotted together to kill Joseph but ended up selling him as a slave, afflicting their father with a deep and inconsolable grief.
- His fourth eldest son committed incest.
- Famine came upon the land.
- In order to survive, Jacob sent his sons to Egypt to get food. No sooner had he done this than he discovered another of his sons had been put into prison. To get him back Jacob was compelled to commit Benjamin, his one and only remaining joy, to the care of others.

It is undoubtedly true that many of the things that happen to Jacob are the result of his own sin but this is not the point here. The point is that his life has been a flood of misfortune, a catalogue of disaster, an overwhelming strife. This is what this elderly man is saying to Pharaoh—life has been something of a personal hell.

Fortunately, Jacob's focus in life was not the here and now. If it was, he would have been sorely disappointed. Jacob's hope was in the future, and so it is that at the end of this story we find him standing with a maimed hip and leaning on his staff, worshipping the God who made him and with whom he had struggled. As he does, he gives instructions to his son about his burial, clearly looking forward in hope to God bringing his children out of Egypt and into the Promised Land. He is looking a long way down the track, looking for something better than this life of 'fewness and badness' offered him.

From our perspective, we know that in Christ God has guaranteed his hope. Because of the descendant of Jacob—Jesus Christ—God offers a new existence without pain, without old age, without strife, without deceit, without tears, without fewness, and without badness.

Many of us think that belief in God must pay off in the here and now to be worth it. The testimony of the Bible is that this is not always the case. For some of us, life will be like it was for Jacob. However, God wants us to look beyond this life and into the future. In the future there is hope. This hope is assured by the life, death, resurrection, and ascension of Jesus.

Repentance

In Genesis 42:19 Joseph says that if the brothers are indeed honest men and not spies, then one of them should remain a prisoner while the others carry home grain and bring back Benjamin. Their response is particularly interesting and important. The narrator has us overhearing these words:

> **They said to one another, 'Surely we are being punished because of our brother. We saw how distressed he was when he pleaded with us for his life, but we would not listen; that's why this distress has come upon us.'**
>
> **Reuben replied, 'Didn't I tell you not to sin against the boy? But you wouldn't listen! Now we must give an accounting for his blood.'**
>
> *(Genesis 42:21–22)*

In Chapter 43, the family is faced with the prospect of sending Benjamin back to Egypt. Such a prospect tears Jacob apart. Judah moves in to reason with Jacob, eventually taking a responsibility that could threaten his status as next in line for the inheritance. He says:

'Send the boy along with me and we will go at once, so that we and you and our children may live and not die. I myself will guarantee his safety; you can hold me personally responsible for him. If I do not bring him back to you and set him here before you, I will bear the blame before you all my life.'

(Genesis 43:8b–9)

In Chapter 44, Joseph threatens to keep Benjamin. In other words, he places the brothers in the situation they had been in 20 years earlier with him. Judah responds, and his remarkable speech represents a point-for-point undoing of their previous sin:

Then Judah went up to him and said: 'Please, my lord, let your servant speak a word to my lord. Do not be angry with your servant, though you are equal to Pharaoh himself. My lord asked his servants, "Do you have a father or a brother?" And we answered, "We have an aged father, and there is a young son born to him in his old age. His brother is dead, and he is the only one of his mother's sons left, and his father loves him."

'Then you said to your servants, "Bring him down to me so I can see him for myself." And we said to my lord, "The

boy cannot leave his father; if he leaves him, his father will die." But you told your servants, "Unless your youngest brother comes down with you, you will not see my face again." When we went back to your servant my father, we told him what my lord had said.

'Then our father said, "Go back and buy a little more food." But we said, "We cannot go down. only if our youngest brother is with us will we go. We cannot see the man's face unless our youngest brother is with us."

'Your servant my father said to us, "You know that my wife bore me two sons. one of them went away from me, and I said, 'He has surely been torn to pieces.' And I have not seen him since. If you take this one from me too and harm comes to him, you will bring my grey head down to the grave in misery."

'So now, if the boy is not with us when I go back to your servant my father and if my father, whose life is closely bound up with the boy's life, sees that the boy isn't there, he will die. Your servants will bring the grey head of our father down to the grave in sorrow. Your servant guaranteed the boy's safety to my father. I said, "If I do not bring him back to you, I will bear the blame before you, my father, all my life!"

'Now then, please let your servant remain here as my lord's slave in place of the boy, and let the boy return with his brothers. How can I go back to my father if the boy is not with me? No! Do not let me see the misery that would come upon my father.'

(Genesis 44:18–34)

Within the speech there is a tacit acknowledgement of the painful reality of their father's favouritism. It may not be right, but it is reality. Moreover, Judah's speech demonstrates that he has come to grips with this reality. He now understands and loves his father and will do anything to protect him. He, the son of Leah, will now even offer himself in lifetime servitude so that the other son of Rachel can be set free.

In this poignant speech, Judah lets us into the drama of repentance. Here is a man in anguish over his past and who regrets that past. However, he is more than that. He is also a man who is willing to demonstrate his remorse and regret in action.

Such resolve is true, biblical repentance. Biblical repentance is about grief and pain, alarm and indignation. It is also about changed actions, a zeal to right the wrong and an eagerness to put things straight. Real repentance is a decision that you were wrong and that God is right. It is the realisation that what God wants from you and what you want from God are not going to be achieved by:

- thinking the same old thoughts;
- doing the same old things;
- walking down the same old tracks; and
- living in the same old ways.

Each of us needs to learn from such examples of repentance. We all have ways of thinking, doing, and living that we know are not of God. We often feel remorse over them and acknowledge our guilt before God. Nevertheless, deep inside we continue to be fascinated by these things and want to keep them and keep returning to them. Such repentance is not true. True repentance is about pain and action—facing the reality of life like Judah and his brothers, acknowledging that there are deep reasons for what we do, and yet determining that because we live before God these things can have no ongoing part in our lives. It is resolving that no matter how great the pain, we will turn from these things and turn to the things of God.

Reconciliation

> Then Joseph could no longer control himself before all his attendants, and he cried out, 'Have everyone leave my presence!' So there was no one with Joseph when he made himself known to his brothers. And he wept so loudly that the Egyptians heard him, and Pharaoh's household heard about it.
>
> Joseph said to his brothers, 'I am Joseph! Is my father still living?' But his brothers were not able to answer him, because they were terrified at his presence.
>
> Then Joseph said to his brothers, 'Come close to me.' When they had done so, he said, 'I am your brother Joseph, the one you sold into Egypt! And

now, do not be distressed and do not be angry with yourselves for selling me here, because it was to save lives that God sent me ahead of you. For two years now there has been famine in the land, and for the next five years there will not be ploughing and reaping. But God sent me ahead of you to preserve for you a remnant on earth and to save your lives by a great deliverance.

'So then, it was not you who sent me here, but God. He made me father to Pharaoh, lord of his entire household and ruler of all Egypt. Now hurry back to my father and say to him, "This is what your son Joseph says: God has made me lord of all Egypt. Come down to me; don't delay. You shall live in the region of Goshen and be near me—you, your children and grandchildren, your flocks and herds, and all you have. I will provide for you there, because five years of famine are still to come. otherwise you and your household and all who belong to you will become destitute." '

(Genesis 45:1–11)

These chapters in Genesis contain one of the richest examples of reconciliation found in the Scriptures, perhaps only matched in its grandeur by the story of the lost son in Luke 15.

Again, its focus can be found in Genesis 44. For close to three chapters Joseph has tested his brothers, placing them under very searching scrutiny. Finally, he finds what he is looking for—contrition, repentance, and a desire for godliness. In Chapter 45 he can control himself no longer and the emotions of twenty years flow from his body with moans and tears. Amid those tears he reveals his true identity to his brothers. The implication of his words is that all is forgiven and reconciliation is now possible.

However, the story of Chapter 45 clearly indicates that the guilt the brothers feel weighs so heavily that they cannot easily be comfortable with Joseph. He is still in the position of power, and although he may weep they cannot yet because of their fear and guilt.

This fear and guilt becomes evident in Genesis 50. As we saw earlier, by this time Jacob is dead and his sons crave yet another audience with the brother they so severely wronged. They confess their guilt and ask for forgiveness. However, they still feel that their crimes are so great that they cannot ask for such forgiveness for their own sake, and so they ask Joseph to forgive them for the sake of their father. Distraught with guilt, they fall on their knees before their brother.

The repeated breaking down in tears by Joseph and the words with which he responds to them indicate what we already knew—he has forgiven them and has done so for their own sake, not because of his father. For this reason there is nothing to fear from him.

It is apparent that Joseph has gone past bitterness, and has so come to grips with these events that he can see the hand of God in them. He knows the brothers did wrong, but that God has been active through their sin. If God has used such sin for such good, then who is he to hold a grudge? Reconciliation is complete.

If we are God's people because of Jesus Christ then we know all about reconciliation. We have experienced it with God in Christ (Romans 5:1-11). However, as far as God is concerned, we have not come to know reconciliation completely until we know it in human relations. Unfortunately, many Christian people have yet to experience reconciliation fully in this area. Our churches are full of people who have wronged others and not repented of it, and of people who have been wronged by others and felt justified in holding on to hatred and bitterness. The result of this failure to be reconciled is an ongoing destruction of personal life and the lives of others around us. There is nothing so soul-destroying as people who have not yet forgiven as God has forgiven them.

It is here that Judah and Joseph provide examples for us. Judah knew what his father's favouritism had done to his family. Nevertheless, he forgave his father and accepted his favouritism as a reality. Life with his father and his brother then became possible.

With Joseph, a long time passed before the brothers actually came before him and repented of their sin. Nevertheless, Joseph forgave them and accepted them.

No matter who we are, there are people who have wronged and hurt us. Sometimes these people will be real brothers, sisters, mothers, fathers, or children. Others will be our brothers, sisters, or fathers and mothers in the faith. No matter who they are, the word of God is clear to us at this point. We are to forgive as we have been forgiven by God in Christ, and accept as we have been accepted by God in Christ (Colossians 3:13; Romans 15:7). God's nature is to show grace, mercy, and forgiveness, and it must also be our nature. If we have sinned against our brother or sister we are to throw aside our pride and ask for their forgiveness. If we have been sinned against we are to hold out our hands in welcome.

God's people cannot hold grudges and cannot allow bitterness to foul their relationships (compare Matthew 18:15–35). We are the people of God and therefore the people of reconciliation.

26

The final days of Jacob

THE ONGOING STORY

It is important as we survey these concluding chapters of the Joseph narrative that we remember where we started. Genesis 37:2 gave the heading for this section—it is 'the account of Jacob'. It is therefore the account of Jacob's family as well as his own account.

Immediately after this heading we were told of deep family strife caused by Jacob's favouritism toward Joseph. Within one family there was a father who loved one son with a very deep affection, and other sons who responded with deep hatred for the favoured son. In ten chapters this hatred and disharmony has moved to reconciliation and forgiveness. The story of Genesis comes to a close.

Genesis 47:28–31

> Jacob lived in Egypt seventeen years, and the years of his life were a hundred and forty-seven. When the time drew near for Israel to die, he called for his son Joseph and said to him, 'If I have found favour in your eyes, put your hand under my thigh and promise that you will show me kindness and faithfulness. Do not bury me in Egypt, but when I rest with my fathers, carry me out of Egypt and bury me where they are buried.'
>
> 'I will do as you say,' he said.
>
> 'Swear to me,' he said. Then Joseph swore to him, and Israel worshipped as he leaned on the top of his staff.
>
> *(Genesis 47:28–31)*

The events of this section are straightforward. Jacob is ne
the end of his life and so he calls Joseph to him and extract
an oath from him that he will bury Jacob in Canaan. Joseph
readily agrees.

Genesis 48:1–22

Some time later Joseph was told, 'Your father is ill.'
So he took his two sons Manasseh and Ephraim
along with him. When Jacob was told, 'Your son
Joseph has come to you,' Israel rallied his strength
and sat up on the bed.

Jacob said to Joseph, 'God Almighty appeared
to me at Luz in the land of Canaan, and there he
blessed me and said to me, "I am going to make
you fruitful and will increase your numbers. I will
make you a community of peoples, and I will give
this land as an everlasting possession to your
descendants after you."

'Now then, your two sons born to you in Egypt
before I came to you here will be reckoned as mine;
Ephraim and Manasseh will be mine, just as
Reuben and Simeon are mine. Any children born
to you after them will be yours; in the territory
they inherit they will be reckoned under the names
of their brothers. As I was returning from Paddan,
to my sorrow Rachel died in the land of Canaan
while we were still on the way, a little distance
from Ephrath. So I buried her there beside the road
to Ephrath' (that is, Bethlehem).

When Israel saw the sons of Joseph, he asked,
'Who are these?' 'They are the sons God has given
me here,' Joseph said to his father. Then Israel
said, 'Bring them to me so I may bless them.'

Now Israel's eyes were failing because of old age,
and he could hardly see. So Joseph brought his
sons close to him, and his father kissed them and
embraced them.

> **Israel said to Joseph, 'I never expected to see your face again, and now God has allowed me to see your children too.'**
>
> *(Genesis 48:1–11)*

At the point where Jacob is near his death, Joseph ensures that he visits his father with his two sons. Jacob repeats the promises (48:3–4), formally adopts Joseph's two sons as his own sons (48:5–7), blesses Joseph and his sons (48:8–20), and finally instructs Joseph regarding his imminent death and bequeaths a section of land in Canaan to Joseph over his brothers.

Genesis 49
As with his fathers before him, Jacob then gathers his sons together for a final word. He prophesies about the future of each of them. In the process he condemns Reuben, Simeon, and Levi for their past atrocities, and gives extended predictions concerning Judah and Joseph. Finally, he gives them all further instructions about his death before drawing up his feet into the foetal position and breathing his last.

Genesis 50
The depth of the tie between Jacob and Joseph is expressed in Joseph's deep grieving for his father, and is followed by the family taking Jacob's bones to Canaan with great pomp and ceremony. On arriving at the land that Abraham bought from Ephron, Jacob is buried in the family plot.

At some time in all of this, the brothers realise that with their father dead Joseph could exact revenge on them for their sins. They approach him on the matter and he assures them that their concern is unwarranted.

Finally, Joseph himself dies at a good old age and leaves instructions for his bones to be buried back in Canaan.

MEANING

Sovereignty again

The overall interpretation of the Joseph story is clear and has been canvassed in the previous chapter. The story conveys a theology of God's sovereignty. God is not simply the God who created, he also controls all history, in order that his purposes will be achieved. While this has been apparent throughout Genesis, its prominence here is important and acts as a reminder that will be necessary as we move into Exodus, where God will again seem to be somewhat distant from his people.

Looking forward and ignoring the passing pleasures of Egypt

We noticed in an earlier chapter that at one point in the story there seemed to be a real danger that Joseph would become Egyptian. He had a position of prominence, a wife who was the daughter of a sun-worshipping priest, and children by her whose names seemed to indicate that he wanted to forget his past and even forget his roots.

The actions of Jacob in Genesis 47 and 48 appear to be structured so as to move Joseph away from such an orientation. One can't help thinking that Jacob sees his son and the temptations posed by Egypt. Egypt is all about being settled and having wealth, prosperity, and stability. Jacob, however, knows that the life of promise is not about these things. Rather, it is about looking into the future and living the life of a sojourner, refugee, and temporary resident (compare Genesis 12:4-9). With this in mind, it is possible to see that Jacob takes a number of steps in order to educate and secure his son in this future.

First, Jacob stresses with his son that his own hope is somewhere else than in Egypt. This is what is meant when he gets an assurance from Joseph that he will bury him in Canaan. The point is that Jacob's own hope is in God and the promise.

Second, no matter what else is going on in Chapter 48, one thing is certain—Jacob is making clear to Joseph that his future is tied up with the people of God. This is apparent in a number of areas:

- Jacob repeats the promises to Joseph.
- He formally adopts Joseph's sons.
- He gives a blessing which ties them in with Abraham and Isaac and himself.
- He then tells Joseph that God's intention is to bring the family of Israel back to Canaan, and that Joseph will have leadership over his brothers.
- And then finally, he gives him the right of ownership of the only piece of Promised Land that he himself had acquired.

This theme of looking into the future is continued in Chapter 49, where Jacob blesses the sons and tells them what will happen in the days to come. As we noted earlier, two of the brothers are singled out for special mention—Joseph and Judah, the two who have featured most in the story of Genesis 37–47.

Joseph is told a number of things. He is told that his father's blessing clearly rests with him. He is also told that Judah will be like a sleeping lion for some time but that eventually the rule will pass to him. With this education in place, Jacob places his hope in the future, draws up his feet, breathes his last, and is gathered to his ancestors in death.

Jacob is very clear about his orientation on life. He is ultimately a person of hope. In his death he does what he has done all the way through life—he hopes. He has had to wait for his wife, for his son, and for reconciliation and peace. Life has been full of hoping, and it is this legacy that he wants to pass on to his children. He wants them to look forward in expectation, waiting for what is yet to come.

Despite this, we are still in tension regarding Joseph at the end of Chapter 49. Jacob may well know where his future lies and he may well have educated Joseph in the doctrine of hope, but what will Joseph actually do? Will he settle in Egypt and continue to become Egyptian, or will he be satisfied with temporary resident status—settled in Egypt for the moment but really not settled because he belongs to Canaan?

This tension grows as we watch and listen in the ne. section. Joseph honours his father with dignity and respec and buries him according to his wishes. Nevertheless, the burial, while essentially Jewish, has all the accoutrements of an Egyptian burial. Everything Joseph does looks Egyptian.

However, then we have the other side presented when the brothers come before Joseph and we are reminded of how this story began. In Genesis 37 we read of a dream where all the sons of Jacob came and bowed down before Joseph. This dream was from God. It was part of his purpose. Which will Joseph choose—will he become Egyptian and line himself up with the passing world of Egypt, or will he choose to be Israelite, a sojourner, settled but not settled?

The growing tension ends with the last five verses of Genesis where we are told of Joseph's future. He did stay in Egypt and live a rich and fruitful life. However, as he faces death he tells us where his hope lies. Even though he may have been Egyptian on the outside, his heart, his hope and his future, were tied up with God's purposes in Canaan. For this reason, he urges his brothers to make sure that when God brings about his great purpose in rescuing the Israelites out of Egypt they are to make sure that his bones are where his hope is—in Canaan.

A DIFFERENT PERSPECTIVE

Genesis 3:15

It is possible, however, to look at these passages from a much larger perspective and as belonging to a much larger context. Although they are the closing verses of the Joseph story and the closing verses of the Patriarchal story, they are also the closing verses of the whole book of Genesis. Because of this there are inevitably various issues that these passages take up from the rest of the book. One of these begins in Genesis 3:15.

In Genesis 3, God is speaking to the serpent in the garden after it has led Adam and Eve astray and he says to the serpent,

'Because you have done this, "Cursed are you above all the livestock and all the wild animals! You will crawl on your belly and you will eat dust all the days of your life. And I will put enmity between you and the woman, and between your offspring and hers; he will crush your head, and you will strike his heel." '

(Genesis 3:14–15)

Jewish and Christian scholars for over two thousand years have seen this verse as speaking about God's coming Messiah or King. It is a promise that a particular descendant of Adam and Eve will be victorious over Satan at some time in the future. The word used here for 'offspring' is actually the word 'seed' and it is this very word that has played such an important part in the story of the patriarchs.

Genesis 17
In Genesis 13:15–16 Abraham is told to look around the land of Canaan and God tells him that all the land he can see will be given to his 'seed' forever and that his 'seed' will be like the dust of the earth. In Genesis 15:5 God tells Abraham to look up into the sky and count the stars and then says to him, 'So shall your seed be'.

In Genesis 17 God tells Abraham about his descendants to come, and in verse 6 he says that kings will come from Abraham. In verse 16 he says that kings of people will come from Sarah.

Genesis 49
In Genesis 49:10 we are told that the sceptre will not depart from Judah nor the ruler's staff from between his feet. In other words, we are being told again that rulers and kings will come from the line of Abraham, Isaac, Jacob, and Judah.

Genesis 49 therefore lets us into a very important part of God's long term plan. His plan is to have a person who will defeat Satan. This plan is put into effect through Abraham and will reach its fulfilment in a descendant of Judah.

Partial fulfilment

As readers of Scripture we know when this fulfilment came, for we are aware that one of Judah's descendants was King David. He did indeed rule over the people of God just as Jacob had prophesied. This king from the loins of Abraham did defeat many of the enemies of the people of God and bring Israel into the first full possession of the land that had been promised to Abraham.

However, David did not defeat that great enemy of the people of God—Satan. In fact, in his latter days David himself was tempted by Satan to take a census of Israel and buckled just as Adam had done before him (1 Chronicles 21:1–5). His descendants didn't do any better. They too sinned, and eventually God did away with kingship in Israel with the result that, at the end of the Old Testament, the prophecies of Genesis were still waiting to be fulfilled.

Full fulfilment

Into this situation came Jesus. He was of the line of David and Judah and Jacob and Isaac and Abraham. He was also of the line of Adam. He did battle with the spiritual enemies of the people of God and he bound them. However, he did also allow them to bind him to some extent. He allowed them to work with the physical enemies of the people of God to place him on a cross, and there on the cross he defeated Satan and made a public display of his victory (Colossians 2:13–15). He conquered Satan once for all.

In Jesus, full fulfilment of Genesis 3:14–15 came about.

Return to Eden

Now that this has been accomplished, all that remains is a final wrapping up. This process is going on in the world right now. We have a king, a second Adam, who has conquered Satan and crushed him under his feet, and the mopping up is going on at this very moment as we proclaim this Jesus to the world, live as God's people, and resist the evil one.

However, the day will come when the mopping up will be completed, and when God will consummate his victory. At

at time he will throw Satan into the judgment reserved for
m from the beginning of time, and re-establish an Eden
without Satan or his cohorts (Revelation 20–22). We will then
again have a clear, unfettered and untainted relationship
with our God and with each other.

This is where God has been heading since Genesis 1, and
he is well on track.

LIVING IN HOPE

As you can see, hope is a ringing bell throughout the story
of Genesis and throughout the story of Jacob and Joseph.
More than that, Jacob and Joseph are, in some senses,
models for us as Christians. They represent two ways of life.

On the one hand there is Jacob. His life has been that of
the continual traveller or sojourner. He has never really
been settled and life has been about conflict, discomfort, and
difficulty. As such, it has been easy for him to hope—for a
wife, for children, for an end to strife, and for his family's
final deliverance.

Joseph represents another side. Although his life has
been difficult at times, things have generally been all right
for him. Since being dragged out of prison, life has been
comfortable. He has been reunited with his family and
married to a wife who has borne children without any of the
trouble experienced by Sarah, Rebekah, Rachel and Tamar.
He has experienced wealth and security and lived a fairly
settled existence. And for such people hope is not easy.

Hope is not easy when things are okay, when material
things are plentiful and life is comfortable. However, the
book of Genesis and the book of Hebrews tell us that Joseph
was like his dad—he too was a man of faith and hope, who
died looking toward the Exodus in hope.

For us, hope is not about physical descendants or land in
the same way that it was for Abraham and his descendants.
Our hope is for a new heaven and a new earth where
righteousness dwells. It is for a place where:

- our physical bodies will be done away with in all th
  weakness, to be replaced with new bodies that woı
  decay (1 Corinthians 15);
- we will be like Jesus for we will see him as he is
  (1 John 3:1–3);
- sin, the flesh, and the devil will be things of the past
  and not of the present (Revelation 20–22); and
- tears and pain and suffering and aches and illness and
  pain will be done away with (Revelation 21–22).

We are people who hope for the future, and who therefore must be sojourners and temporary residents of this earth. For some of us, life will be physically disjointed and full of 'fewness and badness', while for others, life will be settled and successful, full of good and full of days. No matter what it is, all of us who are God's people are citizens of a different country and only temporary residents of this world.

Living like this can be very difficult. It means no longer pinning our hopes for meaning and satisfaction in the here and now. It spells the end to covetousness, materialism, and acquisitiveness. It causes us to put an end to grasping hold of the things of this temporary and transitory life, and grasp hold of God's future.

Knowing this difficulty, let us look to the examples of Abraham, Isaac, Jacob, and Joseph. Let us fix our eyes on Jesus the author and perfecter of our faith, putting aside everything that hinders us. Let us run with endurance the race that is set before us and not grow weary and lose heart (Hebrews 11:1–12:3).

Reading the Bible Today commentaries

Presenting careful scholarship from respected authors

Genesis—Salvation begins *Andrew Reid*
Romans—Dust to Destiny *David Seccombe*
Proverbs—The Tree of Life *Graeme Goldsworthy*
2 Timothy—Finishing the Race *Christopher Green*
Daniel—Kingdoms in Conflict *Andrew Reid*
Hebrews—The Majestic Son *Peter Adam*
Mark—The Servant King *Paul Barnett*
Revelation—Apocalypse Now and Then *Paul Barnett*
John—The Shepherd King *Paul Barnett*
1 Peter—Living Hope *Paul Barnett*
James—The wisdom of the brother of Jesus *John Dickson*
Numbers—Homeward bound *Martin Pakula*

Order copies directly from
Aquila Press Po Box A287, Sydney South, NSW 1235
Phone: (02) 8268 3344 Fax: (02) 9283 3987
www.publications.youthworks.net
or contact your local Christian bookshop

OR

IVP UK
Norton Street
Nottingham NG7 3HR
Email: sales@ivpbooks.com
Phone: (0115)978 1054